Hiking
Minnesota

by

John Pukite

FALCON®

HELENA, MONTANA

© 1998 by Falcon® Publishing Co., Inc., Helena, Montana.

10 9 8 7 6 5 4 3 2 1

Falcon and FalconGuide are registered trademarks of Falcon Publishing Co., Inc.

Printed in the United States of America.

All black-and-white photos by the author.
Cover photo by Cathy and Gordon Illg.

Library of Congress Cataloging-in-Publication Data
    Pukite, John, 1964-
        Hiking Minnesota / by John Pukite.
            p. cm.
        "A Falcon guide"—T.p. verso
        Includes bibliographical references (p.).
        ISBN 1-56044-565-3 (pbk.)
            1. Hiking—Minnesota—Guidebooks. 2. Trails—Minnesota—
        Guidebooks. 3. Minnesota—Guidebooks. I. Title.
        GV199.42.M6P85 1998
        917.7604'53—dc21   97-41155
                                                                CIP

 Text pages printed on recycled paper.

CAUTION
Outdoor recreational activities are by their very nature potentially hazardous. All participants in such activities must assume the responsibility for their own actions and safety. The information contained in this guidebook cannot replace sound judgment and good decision-making skills, which help reduce risk exposure, nor does the scope of this book allow for disclosure of all the potential hazards and risks involved in such activities.

Learn as much as possible about the outdoor recreational activities in which you participate, prepare for the unexpected, and be cautious. The reward will be a safer and more enjoyable experience.

In memory of my Father.

Contents

Acknowledgments

While traveling around Minnesota doing research for this book, it was encouraging to find people from all walks of life and ages also exploring the state's trails. To everyone who hiked with me, I would like to extend thanks for making the trails even more enjoyable. This book would not have been possible without the guidance and information provided by many local, state, and federal organizations working and caring for the state's natural treasures. Thanks to the Minnesota Department of Natural Resources for the help on the state parks and forests. This includes the countless, and to me, unfortunately, nameless field personnel in the state parks who gave unselfishly of their time and knowledge. Thanks also to the rangers at both Voyageurs National Park and the national monuments for their helpful suggestions and support, the Forest Service rangers at both Superior National Forest and Chippewa National Forest who directed me onto the right paths, the chambers of commerce throughout the state for their assistance, and all of the outdoor clubs that promote long-distance trails and outdoor activities in the state.

Map Legend

Interstate		Campground	▲
US Highway		Cabins/Buildings	▪
State or Other Principal Road	00 000	Peak	2,107 ft.
National Park Route	00	Hill	
Interstate Highway		Elevation	2,107 ft. ✕
Paved Road		Gate	•—•
Gravel Road		Mine Site	⚒
Unimproved Road	========⇒	Overlook/Point of Interest	◻
Trailhead	○		
Main Trail(s) /Route(s)		National Forest/Park Boundary	
Alternate/Secondary Trail(s)/Route(s)			
		Map Orientation	N
Parking Area	Ⓟ		
River/Creek		Scale	0 0.5 1 Miles
Spring	♂		
One-way Road	One Way		

Overview Map

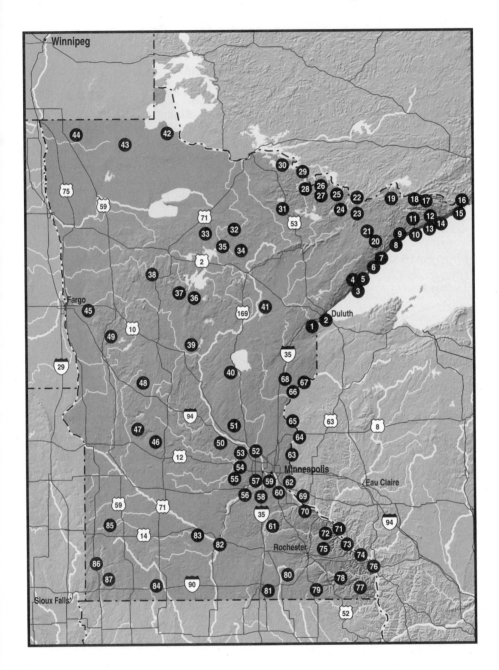

Introduction

To see a world in a grain of sand
And a heaven in a wild flower
Hold infinity in the palm of your hand
And eternity in a hour.
—Blake, *Auguries of Innocence*

Minnesota can be an amazing place. Within the state's boundary, there is a tremendous diversity of terrain and environments. In the northern reaches, trails thread their way around thousands of narrow bedrock lakes and through boreal forests where timber wolves still run wild. In the southern tallgrass prairies, footpaths go by prickly pear cactus and an occasional herd of bison.

Along Lake Superior's North Shore, you can explore the highlands that tower over this magnificent inland ocean and the wild rivers that cut through the rock, forming cataracts and cascades. Down in the southwest, the bluffland's high plateaus rise over the mighty Mississippi River as well as hardwood forests, and clean, flowing trout streams in deep narrow valleys,. At the Mississippi's headwaters you can jump across the river and wander among the huge trees that have escaped the lumber industry. In the northwest, the land lives up to Minnesota's reputation for flatness, but it also offers lakes, forests, and blooming prairies. In the middle swath of the state are rolling hardwood hills, glacier-made lakes, and dense forests, while on the eastern side, along the shores of the wild and scenic Saint Croix, paths traverse geologic wonders. Even in Minnesota's metropolitan areas, trails lead into big woods and deep valleys that hide lush vegetation and beautiful waterfalls or pass into large wildlife preserves only minutes away from downtown.

Hiking is the perfect way to explore these wild and beautiful places. You can find miles of trails, from remote, rugged trails to gentle, easy strolls. A few hikes take you on multi-day backpacking trips, while most are amenable for an afternoon nature walk. Whatever your skill level or wherever you live in the state, you will be able to find a hike and a remote spot to get away from it all.

Fortunately, you can find hiking opportunities within any of the sixty-four state parks, fifty-five state forests, or two national forests. Also, found in opposite corners of the state are Voyageurs National Park and Minnesota's two national monuments—Grand Portage and Pipestone. Minnesota is the envy of many states for its countless county, regional, and city parks. All have hiking trails and ample opportunities to explore parts of wild Minnesota. These eighty-seven hikes give but a sampling of what the state has to offer, but they do allow you to make an acquaintance with the state's diversity.

1

ECOLOGY

Within Minnesota's 84,000 square miles is the intersection of three major biomes or ecological provinces: prairie parkland, eastern broadleaf forest, and laurentian mixed forest. It is these large provinces that give the state its wide-ranging variety. They provide the first impressions, be it the wide open grasslands or the dense rugged boreal forest. Within each of the provinces are also many nuances resulting in over fifty different individual communities. These fascinating habitats range from goat prairies to red pine forests, to white-cedar swamps, to oak savanna, and to black spruce bogs. The following paragraphs give a brief overview of the three provinces.

Prairie: At one time, prairie covered the entire southern and western portion of the state, although now only small fragments remain, with most converted to farmland. Fortunately, a number of parks are working to reintroduce native grasses to regain the look of a hundred years ago. The tallgrass prairie is a species-diverse system with hundreds of flowering plants and deep-rooted grasses. The more common grasses include Indian grass, which grows up to 7 feet tall, little bluestem, which reaches 4 feet in height, and the dominant grass—called big bluestem (no relation to the little one)— which can attain heights of 9 feet and has seeds shaped like turkey feet.

Broadleaf: Between the prairie and the northern boreal forest, the deciduous forest cuts across the state in a narrow diagonal corridor from the southeast corner reaching up to the northwest. The woods, an extension of the eastern deciduous forest, contains a mixture of basswoods, oaks, elms, and maples. The fully mature stands take on the name "Big Woods," or as the early French explorers called them, *Grand Bois*. In these woods maidenhair and lady ferns cover the forest floor, barely making way for a footpath. During different seasons the ground also harbors a profusion of flowers, such as the large-flowered trillium. In the lowlands and river floodplains a different forest takes over, consisting mainly of the towering cottonwoods and silver maples. On the drier plateaus of the state's southeastern corner, oaks and maples dominate the forests, while in the far opposite corner in the northwest, small scrub oak and aspen are more common.

Boreal: Covering the arrowhead and most of the north, mixed or boreal forests make their way down from Canada. Here loons still laugh on the lakes, and footpaths lead to old-growth stands of white and red pine that survived the axe of the lumber industry. This is a rugged, yet fragile, environment, where growth is measured in millimeters. Here, some of the lichens and 2-foot-high white-cedars are hundreds of years old. Any disturbance to the land can take decades to repair.

GEOLOGY

Although Minnesota is a non-mountainous area, its geologic features have a surprising variety. The state's visible geologic history, what can be seen on the surface, can be divided into three parts: the Archaic Era, 3.5 billion years ago; the Paleozoic Era, five hundred million years ago, during which

Minnesota Vegetation

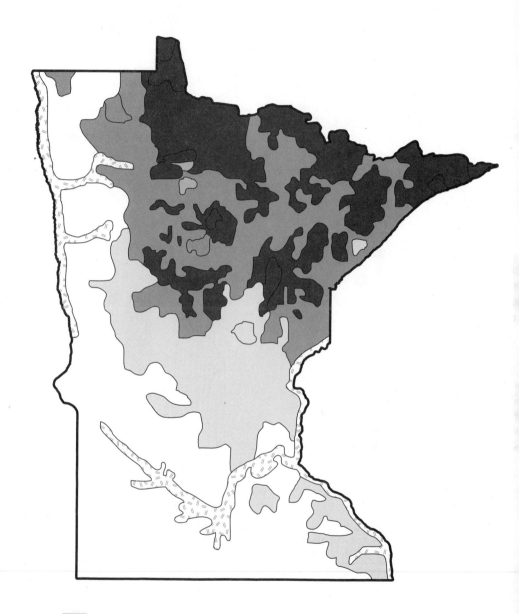

■ SPRUCE–FIR–PINE	FLOOD PLAIN FOREST
■ BIRCH–ASPEN	☐ PRAIRIE
OAK–MAPLE–BASSWOOD	

Minnesota Topography

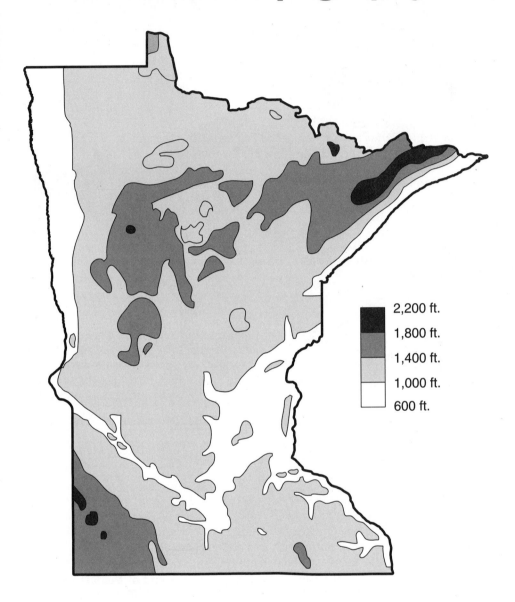

2,200 ft.
1,800 ft.
1,400 ft.
1,000 ft.
600 ft.

inland seas laid down a layer of sediments, and the Pleistocene Era, or ice age, which spanned from 2.5 million years to only ten thousand years ago.

Minnesota contains some of the world's oldest geological features—outcroppings of Archaic and early-precambrian rocks that date close to the earth's origin. In the Minnesota River valley, ancient outcroppings of quartzite and variegated gneiss, among others, appear from underneath layers of glacial soil. In the north, exposed archaic bedrock from the worn-down Laurentian mountain range, which once rose miles high, now covers the land. On the North Shore, slightly younger volcanic and sedimentary rocks are found along Superior's edge.

The blufflands are a result of the Paleozoic Era, the effects of which were largely erased by the glaciers flowing through the rest of the state. Fossils buried in the rock layers record a tropical climate and a warm-water sea. In the Mississippi and Saint Croix river valleys, the rivers cut and exposed the earth, giving hikers opportunities to examine the layers and search for small fossils. Here, in the rocks, you can follow the progression of life over time; while hiking you may observe small, ancient life forms, such as coral and the occasional trilobite.

The Pleistocene Era had the greatest geologic influence on the state's land features, since only the southeastern blufflands escaped being covered with ice during the full time span. During four major glaciations, an ice sheet hundreds, and perhaps many thousands, of feet thick covered the state in places; the Wisconsin glaciation, the last to leave, ended about ten thousand years ago. The glaciers periodically scraped away to the bedrock, leaving it exposed in places or covering it with hundreds of feet of glacial sand and gravel, forming hills and swales. During their melting and retreating, glaciers left behind thousands of lakes, wide river gorges and huge, flat lake bottoms. Unique remnants of this era are scattered around the state—erratics, huge and small boulders which were ignominiously dropped by the ice, and sinuous eskers, which formed from glacial rivers.

HUMAN HISTORY

Minnesota has its share of historical and archeological sites that go back centuries as well as thousands of years. Many parks have interpretive centers on the state's early history. A couple of hikes follow age-old paths and portages used by both native cultures and early explorers.

Throughout the state, archeological finds have demonstrated that human habitation began ten thousand years ago, near the end of the last ice age. Burial mounds and early stone tools and pottery record this earliest time of human habitation in Minnesota. Before European settlements, two major native cultures occupied the region. Briefly, the Dakota (alternatively called the Sioux) lived on the plains, hunting large game as a prime source of subsistence. And the Ojibwe (also known as the Chippewa) lived in the woodlands, where fishing and harvesting wild rice from lakes provided the means of survival.

A brief early timeline of European exploration and other notable happenings in the state:

1679   Sieur du Luht plants a flag for France near Duluth and Mille Lacs.
1695   Pierre le Sueur builds a fort near Red Wing.
1731   Verendrye builds a fort on Lake of the Woods—the start of the Voyageurs era.
1803   The Louisiana Purchase.
1820   Cornerstone for Fort Snelling is laid.
1832   Schoolcraft finds the source of the Mississippi.
1834   First Minnesota summer cabin on the shores of Lake Calhoun.
1836   Commercial logging begins in the Saint Croix River valley.
1849   Minnesota becomes a Territory.
1858   Minnesota becomes a State.
1872   Mesabi open pit mine opens.
1891   Itasca State Park established, Minnesota's first state park.
1908   Minnesota National Forest (Chippewa National Forest) established.
1909   Superior National Forest established.
1926   Sections of Superior National Forest turned into a roadless area (later the Boundary Waters Canoe Area Wilderness).

FUNDAMENTALS

Hiking is one of the most basic of all outdoor activities; and people go hiking for many reasons—to find a beautiful, relaxing spot, to access a remote fishing lake or trout stream, to discover the intricacies of nature, to go bird watching, or just to enjoy some physical activity outside. Whatever your reason, one absolute essential to take along is some common sense. This means planning ahead for the trip, doing a hike within your abilities, and telling someone where you are going.

For day hikes, little gear is needed. In fact, all that is really needed during the warmer seasons is a sturdy pair of shoes, maybe a snack, and water. For longer trips, of a couple days or more, a fully loaded backpack will be necessary. To plan properly, look over the hike descriptions and maps, paying close attention to the difficulty and the terrain description. Most of the trails are well marked with trail maps and signs, especially in the state parks, but in the state and national forests this is not always the case. On the more remote trails, take along either USGS topographic maps, or for the Boundary Waters Canoe Area Wilderness (BWCAW) at least, one of the commercially produced maps, like the Fischer or McKenzie maps.

Know your fitness-level and test it out on some of the easier hikes, maybe trying out some equipment you might carry on a longer hike. Watch out for fatigue. On rolling terrain, the trip back doesn't get any easier, so if you do get tired, turn around. Hiking with young children can often be done on the easier trails, usually found in the state parks, which sometimes offer backcountry campsites fairly close to the trail center.

Devil's Cascade.

Tell someone where you are going, even on the easier hikes. Also check out the weather forecast to see what the conditions might be on the trail. A long hike can become much longer, as well as potentially dangerous, if you are caught unprepared in a drenching rain.

As a final comment, follow the "leave no trace ethic," IF YOU PACK IT IN, YOU PACK IT OUT. Some places like the BWCAW mandate it, but it holds true wherever you hike. With the increased use and encroachment on our state's land we should ensure that nothing distracts from its beauty. Although this is mostly rugged country, some areas are also fragile and can easily be damaged. The blufflands in the southeast are especially susceptible to erosion. Taking shortcuts on switchbacks can create gullies and destroy rare plant habitats. In the north, walking on lichen can kill it and leave a ghost of a footprint that can last for years. Hikers should take extra care with the land and leave it wild for the person who will hike the trail the next day or next year.

CLOTHING

Thoreau once said, "Beware of enterprises requiring new clothing." But, if you have ever survived a winter in Minnesota, you probably already own at least a few things necessary for outdoor adventure.

The basics, even for a short hike, can vary dramatically. Under the sun on a prairie hike, sunscreen and a wide-brimmed hat may be necessities. However, I might carry a jacket in my pack even for a midsummer hike in the north woods; rain gear, a long sleeved shirt, and long pants should be in your pack, no matter what the season. On a shorter hike, your rain gear can simply be a light jacket, but on a longer hike, a full outfit is essential. Long sleeves and long pants come in handy, not only for warmth and protection from the sun, but also as an effective barrier against biting insects and poisonous plants (for those times you don't want to drench yourself in bug spray or anti-poison ivy lotion). In spring and fall, bring clothes appropriate for both summer and winter weather.

Outdoor stores carry a wide selection of breathable, water-resistant fabrics appropriate for most weather conditions. Whatever type of clothing you wear, even with waterproof/breathable fabrics, dress in layers. Layering allows you to fine-tune your own personal climate. When it starts to get too warm, shed a layer. As it gets colder or when you take a break, put a layer back on. Gore-tex or waterproof boots will also help on many of the trails. They keep your feet dry, which helps prevent blisters.

WEATHER AND SEASONS

Experiencing all four seasons is one of the joys of living in Minnesota. Each has its own distinctive feel. The temperature can vary from bone-chilling subzero winter days to the occasional hundred-degree day in summer. Fortunately these extremes don't happen in the same day. However, the temperature does vary enough to go from short sleeves in the afternoon, to sweater conditions at dusk. It can vary with the region, especially in the fall and spring. In northern Minnesota, snow can come a month before it starts in the southern part of the state.

Unpredictable weather conditions mean a few cautions are in order. Some weather, like the cold, should not be taken for granted. Hypothermia can result even on what was a warm day, if you find yourself in a chilling wind or stop for a rest after building up a sweat. Other severe weather conditions are more obvious, such as the occasional tornado or thunderstorm. In these circumstances you need to seek shelter, which could mean lying down in a ditch; stay away from lone trees or granite outcroppings.

Spring: The trails might be frozen or water-logged, and unexpected winter storms can strike unexpectedly. Watch the weather conditions carefully, since you never know what might get thrown at you. This is an excellent time for bird watching; the migrating flocks arrive, and the absence of leaves allows for good sightlines through the trees. Many wildflowers bloom at this time of year; usually in such profusion that you might consider a special trip just to see them. Another advantage to a spring hike: most bugs have yet to make an appearance.

Summer: In Minnesota, only three months are on record for never having received snow: June, July, and August. Take advantage of it. The longer days make this time of year ideal for an extended hike, allowing enough time for you to spend a full day hiking, set up camp, and relax, all before the sun goes down. Note that while Minnesota's southern half may be hot, the northern region usually stays relatively mild. The lake effect from Lake Superior acts to keep the temperature cooler and more constant. On the prairie, the grasses are reaching their full height. Also during this season, thunderheads might roll in over the grasslands—one of nature's most powerful sights. On the down side, bugs are in full force.

Fall: A favorite season of many people, fall means cool, crisp days and forests flaming up in color. However, the shorter days mean less time to hike before dark. Plan accordingly. Rain showers are more likely to linger all day; this is the time to make sure you have full rain gear along. The North Shore and hardwood forests are always favorite spots for fall colors, generally seen from mid-September to mid-October. A hike to a peak during this season can provide an amazing panorama, while the river valleys and the Big Woods offer the rich, mellow colors of oaks and other hardwood trees. This is also the end of bug season; many hikes that were swarming with bugs are now comfortable as can be. Fall is the start of hunting season, so wearing some blaze orange, even just on a cap, might not be such a bad idea.

Winter: This is not traditionally a hiking season, but many of these trails can be travelled on cross-country skis, snowshoes, or on walking paths found in some parks. If you are one to test the limits of your sleeping bag, a snowshoe hike and ice-fishing in the BWCAW can be an amazing treat. Winter is the only season to visit some areas, where trails lead over marshes and wetlands. A few metro-area parks even keep paths clear for winter walking.

BUGS

Minnesota has its share of irritating bugs. They are an integral part of the ecosystem, providing food for fish and birds, but since many of them bite, they can ruin the day for the unprepared hiker. Know your enemies, namely: mosquitoes, gnats, horse flies, deer flies, black flies, wood ticks, and a true threat, deer ticks.

Mosquitoes: Probably the most common biting insect, and everyone's favorite enemy. The description is probably well enough known: about 0.2 inch long with a long proboscis and skinny abdomen. The female mosquito does the biting, at any time of day, though they seem less aggressive in the early morning.

Gnats or no-see-ums: Small, less than 0.1 inch, black with brown legs and gray-brown wings.

Horse and deer flies: Two similar, almost sluggish flies that differ in size. The horse fly, at up to 1 inch, is the larger of the two. The deer fly has a v-shaped pattern on its abdomen.

Black flies: These stout, small (0.1 inch) black nuisances come out for a couple weeks in spring and again in summer, usually near running water. One of the most hated bugs, they travel in thick swarms.

Wood ticks and deer ticks: Wood ticks (0.1 inch) are brown with a spot of white near the head. Deer ticks are orange-brown with a black spot near the head and are half the size of the other tick at a tiny 0.0625 inches. Deer ticks carry Lyme disease, which has been reported in Minnesota. If you develop a ring-shaped rash within four to twenty days of a bite, have it checked out by a doctor.

Stinging bugs find us, their victims, through a number of methods. They can detect our body heat, chemicals in our sweat, even carbon dioxide in our breath (most of these increase with physical activity, like hiking). Colors also attract them—bee keepers wear white for a reason. Odors, especially fruity ones from soaps, perfumes, and lotions, will also attract insects.

The best repellents against mosquitoes and ticks contain either of two active ingredients: N,N-diethyl-meta-toluamide (DEET) or the slightly less effective ethyl hexanidol. DEET comes in several concentrations. DEET of 10–35 percent, often used for direct application to the skin, should last about an hour if not washed off by sweat or rain. Higher concentrations are usually applied to clothing. Avoid repeated application of greater than 50 percent concentrations of DEET to skin over a short period of time, especially with small children.

Other repellants include oil of citronella, which has been used as a mosquito repellent since 1882, and mineral oil based lotions. The lotions work best against no-see-ums and other biting insects with short mouthparts, since the lotions do not actually repel bugs, but form a barrier preventing the insect from biting the skin. Petroleum jelly works the same way, and is a sure method to keep black flies from biting your ears.

Another barrier is a head net, long pants, and a long-sleeved shirt. Long pants tucked in the socks or drawn shut, the standard recommended defense against ticks, are also effective against poison ivy. Poison ivy can linger on clothing until it is washed, so be careful. Horse and deer flies seem attracted to the highest point of a person; a hat seems to keep them off, but not necessarily away. Black flies seek out crevices; some people duct-tape their shirt sleeves closed and wear high collars to help combat them.

ANIMALS

Minnesota is a land of diverse habitats and large animal populations, so spotting a large animal is possible and can be a thrill for everyone. Use common sense and care around animals, especially those with young. This holds especially true for moose and black bears, which are normally shy and retreating if a human is nearby. However, with young they may become aggressive if they feel enclosed or threatened. Give them room.

The biggest problem with bears is not the risk of being attacked, but the nuisance they can cause in a campsite. To avoid these visitors, keep your campsite clean and put food away. Bears have an excellent sense of smell and will find any food stashed in a tent. While you're off hiking, use a food bag in camp, hanging it well out of reach from above as well as below. If you can reach the food sack, a bear probably can too. A Minnesota company called Granite Gear makes a food bag with a long-enough cord, or you could use a stuff sack with a rope. Some developed campsites have strong boxes to keep the critters out, or if you are car camping, a cooler will do the trick as well. If a bear does come into the campsite, try banging pots or yelling; this should, in almost all cases, chase them away.

Other animals, such as raccoons and ground squirrels, can also cause a ruckus by tearing into gear or a food bag. Needless to say this can be a problem, particularly on a long hike. If your next breakfast, lunch, or dinner is cached away for winter by a squirrel, you are simply out of luck. Making food accessible to animals also encourages future visits, and the next campers may lose their food supply. Remember human food is not part of a wild diet, so lock it away, and don't feed the animals.

For southeastern Minnesota only, there is one final caution—the timber rattlesnake. This snake makes its home in the crevices and cracks of the blufflands, usually in spots off the beaten track. Snake bites are rare, but if it does happen to you, get to a local hospital as soon as possible.

PREPARATION

Most of the day hikes in the book are rated easy to moderate (see descriptions below). The few trips rated difficult either lead farther back into the woods or are more physically strenuous due to more rugged trails.

Easy: Many of the easy hikes are on well-maintained paths in the state parks. For these, the distance back to the trailhead is usually short and any sturdy shoes, or even tennis shoes, will do. Take along insect repellant, a water bottle, a snack, and a jacket.

Moderate: Depending on a person's experience and conditioning, these hikes can be in either of the other two categories. Moderate trails have rougher, rockier paths; they may be on a rolling course with a number of hills to climb. There may also be some windfall to climb over, or just a longer distance to travel. These paths also vary more with the weather conditions, getting muddier than the easy trails when wet.

Difficult: These are long-distance trips requiring a few days or trips that travel into remote areas on rugged trails. Most of them are in the Boundary Waters Canoe Area Wilderness. Help can be miles away, so for a safe trip, planning is essential.

What to take really depends on the hike and the season. Listed below are some of the essentials that you should either take along with you on a longer hike or have readily available on shorter hikes. The first aid kit can be a do-it-yourself assemblage with items collected individually. This whole kit is fairly small; even in a small rucksack plenty of room is left for those other essentials like binoculars, a camera, and lunch.

Essentials: compass, first-aid kit (antibacterial ointment, aspirin or acetaminophen, bandages, elastic bandage, gauze, biodegradable soap for washing off poison ivy, and tape), flashlight, insect repellent, knife, map, matches, rain gear, sunscreen, sweater, water bottles.

BOUNDARY WATERS CANOE AREA WILDERNESS (BWCAW)

By definition, a wilderness area has no roads. While this is true of the BWCAW, it is crisscrossed by water routes, which allow thousands of people to visit the most popular wilderness area in the country. Although the BWCAW is mainly used by canoeists, several superb trails also exist in the area, some of which lead to isolated lakes accessible only by foot.

Because of the BWCAW's popularity, the Forest Service has developed a registration system to keep it from being overused and abused. All users need to obtain a permit. For day hikes, this is simply a self registration, which can often be done at the trailhead. For overnight camping during the peak season, a permit is required from a ranger. Advance registrations can also be made, although a fee is charged.

The rules for hiking in the wilderness begin with the basic motto "no-trace hiking." Another way to say it, is "leave the place as wild as you found it." A few more rules apply specifically to a wilderness area to help keep it as pristine as possible:

- Use no cans or bottles.
- Don't cut live trees or brush for fires.
- Pack out food containers (only reusable allowed).
- Camp either at designated campsites or at least 150 feet from the trail or lake shore.
- Limit group size to nine people or fewer.
- Write or call the Forest Service for a complete set of rules and regulations.

LONG-DISTANCE HIKES

Even though the majority of hikes described in this guide are short enough to cover in a day or a weekend, several long-distance trails in the state can make for multi-day extended hikes. Currently, four major point-to-point trails are in the state; three of them link to form a nearly compete loop of the Minnesota Arrowhead Region. This book covers sections of these hikes, just to give a flavor of some of their attractions.

Superior Hiking Trail: 200 miles—Follows the North Shore of Lake Superior from Two Harbors up to Canada at the tip of the Arrowhead. Hikes 3, 4, 5, 6, 8, 9, 10, 13, and 14 all cover short sections of this trail. *Backpacker Magazine* voted Superior one of the country's best long-distance hikes. It runs atop the Superior Highlands for most of its distance, jumping from state park to state park, all the while offering magnificent views of Lake Superior, cascading rivers, and surrounding forests. To allow you to hike either sections or the whole length of the trail with just one car, the Superior Hiking Trail Shuttle offers bus service along Minnesota Highway 61. With the help of the bus, you can hike stretches of any length on any portion. A published schedule lists pick-up and drop-off spots and times. The hiking guide written by the Superior Hiking Association has more information on the full length of the trail; proceeds from sale of the book go to trail upkeep.

Border Route Trail: 75 Miles—Gunflint Trail to Pigeon River. Also located at the tip of the Arrowhead, this trail leads to Grand Portage National Monument. Hikes 18 and 19 in this book give a flavor of the trail, which begins at Loon Lake on the Gunflint Trail and ends at Little John Lake. Additional access points along the way are at South Lake Trail and the Caribou Rock Trail. Most of the Border Route Trail is in the BWCAW as it parallels the voyageur's water routes and follows the border between the United States and Canada. The trail leads to sweeping overlooks and bare bedrock ridges in the boreal forest. Minnesota Rovers Outing Club offers a trail guide and a map, which cover the trail from end to end; proceeds go to trail maintenance.

Kekekabic Trail: (pronounced Kek-a-kabic or 'Kek' for short) 38 miles—Fernberg Trail to Gunflint Trail. A 1930s fire fighting road is the trail's main path through a rugged remote section of the BWCAW. The Kekekabic Club helps with its upkeep; however, the trail is still a minimum-maintenance trail requiring good navigation skills. The trail ends on the eastern side of the lake at the Gunflint Trail, which happens to be right across the road from the start of the Border Route Trail. Hike 23 covers the easy section as it goes along the south side of Snowbank Lake.

North Country Trail: 68 miles—From near Walker to near Remer. Three hikes in this book cover sections of the North Country Trail. Hike 36 and Hike 37 do short, rolling sections in the Chippewa National Forest, and there is also a section that runs through Itasca State Park. Today, just a small section exists of a planned elaborate trail that will cross the United States and more than 3,000 miles. Minnesota's longest section is in the Chippewa

National Forest, where the trail threads its way between a cluster of lakes and through a mixed evergreen forest. In the future, this trail will enter the state, bridging the Saint Croix from Wisconsin, veer north, and hook up with the above three trails for what will be an exhaustive loop. After this, the trail will run alongside the Mesabi Trail (a planned crushed-limestone bike path), to Chippewa National Forest, Itasca State Park, and on west into the prairie and North Dakota.

NAVIGATION AND GLOBAL POSITIONING SYSTEM (GPS)

The basic tools for navigating on a hike are a map and compass. For all the hikes in this book these are the only tools you need to bring along to follow the path. Since most of the trails are well maintained, especially the ones in the state parks, even the use of navigation tools is often limited to the intersections. However, wilderness trails can be confusing, especially on longer hikes, which wind their way through thickets or dense forests with few landmarks. It is on these latter trails that a GPS receiver can come in handy, to help you determine your course and your exact location, whether along a lake shore or deep in the woods.

GPS receivers act like radios. They pick up faint signals that originate, not from radio land-based transmitters, but from twenty-four solar-powered satellites. These satellites, 10,900 miles away in space, send out a code that the receiver uses to find its position, time, and velocity. A GPS receiver makes its calculations based on simple trigonometry after it obtains at least three satellite signals. There are minor errors built into the machine, one caused by the government and the other by the atmosphere. The government introduced an error of position, mainly because it wants to keep critical accuracy out of non-military hands. This induced error is called Selective Availability or S/A, and it randomly places the real position off by up to 200 feet. When the atmospheric error is included, the error increases up to 300 feet, still a close enough mark for hiking and general use.

Maps are still needed to make sense of the GPS reading. Any map can be used that has a labeled coordinate system on the sides or corner. These coordinates are most often in latitude and longitude—even the state's official highway map has them on its 1:1,000,000 scale projection or Delorme's Minnesota State Gazetteer at a 1:190,000 scale. However, the maps most commonly used with a GPS are the USGS topographic maps at a 1:24,000 scale. You should use these on the hikes themselves. The larger scale statewide maps don't help much on hikes; but they can help get you to the trailhead.

Since there is always an S/A error in the GPS positions, locating your position on a map results in only an estimated position. The average 300-foot error translates to plus or minus four seconds, or put another way, a circle about the size of a pencil's eraser on a 1:24,000 scale map. Unless you are looking for buried treasure, this is more than accurate enough. Some receivers, like the Trimble Scoutmaster, give positions in inches, allowing

GPS, compass, and pedometer.

you to use a ruler to find your position on a map. Most receivers can also use the UTM grid system (the blue tic marks on the edges of USGS topographic maps). Since the UTM grid is uniform across the map, this is also a good way to locate your position.

In general, the units work best with a clear sky, though multi-channel receivers work fine in deeper woods. The biggest reception problem comes in dense forest with a wet canopy, which can cause the satellite signal to be reflected by water on the leaves. In these conditions, finding a location might be impossible. Don't rely on one navigation system. Also, as with any electronic device, the batteries might go dead or the unit could break. So you should still take a compass and use it to point the way, while letting a GPS tell you exactly where you are at any given moment. Other navigation devices, such as a pedometer, which measures the distance you cover hiking, can also help.

North Shore Highlands

1 Jay Cooke State Park

General description:	A short trail through a large park that follows the Saint Louis River from the rocky gorge to the high, red, clay banks.
General location:	West of Duluth.
Length:	About 4 miles, round-trip; there are about 50 miles of listed trails in the park.
Difficulty:	Easy to moderate—rocky trail along the river.
Elevation differential:	About 180 feet.
Special attractions:	The Saint Louis River Gorge, the swinging bridge, and overlooks of the river valley; also backcountry camping.
Maps:	State park trail map; USGS quads: Esko and Cloquet.
Camping:	80 drive-in, 3 walk-in, and 4 hike-in sites.
For more information:	Department of Natural Resources Information Center; see Appendix B.
GPS:	46 39.368 N 92 22.224W.

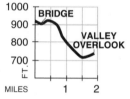

Finding the trailhead: The park is about 10 miles west of Duluth and 5 miles southeast of Cloquet. From Interstate 35 take Minnesota Highway 210 east, which passes through Carlton and Thomson, and then goes to the middle of the park. Or from Duluth, take MN 210, a winding road from this direction. Park signs lead the way. The trailhead is accessible from the paved Willard Munger Bike Trail, which passes along the north edge of the park.

The hike: For most visitors, the Saint Louis River Gorge is Jay Cooke State Park's main draw, though it was not always as appreciated as it is today. As the western terminus of the Great Lakes trade route, it was an impediment for early explorers and voyageurs who were forced to portage around the rapids, going up steep slopes and over sharp rocks. From here they were able to access the wild interior and link the east coast with the Gulf of Mexico—by way of the Mississippi River and one more portage. Now, fortunately, visitors do not have to carry hundreds of pounds of supplies and a canoe, that is, if you do not want to, to enjoy the park's rugged scenery.

The park's trail center is at the picnic grounds, right behind the huge stone building built by a 1930s government work project. Trails lead off across the road connecting to the Munger Trail and also behind the building

Jay Cooke State Park

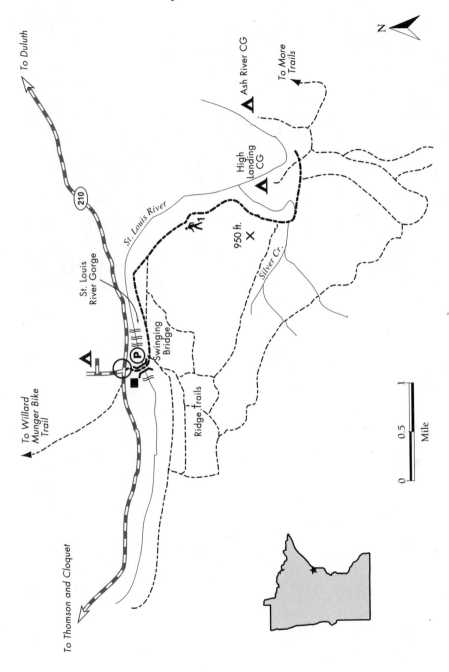

N

To Duluth

Ash River CG

To More Trails

210

High Landing CG

St. Louis River

950 ft. ✕

Silver Cr.

St. Louis River Gorge

Swinging Bridge

P

To Willard Munger Bike Trail

Ridge Trails

To Thomson and Cloquet

0   0.5   1
Mile

St. Louis River Gorge, looking upstream from the swinging bridge.

to the main portion of the park. MN 210 intersects the park, where the majority of the park's land and trails lies south of the road, alongside the river. On the northern side, across the road, a smaller trail system hooks up with the Munger Trail—a bike trail, which leads down into Duluth. On the southern side by the big works building, there is a short path that leads to the park's main attraction. This spot makes a good place to relax and explore. In the early morning, the gorge fills up with mist coming off the water for an especially striking scene. Sharply slanted rocks, called Thomson slates, divert the water in this intensive, long stretch of frothy rapids. The slates were formed about 2 billion years ago, and in places they reveal ripple marks left by an ancient ocean, still frozen in time.

Across the bridge, you will find a large network of trails leading into every corner of the park, with miles of hiking through open fields, deep woods, and marshes. For a short overview of the park try the riverside trail that leads a couple of miles downriver to a valley overlook. The trail starts on the other side of the bridge with a quick left that goes up a few steps and then heads downstream. Stay to the left for the hiking path and the rockiest section of the trail along the rapids, which continue for about 0.5 miles downstream (a cross-country skiing bypass also veers off to the right for an easier and less scenic path around the rapids).

Beyond the rapids, the next section continues to parallel the river, now away from the bank, as the river winds to the south. The path then reaches a small tributary named Silver Creek. You follow this creek up to an intersection with the aptly named Silver Creek Trail where you head south over a footbridge. After another intersection with some cross-country ski loops, which go up into the hills, you come to a trail shelter. Behind the shelter is the destination of this hike: an overlook of the Saint Louis River valley. This vista, which sits on a 60-foot bluff on the bend in the river, looks toward the northeast to a high, narrow valley. The bluffs rise steeper and higher, looking farther down the valley, where the sides rise nearly 200 feet. Here the soft and muddy red clay valley is completely opposite in character from the hard slates rapids at the swinging bridge. While valley composition is less rugged, it also originated fairly recently from Lake Superior bottom sediments, which were laid down by glaciers around ten thousand years ago.

For the return trip, either go back the same way for another view of the rapids or return to the Silver Creek intersection and take a left for the Silver Creek Trail (this route can get a bit wet). If you're ready for more hiking, there still are miles of trails left in the eastern part of the park and connections to the Willard Munger Bike Trail.

2 Park Point

General description:	Long sandy beach walk along a sandspit that juts miles out into Lake Superior.
General location:	Duluth; at the end of Minnesota Point.
Length:	4 miles, round-trip.
Difficulty:	Easy, hiking on a sandy beach.
Elevation:	Nominal.
Special attractions:	Sand, wind, and waves of Lake Superior, beach combing, and barge traffic.
Maps:	USGS quads: Superior, Wisconsin, and Minnesota
For more information:	Duluth Convention and Visitors Bureau; see Appendix B.
GPS:	46 43.782N 92 02.998W.

Finding the trailhead: From the waterfront in downtown Duluth, take Lake Avenue to the Aerial Bridge and cross to Minnesota Point. Continue about 4 miles until you reach the park and beach facilities near the road's end, right before the airport.

The hike: The whole of Minnesota Point (and of Wisconsin Point on the south shore) is a sandspit that forms Duluth and Superior harbors. These sandspits, stretching for 6.5 miles on the Minnesota side and 2.5 miles on the Wisconsin side, are the largest occurring freshwater spits in the world. The wave action of Lake Superior pounded them into shape, and river runoff from the Saint Louis River added sand for their makeup. A peninsula for most of its existence, Minnesota Point was transformed into an island in 1870. It seems Minnesotans wanted closer access to the open water and dug

Park Point

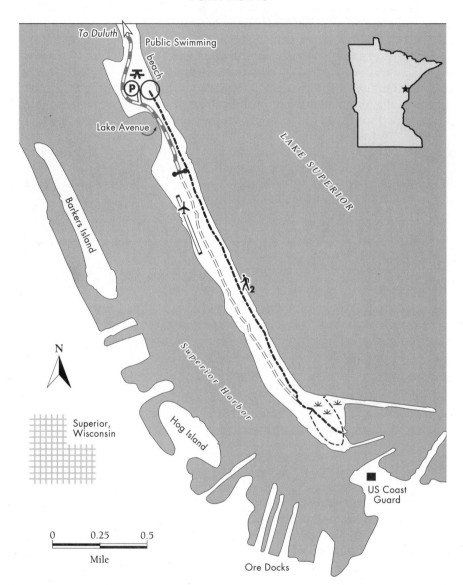

To Duluth

Public Swimming

beach

P

Lake Avenue

LAKE SUPERIOR

Barkers Island

N

Superior, Wisconsin

Superior Harbor

Hog Island

2

US Coast Guard

0   0.25   0.5

Mile

Ore Docks

Near the end of the point on the Lake Superior side, looking towards Duluth.

a channel through the point. This was opposed by Wisconsin, whose citizens got a court injunction to stop it, but by the time the injunction arrived from Washington the channel was already dug and boats were sailing through. Today, an aerial bridge crosses this 300-foot channel.

This beach, with miles of sand and shoreline to explore, is quite unlike any other in Minnesota. It could easily be on either coast of the United States—salt water is the only missing ingredient. Everything you could want in a beach is here, at least on a windy day, with the wind-induced waves crashing into the shore, sea gulls cackling above, and sand in your shoes. The beach itself, varying in width from about 10 to 20 feet, consists of a fine, light-colored sand, and is bordered by a pine forest which runs down the middle of the point. I visited the park in the fall when the crowds were nonexistent, but I have the feeling that the place fills up on hot summer days (a rare occurrence in Duluth).

Start hiking at either the beach headquarters or a bit farther up by the airport where there is a sign indicating the Park Point Nature Trail. On the beach, a right turn (southeast) takes you toward the end of the coast guard lighthouse jetty. From this side of the point (the Lake Superior side) you can look back, beyond a sweeping view down the shore, and see the city of Duluth.

The beach almost stretches to the first boulder jetty. To reach the channel separating the two points, head to the middle of the point and follow the doubletrack to its end. Poison ivy is common here, so remember, "leaves of three, let it be." The road runs the length of the park and functions as an interpretive trail with nine sign posts. A pamphlet is available from the visitors bureau. Alongside the road are the remains of old military buildings—the shell of an old lighthouse and a warehouse for the Army Corps of Engineers. Continuing down the trail, you will go through a virgin pine forest and pass by one, and only one, private cabin, located on the point, right before the pump houses. The beach's southern side looks over to Superior, Wisconsin, with its huge ore docks.

In the middle of the spit there are sand dunes, sparsely covered with wildflowers in the fall, that tower over 7 feet. At the end of the point, long cement jetties line the Superior Harbor Channel. The channel separates the two sandspits and is the best spot to watch the unbelievably long ore ships as they come into port. Looking to the Wisconsin side you can see a lighthouse and the coast guard station.

3 Gooseberry Falls State Park

General description: A beautiful hike from the agate beach at the mouth of Gooseberry River, along its shores, and to the popular waterfalls.

General location: Northeast of Two Harbors.

length: About 5 miles, round-trip. The trail network contains about 18 miles of trails.

Difficulty: Easy around the beach and the falls, moderate on the sometimes rugged path up to Fifth Falls.

Elevation differential: A rolling trail that climbs a total of 240 feet from the beach to fifth falls bridge. From the beach to the road it is a 90-foot climb.

Special attractions: The falls, the nature center, stunning views of Lake Superior, and an agate beach.

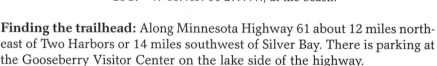

Maps: State park trail maps; USGS quad: Split Rock Point.

Camping: 70 drive-in sites.

For more information: DNR Information Center; see Appendix A.

GPS: 47 08.46N 91 27.44W, at the beach.

Finding the trailhead: Along Minnesota Highway 61 about 12 miles northeast of Two Harbors or 14 miles southwest of Silver Bay. There is parking at the Gooseberry Visitor Center on the lake side of the highway.

The hike: Gooseberry Falls is one of the most popular attractions along the North Shore. Almost everyone traveling along Minnesota Highway 61 stops here to do a little exploring around the falls. This is a time-honored tradition, going all the way back to the 1670s when the falls first appeared on the

Gooseberry Falls State Park

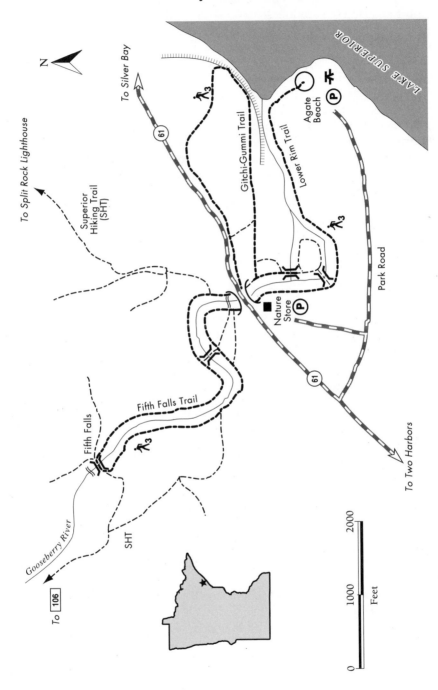

maps of French explorers. The explorers also gave the river its name. It was not named after the gooseberry bush, at least not directly, but after the explorer Seuir de Grosseilliers. Most of the trails and buildings in the park were built by the Civilian Conservation Corps (CCC) after the logging era was over in the region. The park was officially formed in 1937.

Trails go to every nook and cranny in the park, starting from the beach at the lake front, to the cascades below the bridge, to the rough, rolling trail up the river, and onto the high bluff above the lake. The park is undergoing some construction—a new highway bridge is being built over the river and a larger nature center is in the works. The old center is reverting back to its first use as a historic CCC camp.

The hike combines three separate loops, providing a taste of the entire park. A good place to start is at the picnic grounds and beach—that is if you can hold off visiting the cascades for a little bit. Along the less crowded shoreline, you can explore the lava flows and agate beaches alongside the crashing waves of Lake Superior. The lava poured out of the earth some one billion years ago, covering the land with layers of volcanic material over time. These flows, said to be similar to the lava flows of present-day Iceland, look like hard black tongues jutting into the water. Next to the flows are a couple of small pebble beaches, where, if you have a sharp eye and some patience, you can find some agates, small multi-layered and multi-colored pebbles. Please do not keep the rocks; leave them for others to find and enjoy. (Agates, by the way, are formed when minerals seep into small gas cavities found within the flows.) If you can pull yourself away from beachcombing, follow the calm lower stretch of the Gooseberry River up to the falls, about 0.75 mile from the mouth of the river.

The Gooseberry River flow rate varies with the season—early spring provides the greatest rush of water, later in fall it is sometimes reduced to only a trickle. There are actually five sets of falls, with the largest three within easy reach of the bridge. At the bridge, lava-flow layers spread out to form a 200-foot-wide platform for the falls. Running over the flat platforms, the river splits apart and braids back together before plunging over the ledges. Needless to say, this is the park's most visited section. You will see people of all ages jumping around the puddling pools of water or peering over the falls themselves. Trails go along both sides of the river and also out onto the lava flows. There are several viewing places which allow a shot of the cascade from every conceivable angle, but be careful on the ledges, as they can be slippery.

On the other side of the river, crossing MN 61, is an optional loop of the Gitchi Gummi Trail. This 1-mile loop extends to the edge of a vertical cliff to give an eagle's eye viewpoint on the ocean-like expanse of Lake Superior. Exercise caution with this trail as it goes right along the cliff and no fences or guards warn of the edge and a vertical drop of about 100 feet. The Gitchi Gummi Trail comes out across the highway from the CCC camp and provides access to the start of the Fifth Falls Trail.

The path, as shown on the map, makes a loop around Gooseberry River up to Fifth Falls. Here the trail is rougher, rockier, and rootier as it shares a path with the Superior Hiking Trail. First you will find the Upper Falls, right above the high bridge and worth a look before traveling upstream. The trail closely hugs the river up to the first cross-over bridge at the 0.3 mile mark. Continue going upstream for nearly 0.6 mile to reach Fifth Falls and a foot bridge. If you're looking for more hiking, the Superior Hiking Trail veers off to the northwest, goes up a hill after the bridge, then continues up the river. Otherwise follow the riverside trail back to the highway.

4 Split Rock Lighthouse State Park

General description:	A lakeside hike from the lighthouse to the summit of a small hill overlooking the lake with views back to the lighthouse.
General location:	Northeast of Two Harbors.
length:	About 3 miles, round-trip. Total of 12 miles in the trail network and more on the SHT.
Difficulty:	Easy; well-groomed path with a moderate climb going up Day Hill.
Elevation differential:	240 feet from the beach level to the top of the hill.
Special attractions:	Split Rock Lighthouse, beach, and a fireplace on top of the hill.
Maps:	Split Rock State Park map; USGS quads: Split Rock Point and Split Rock Point NE.
Camping:	24 camping sites. All the sites are walk-in only, though the park supplies push carts to haul your camping gear to camp.
For more information:	DNR Information Center; see Appendix B.
GPS:	47 12.117N 91 22.182W.

Finding the trailhead: Along Minnesota Highway 61, about 6 miles past Gooseberry State Park, 19 miles past Two Harbors, and 8 miles before Silver Bay. Parking is available at either the State Park or at the lighthouse (a ticket is needed to visit the lighthouse). Superior Hiking Trail parking is also available along the northwest side of the road right by Split Rock River.

The hike: Hike 4 starts near the front entrance, with the trail leading downhill. A side loop, which has steps following an old tramway, leads to the former location of a boathouse on the water. On the main trail, you will pass the trail center for the state park and the cart-in campgrounds. A few paths

Split Rock Lighthouse State Park

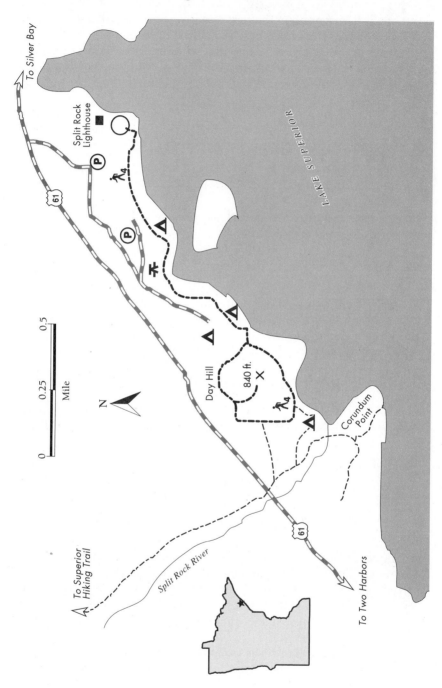

Split Rock Lighthouse.

lead to the beach for picture-postcard shots of the lighthouse. The park road ends and after 0.1 mile, you will come to the intersection with the Day Hill Trail which climbs to the top of Day Hill.

This quick, steep climb rises about 100 feet over a distance of 500 feet, and gives you one of the better views of Lake Superior. Look to the left (east) to take in the majestic lighthouse sitting on top of its scrapped, clean bedrock (diabase sill, actually). If the conditions are not too hazy, you can see the Apostle Islands, which lie off the coast of Wisconsin about 20 miles away to the southeast. The top of this big bald rock is a perfect spot to lounge about—there is even a sizeable fireplace (BYOW—bring your own wood) making this a fine site for a late night stargazing session. Heading back down the trail, either finish off the loop on the lake side of Day Hill or continue on and check out the trails farther on in the park. If you stay on the trail, you pass by Corundum point and a turn-of-the-century mine. Miners dynamited the rock here—anorthosite, a hard igneous rock—mistaking it for the very hard corundum, which is used as an abrasive in sandpaper.

If you have ever shopped for a postcard with a Minnesota theme, then in all likelihood you have already seen this lighthouse, which has been immortalized on a U.S. Postal Service stamp. When the structure was first built, it was an outpost in the wilderness accessible only by water. While today it is easy to get to, it has a rugged charm equaled by few other places in the state. Construction of the lighthouse was initiated after the especially stormy year of 1905—the year in which six ships sank off the coast. The lighthouse's kerosene lamp was first lit in 1910. The light was later converted to electric power, operating until 1969, when radar and other navigation techniques took over the job of warning boats of coastal dangers. The Minnesota Historical Society is now responsible for the upkeep of the grounds. This trail takes you along some picture-postcard spots for viewing the lighthouse.

The lighthouse building itself is not overwhelming or imposing, but the vertical gabbro cliff the house sits on makes for a commanding overlook— what a great spot for a warning beacon! Inside the cramped lighthouse you can examine the original huge glass lenses used to magnify the light, imported from France. Outside, at the edge of the precipice is a panorama of the lake, the nearby scalloped shoreline with points and bays that stretch to the horizon. Looking west (right) you see the final destination of this hike— the top of Day Hill. Also visible is Corundum Point, a rocky point reaching out into the bay just past the hill.

Note: Also accessible from the southwestern end of the park is the Superior Hiking Trail, which has a beautiful section following a loop up and around Split Rock Creek and Split Rock River. The Superior Hiking Trail itself starts across MN 61 at the parking lot by the road. This trail is a bit more rugged, but allows views of cascades, waterfalls, rock pillars, and an overlook of Lake Superior. The loop is about 4.5 miles long. Split Rock State Park and Gooseberry State Park, not too far apart, can be linked by following the Superior Hiking Trail.

5 Bean and Bear Lakes

General description:	A day hike to the bluffs and overlooks 300 feet above these 2 alpine-like lakes.
General location:	Just west of the city limits of Silver Bay.
Length:	A 6.4-mile round trip for the big loop.
Difficulty:	Moderate. Caution; steep, high cliffs.
Elevation gain:	About 400 feet from start to the overlooks.
Special attractions:	Scenic vistas of the two lakes and camping along their shores.
Maps:	Superior Hiking Trail map; USGS quad: Silver Bay.
Camping:	3 hike-in sites.
For more information:	DNR Information Center; see Appendix B.
GPS:	47 17.463 N 91 17.826W.

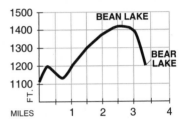

Finding the trailhead: From Minnesota Highway 61 and the turnoff for Silver Bay, take Outer Drive, which becomes Edison Boulevard. Continue for nearly 2 miles, then turn left onto Penn Boulevard (County Route 5). After 0.5 mile park off road in a large lot. A Superior Hiking Trail sign marks the trailhead.

The hike: This short section of the Superior Hiking Trail lies right outside the city of Silver Bay. Surprisingly, in spite of its proximity to town, this is a great little hike that leads to a pair of unexpectedly scenic lakes walled in by towering bluffs. For people hiking the full length of the Superior Hiking Trail, this is another one of the gems that makes the trail so special, but it can also be recommended in its own right as a day hike. The trail also has several campsites amenable for an overnight stay.

The main trail is well groomed, but offshoot trails, like Twin Lakes Trail, which drops down to Davis Drive, may be overgrown and muddy. The lakes themselves, actually within the boundaries of Tettegouche State Park, are also accessible from the park's main entrance using the Mount Trudee Trail.

For the first mile, the trail does not have much to offer. The encroachment of civilization—a number of dirt bike trails and access roads crossing the trail—can dampen your enthusiasm at first. However, a couple of glimpses of Lake Superior and Silver Bay through this mixed-hardwood section of the hike make it more interesting. At 1.8 miles the path intersects with the Twin Lakes Trail. Going to your left toward the lakes, head down the hill and you

Bean and Bear Lakes

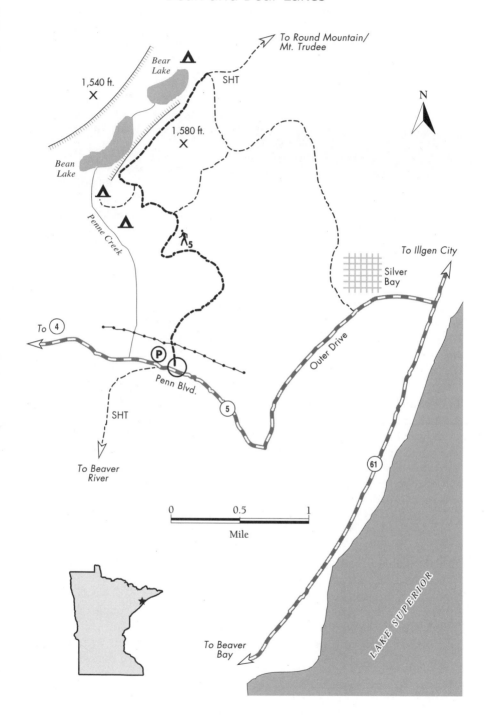

To Round Mountain/
Mt. Trudee

Bear
Lake

1,540 ft.
X

SHT

1,580 ft.
X

Bean
Lake

Penne Creek

5

To 4

P

Penn Blvd.

5

SHT

To Beaver
River

To Illgen City

Silver
Bay

Outer Drive

61

N

0   0.5   1
Mile

LAKE SUPERIOR

To Beaver
Bay

The Bear Lake overlook.

will shortly come to a campsite spur leading toward Penn Creek (a recent campsite addition) and then the spur for the Bean Lake campsite. The main path turns a corner and comes to a bean-shaped lake (appropriately named Bean Lake). The view is stunning. About 300 feet below the rock ledge, the tranquil lake sits snuggled between two high forested ridges. At this overlook, if the weather is cooperating, you might also get a peek of Round Mountain and the anorthosite dome of Mount Trudee, covered in pines, about 4 miles away to the east.

At 3.4 miles you come to Bear Lake, where I liked the view almost better than the view of Bean Lake, even though it is not as high off the water. The path follows the jutting ledge around a spot where the panorama includes not only the lake but also the cliff face. With the sheer cliffs in the scene, you get a new perspective of the cliffs' height and steepness and the drop down to the water. The place has an almost mountainous feel, a feeling that is increased if you go down by the lake where the ridges of the V-shaped valley reflect off the water. At the eastern end of the lake, the trail drops down to the rustic Bear Lake campsite. Both of the lakes are said to be remnants of glacial rivers that tore through this area and carved out the valley. Return to the Superior Hiking Trail to continue on toward Mount Trudee.

To head back, either retrace your steps or try the Twin Lakes Trail, which starts about 0.2 mile past the spur going to the Bear Lake campsite. When I hiked it, this trail was cluttered with windblown trees, making it hard to follow, at least compared to the well-maintained section leading to the lakes.

Still this loop carries you off the beaten trail. It connects about 1.5 miles down the Silver Bay access spur.

Note: After Bear Lake, the Superior Hiking Trail leads to overlooks on Mount Trudee of Palisade valley and the rest of Tettegouche State Park. This would make a fine continuation of the hike; see the next hike for possibilities within Tettegouche State Park.

6 Tettegouche State Park

General description:	A rugged full day of hiking among the alpine-like lakes and their surrounding hills, with overlooks of the park lakes and Lake Superior.
General location:	Just northeast of Silver Bay.
Length:	About 9 miles; 23-mile trail network in the park.
Difficulty:	Difficult. A long, rugged trail for the full loop. Easy trails lead to the High Falls and Shovel Point.
Elevation gain:	About 1,000 feet From Lake Superior up to the top of Mount Baldy.
Special attractions:	More than a dozen overlooks of Lake Superior and interior lakes, Shovel Point, which has at least half a dozen overlooks itself, and Baptism High Falls.
Maps:	State park trail map; USGS quads: Silver Bay and Illgen City.
Camping:	28 drive-in and 6 walk-in sites
For more information:	DNR Information Center; see Appendix B.
GPS:	47 20.159N 91 12.384W.

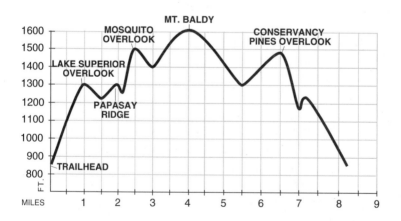

Finding the trailhead: Along Minnesota Highway 61, about 4.5 miles northeast of Silver Bay. The park is alongside Baptism River and Shovel Point. Follow state park signs. Park near the campground.

Tettegouche State Park

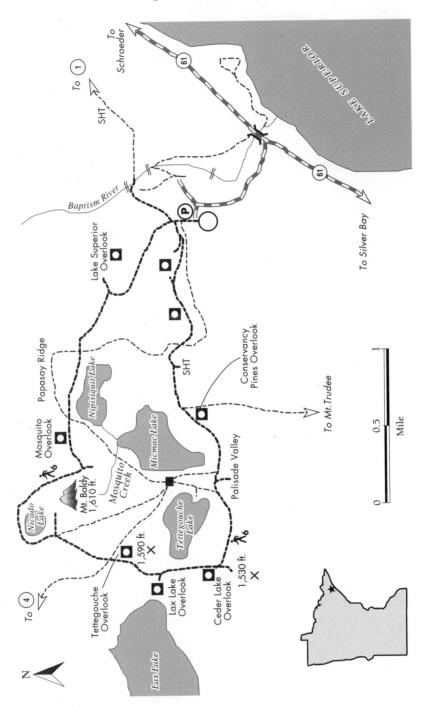

LAKE SUPERIOR

To Schroeder

To 1

61

SHT

61

To Silver Bay

Baptism River

P

Lake Superior Overlook

SHT

Conservancy Pines Overlook

To Mt. Trudee

Papasay Ridge

Nipisiquit Lake

Mosquito Overlook

Micmac Lake

Palisade Valley

Mt. Baldy 1,610 ft.

Mosquito Creek

Nicado Lake

Tettegouche Lake

1,590 ft. X

To 4

Tettegouche Overlook

Lax Lake Overlook

Ceder Lake Overlook

1,530 ft. X

Lax Lake

N

0   0.5   1
Mile

33

Mosquito Creek and Micmac Lake.

The hike: Tettegouche State Park presents a little of everything the North Shore has to offer. The park has miles of rugged trails, high waterfalls, and stunning cliffs along the lake front. In the late nineteenth century the park was the center of a logging operation that had its main base along the shores of Micmac Lake. This operation lasted only a few decades, until the tall pines were cut down. Next, a Duluth business club bought the land for a retreat—exactly the kind one imagines executives have far off in the woods— and named the place *Tettegouche*. The name comes from an old French-Canadian phrase meaning "meeting place." Today, the park offers a remote retreat, open to the public.

Trails in the park lead to remote spots that are alongside lakes (where the fishing is said to be good) and up to high overlooks that scan the interior lakes or Lake Superior off in the distance. Fortunately, not all of the land was logged; you can still find prime examples of natural forests: northern hardwood forest in between the lakes, cedar groves in the lowlands, red oaks on the hills and ridges, and, at least in one spot called Conservancy Pines, some tall, stately red pines.

Four main paths traverse the park: The High Falls Trail, Shovel Point, Superior Hiking Trail to Mount Trudee (which continues on to Bean and Bear lakes), and a big loop that rounds the park's circumference. The last loop, described here, is a good way to bag all of the park's peaks and over-looks. Off the loop are the side trails going to the High Falls and to Mount Trudee, which can serve as side trips or hikes in themselves.

The main trailhead is behind the parking lot, located just past the camp-grounds. Once on the trails, lettered posts mark the intersections; for the hiking loop the letters go roughly in alphabetical order. Alongside the big park trail map at the trailhead, the hike starts off heading north into a birch-aspen forest and continues straight past the first intersection. The intersection with the Superior Hiking Trail, at a post marked B, pops up at about 0.2 mile, where you can take a right for a short, worthwhile detour leading to Baptism High Falls. The falls drop 70 feet, which makes it the highest waterfall in the state; Pigeon Falls is higher, but it is shared with Canada.

After this side trip, backtrack to intersection B and head north to the Lake Superior overlook and the rest of the big loop. Some parts of the trail's lower sections can be muddy. The first overlook of Lake Superior is a view from a small ridge about 500 feet above the lake. Back on the main trail, continue past the overgrown snowmobile trail to the five-way intersection near the shore of Nipisiquit Lake, 1.8 miles from the start. With a picnic table along the mountain-like lake, this would make a relaxing spot for a break and maybe some fishing—walleye and northern pike are found in the waters here. A narrow hiking trail leads up the hill to Papasay Ridge, while a poison-ivy infested cross-country skiing bypass veers off to the right. On the ridge, an overlook takes in the dense canopy of the Finland State Forest.

Stay to the right at intersection E where our route goes straight west up a hill toward the Mosquito Creek overlook, and farther on to Mount Baldy. Intersection F leads to Mount Baldy, which, at 1,610 feet, is the highest point on the trail. The top of this hill has a clearing on bedrock and plenty of room to stretch out and take in the view. After the peak, drop back down onto the wide cross-country skiing trail to a three-way intersection. A left goes to the camp at Micmac Lake and a right (southwest) leads to a series of overlooks above Tettegouche Lake, Lax Lake, and Cedar Lake. Traveling to these overlooks, the trail turns back into a footpath at the next intersection J. Lax Lake borders the park so some private cabins are visible along its shores. A few unmarked side trails also lead down to this lake.

At the southern part of Tettegouche Lake, follow post K to I where between the two posts a spur goes to a scenic Palisade Valley overlook, with views of Mount Trudee. Another spur worth taking—it seems they are all worth it—is to Conservancy Pines, located on a small ridge where towering red pines shade the ledge. Only 0.2 mile after the pines, the Superior Hiking Trail enters the trail system coming from Mount Trudee. For those ambitious enough, a 0.75-mile detour to Mount Trudee leads to another Palisades Valley overlook.

Next up is a perch called the Raven Rock overlook. Having finished off the alphabet, you are now near the beginning, at intersection C. Here one trail goes north back up to Nipisiquit Lake and the other two lead east back to the trailhead. The path shown is the Superior Hiking Trail, the more scenic and definitely the more rugged. Taking this trail you go down the "Drainpipe," which follows rock steps down a narrow crack in the rocks, dropping 150 feet. Then pass an overlook on a ledge with two rocks almost touching (an unofficial name is the Romeo and Juliet overlook). A final overlook, sitting on a wide, open ridge, occurs near the end of the loop; the panorama takes in Lake Superior and all its jutting points.

7 George H. Crosby–Manitou State Park

General description:	A rugged state park, leading hikers and backpackers to remote trails alongside Manitou River.
General location:	Northeast of Finland.
Length:	2-mile loop. 24-mile network in the park.
Difficulty:	Difficult. A smoother path upon the humpbacks; a rugged trail alongside the river.
Elevation gain:	About 150 feet from the top of the knolls to the first river overlooks. Drops about 900 feet on the path to Lake Superior.
Special attractions:	The cascades of Manitou River, northern hardwood old-growth forest.
Maps:	State park trail map; USGS quad: Little Marais.
Camping:	21 hike-in sites.
For more information:	DNR Information Center; see Appendix B.
GPS:	47 28.715N 91 06.688W.

Finding the trailhead: This park borders Minnesota Highway 61, but access is limited to the park's western side from County Road 7. To get there, take Minnesota Highway 1 from Illgen City to Finland, where you turn east at the intersection with CR 7. The park road is about 8 miles from the intersection.

The hike: Crosby-Manitou is one of the most remote and rugged state parks along the North Shore. The park first came into existence when George Crosby, a mining entrepreneur, donated the land with the stipulation that it remain a truly wild place, offering only backpack camping within its boundaries. Following his wishes, today there are twenty-one campsites, most of which are along the rugged river, though several are on the more accessible shores of Benson Lake. The trails leading to the river sites are the most traveled, the most rugged, and the most scenic. The easiest trail is the short loop around Benson Lake where you can also find a picnic table.

The major focal point of the park is the Manitou River. The *Manitou*, which means "spirit" in Ojibwa, runs for 18 miles, drains eleven small lakes, and covers 10 square miles of swamps containing alder, cedar, and tamarack. The river's lower 7 miles have 8 major waterfalls of which the last spills right into Lake Superior. Unfortunately, this last one can be seen only by paddling in a kayak, as the land is on private property. A spring feeds the river, providing a consistent water flow and making it one of the finest trout fishing rivers on the North Shore. The rest of the park offers a chance for some wildlife viewing—especially from the granite outcrops rising up from the forest.

The short hike follows the Humpback Trail, taking in the granite hump-

George H. Crosby–Manitou State Park

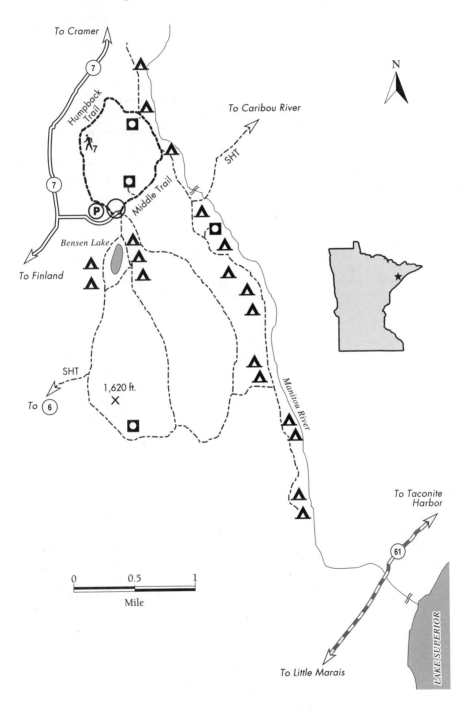

backs and the rapids. At the parking lot, trails from all sides head for the trail access on the western side of the parking lot (see map). The clockwise loop trail, visits a number of humpbacks, which are shorter versions of the bare domes at Tettegouche. Hiking for the first mile is fairly easy, passing through the forest with a few minor views of the surrounding landscape. On the northeast part of the loop the trail hooks up with the Manitou River for the 0.5-mile River Trail along the rocky bank. The first overlook, near campsite 2, gives some of the best views of the turbulent cascades. These rapids were formed by a glacial river cutting through the layers of Keweenawan lava flows. Today, the river is fed by a copious spring, making for an always-energetic flow. Near campsite 3, the trail loops back following the Superior Hiking Trail (SHT) toward the parking lot, 0.5 mile away. Another fine hike would be to follow the SHT across the river to Caribou River gorge.

8 Temperance State Park and Carlton Peak

General description:	From the shores of Lake Superior, along the narrow tumultuous river gorge, and up to Carlton Peak for a magnificent overlook of Lake Superior and the forests.
General location:	Just southwest of Tofte.
Length:	6 miles, round-trip. 22-mile trail network in the park.
Difficulty:	Moderate. A short difficult section at the base of Carlton Peak. Caution—steep bluffs along the river.
Elevation differential:	924 feet.
Special attractions:	Temperance River gorge and overlooks of Lake Superior.
Maps:	Superior Hiking Trail map, state park trail map for the Temperance River section. USGS quads: Schroeder and Tofte.
Camping:	55 drive-in and 3 cart-in sites at the state park.
For more information:	DNR Information Center; see Appendix B.
GPS:	47 33.270 N 90 52.480W.

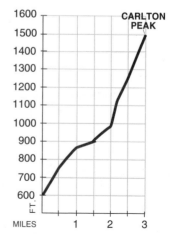

Temperance State Park and Carlton Peak

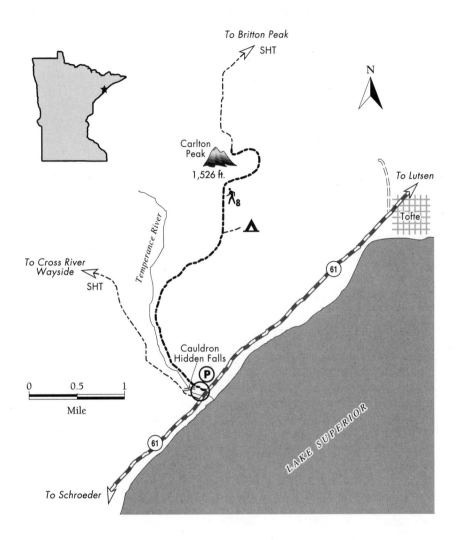

Finding the trailhead: About 2 miles southwest of Tofte, on Minnesota Highway 61. Parking is at Temperance River State Park, near the Cauldron Trail sign. The park is just past Cross River Wayside.

The hike: Native Americans in the area descriptively named the river here *Kawimbush*, "deep-hollow," for the gorge that cuts through the basaltic rocks. Its current name, Temperance River, was bestowed later, when the voyageurs—probably jokingly—referred to the fact that the river lacked a bar (a sand bar) at the mouth of the river.

Carlton Peak, one of the most prominent peaks along the shore, was named after Reuben Carlton who took part in an early geologic survey of the area. The peak is actually made up of a large inclusion, or block, that arose from deep within the Earth's crust. This rock, anorthosite, is composed of the mineral Labradorite, which is light green when freshly broken and then turns a whitish color. The quarry on the south side of the mountain has supplied rocks for water fountains, a breakwater in Taconite Harbor, and the ranger station in Grand Marais. This hike begins with a tour along the river gorge, then veers off, leaving the river to climb the peak.

The trail starts off at the "Cauldron Trail" sign along Highway 61. This leads right up the river's cascade, but first take a quick side trip to the lakeshore to see for yourself whether or not the river really lacks a bar. The trail leads down to a footbridge over the canyon-like gorge and on down to the picnic grounds. Retrace your steps, heading back up the trail and cross over the road to see the river's cauldron.

This section, an interpretive trail, closely follows the cascade. Exercise caution along the steep and slippery edge. Posted signs along the trail explain the geologic details of the river gorge, and how it was formed by rock types of differing strengths. The sight is amazing, with or without an explanation.

The river has cut a tunnel through the rock, leaving the back-up water barely enough room to rush through a crevice. This action creates a chute called Hidden Falls. Behind these falls lies the twirling maelstrom called the cauldron, which is a huge, swirling whirlpool. It is no wonder that kayakers stay off the river, for this tempest could probably swallow a Volkswagen whole and not leave a trace. After this treat for the eyes and ears, the trail takes off to the right on a much more gentle cross-country ski path at the 1.25-mile mark.

Entering a mixed birch forest at 2.5 miles, a short side trail leads to an overlook of the lake and river valley. Near the 3-mile mark you come to the massive 100-foot rock wall of the summit. The trail circles around the wall to your right, where it climbs through the boulders to reach the peak's lake-facing side. This is said to be a popular rock climbing area; you may have to do some scrambling to get around the boulders. Right before the summit, the Superior Hiking Trail continues on to Britton Peak, while the trail for Carlton Peak makes a sharp left to climb to the summit. On top, a sparse covering of scraggly trees finds a foothold on the sloping bedrock.

A few cement foundations are all that remain of a fire tower, which closed up shop in the 1950s. The view is superior. No obstructions block the panorama across the lake, over to a secondary peak (1,410 feet) and off to Britton Peak to the northeast.

Note: Trails from Temperance State Park also lead into the neighboring Cross River Wayside. After Carlton Peak, the Superior Hiking Trail continues on to Britton Peak and then Leveaux Mountain.

9 Oberg Mountain and Leveaux Mountain

General description:	Two short scenic hikes with views of surrounding hills and Lake Superior.
General location:	Between Tofte and Lutsen.
Length:	2.25-mile loop to Oberg; 3.4-mile loop to Leveaux.
Difficulty:	Easy to moderate. Short steep climb up the loop for Oberg and more gradual climb for Leveaux.
Elevation gain:	Oberg: 315 feet. Leveaux: 310 feet. 1,000 feet above Lake Superior.
Special attractions:	Overlooks galore and a picnic table atop Oberg.
Maps:	Superior Hiking Trail map. USGS quads: Honeymoon Mountain and Tofte.
Camping:	1 hike-in site off the Leveaux trail.
For more information:	Tofte Ranger District, Superior National Forest; see Appendix B.
GPS:	47 37.714N 90 47.176W.

Finding the trailhead: From Minnesota Highway 61, travel 2.5 miles northeast of Tofte to Forest Road 336. Continue for 2 miles on the dirt FR 336 up the steep hill to the large parking lot situated between the peaks. Oberg Trail starts to the east (right) and Leveaux Trail starts to the West (left).

The hike: While these two hikes share a common starting point, they each have their own unique pleasures. The shorter Oberg loop, the more popular of the two, seems to have overlooks at every couple of steps, as the trail circles the peak. The longer Leveaux trail has more solitude, wilderness, and what might be a muckier trail, as well as a couple of panoramic overlooks of its own. Both of these trails are in the Superior National Forest, which means no facilities, just no-frills hiking.

Starting with the Oberg Mountain loop, head back out of the parking lot toward Forest Road 336 and cross to the other side. A small gap in the woods, indicated by a sign, points to the trail's start. Another sign provides you with a short history of the trail and its construction in 1974–1975 by the Youth Conservation Corps. This first brief section of the Superior Hiking Trail branches off at the 0.2-mile mark to the northeast (left), while the loop continues on to the east (right). At about 0.4 mile up the grade you begin a series of switchbacks that take you to the 1.8-mile main loop.

The loop has eight overlook spots where the maples give way to spec-

Oberg Mountain and Leveaux Mountain

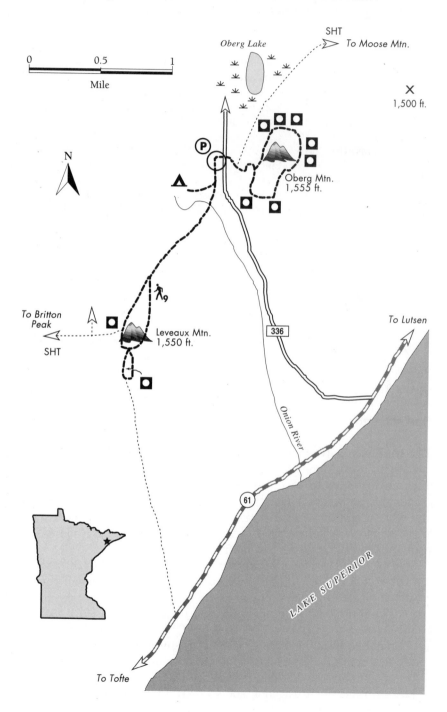

SHT
To Moose Mtn.

Oberg Lake

X
1,500 ft.

0   0.5   1
Mile

N

P

Oberg Mtn.
1,555 ft.

To Britton
Peak

SHT

Leveaux Mtn.
1,550 ft.

To Lutsen

336

Onion River

61

To Tofte

LAKE SUPERIOR

Overlook from Leveaux Mountain.

tacular views in every direction. The first and lowest overlook gives views of the big lake and Leveaux and Carlton peaks about 3 miles to the southwest. The three overlooks on the east side look off to Moose Mountain.

On this side, a rustic picnic table hewn out of huge logs makes a perfect destination for a lunch. The last three overlooks along the north part of the loop sit almost on top of Oberg Lake and the Superior Hiking Trail. Another 0.5 mile brings you back to the end of the loop and the trail down to the road.

The Leveaux Mountain Trail starts off at the western end of the parking lot, once again sharing trail with the Superior Hiking Trail. One campsite is just past the Onion River Bridge at 0.5 mile.

The trail begins on a level path; this changes slightly after the river starts climbing an easy grade. There are actually a couple of connected loops on Leveaux Mountain, each one basically covering a side of the hill. In another 0.5 mile you start on the first Leveaux loop, after a left turn and a climb of 100 feet. At the southern part of this trail, a short, connecting spur leads to the second loop. This loop has a few openings on the hillside that provide overlooks of Lake Superior and, off in the distance, Carlton Peak. A trail also goes straight down from this loop, hooking up with Highway 61 right in front of Chateau Leveaux. Finish off this 0.2-mile loop and head back to the first loop in the woods, then back to the Superior Hiking Trail for a return to the parking lot.

10 Cascade River State Park

General description:	A rugged loop around Cascade River visiting the namesake cascades, high overlooks, and riverside cedar forests.
General location:	Between Grand Marais and Lutsen.
Length:	7.7 mile, round-trip; 18-mile trail network in the park.
Difficulty:	Moderate to difficult. Long trail with a few steep sections.
Elevation gain:	Climbs almost 740 feet from Lake Superior to County Road 45. The actual cumulative climb ends up being much longer after dropping down into and climbing out of the valley a couple of times.
Special attractions:	Waterfall and cascades, overlooks above the river, and in the park 1.5 miles of easy hiking along Lake Superior.
Camping:	40 drive-in and 5 hike-in sites.
Maps:	State park trail map; USGS quad: Deer Yard Lake.
For more information:	DNR Information Center; see Appendix B.
GPS:	47 42.503 N 90 31.401.

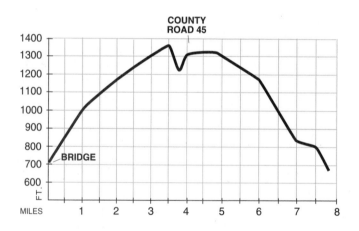

Finding the trailhead: The park is alongside Minnesota Highway 61 about 7 miles northeast of Lutsen or 9 miles southwest of Grand Marais. Also Superior Hiking Trail parking is available by the Cascade River bridge on County Road 45, off County Road 7.

The hike: Cascade River drains a watershed of 150 square miles over its 15-mile run to Lake Superior. During the last 3 miles of its journey, the river drops 900 feet; in the last 0.25 mile it drops 120 feet in a series of cascades through a twisting, turning gorge, cutting through ancient lava flows.

To explore this region, you can choose among a sizeable number of trails,

Cascade River State Park

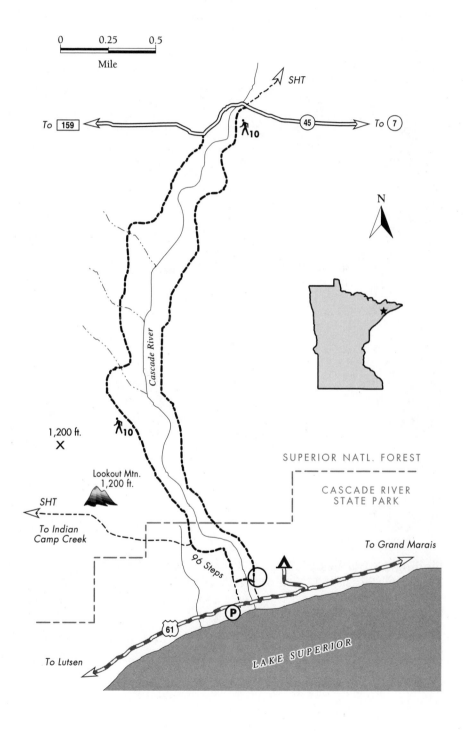

0   0.25   0.5
Mile

SHT

To 159

45

To 7

N

Cascade River

SUPERIOR NATL. FOREST

CASCADE RIVER
STATE PARK

1,200 ft.
X

Lookout Mtn.
1,200 ft.

SHT

To Indian
Camp Creek

96 Steps

To Grand Marais

P

61

To Lutsen

LAKE SUPERIOR

The cascades in Cascade River State Park.

many of them first built in the 1930s. Not all of them lead through the state park. This trail leaves the park's boundaries to follow a rolling riverside trail up to County Road 45, returning on the east side along the Superior Hiking Trail (SHT). Sections of the trail get steep and also cross numerous soggy areas on log bridges or boardwalks.

Locate the park's trailhead at the far end of the campground. Take the trail leading to the cascades, where a footbridge crosses the river right below the falls. This provides a good upriver view of the twisting rapids.

On the bridge's other side, follow the SHT to 96 steps—a staircase down to the river's edge. At the top of the stairs, the SHT turns left toward the unremarkable Lookout Mountain, and continues farther west. Instead of following the SHT, descend the steps to the river and follow it upstream. At the 1.4-mile mark, a short spur leads to a small waterfall at the end of a sheltered valley. The main trail crosses the creek above the falls as it veers away from the river banks.

The trail could best be described as gently rolling, as it crosses three creek valleys, following their contours, on its way north. Just before reaching CR 45 (at 4.1 miles) the trail veers back near the river's bank to give an elevated view of the Cascade River valley. This is an almost mountainous view that looks down on the bends in the rumbling river, with its rapids, and on the forested valley. Exercise caution, as there is about a 150-foot drop from the bluff, straight into the water. Continue up to the road and cross the vehicle bridge going east (right) to the other side of CR 45, to the parking area for the SHT, and the Cascade Trail south. The return trail follows the river downstream, looping back under the bridge.

Immediately after emerging from under the bridge, you get a bottom-up view of the rock face and your former vantage point on the high bank. Starting here, the trail enters private land for 1.5 miles, passing though a cool, moist cedar grove alongside the river— please respect the land and stay on the trail. Then the trail climbs the steep bank to follow the upper plateau above the river. It is smooth going to Bally Creek, after which you are near the end as indicated by numerous intersections with the main trail. From here keep the river to your right all the way back to the footbridge.

11 Eagle Mountain Trail

General description:	The highest point in Minnesota. This rugged trail passes a scenic lake and climbs to a summit where panoramic views take in the surrounding wilderness.
General location:	In the Superior National Forest northwest of Grand Marais.
Length:	About 6 miles, round-trip.
Difficulty:	Difficult. Rugged path, extremely rocky in sections.
Elevation gain:	554 feet.
Special attractions:	Spectacular views of surrounding lakes and forest.
Maps:	USGS topographic maps: 1:24,000 Eagle Mountain and Mark Lake and 1:100,000 Grand Marais for a overview; also Fischer Map number F-6.
Camping:	2 hike-in sites.
For more information:	Gunflint Ranger District, Superior National Forest; see Appendix B.
GPS:	47 51.68N 90 32.85W.

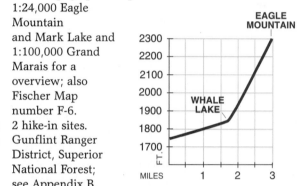

Finding the trailhead: Primary access is from Grand Marais, where Forest Service signs lead the way. Travel north on County Road 12 (the Gunflint Trail) for about 3.5 miles to County Road 8. Turn left and continue for a little less than 6 miles, to the intersection of County Road 57 and County Road 27 on the north side of Devil Track Lake. Take a right on CR 27 and follow it for 5 miles to Forest Road 153; turn left. Another 5 miles brings you to the trailhead's large parking lot, on the right side of the road across from Forest Road 158. The trail starts behind the trail sign. A secondary access route, rougher and more winding, starts from Lutsen. Take County Road 4 (Caribou Trail) north for about 17 miles to Forest Road 153. Travel east on FR 153, about 4 miles, to the parking area.

The hike: For more than seventy years, Minnesota's highest point was thought not to be Eagle Mountain, but a point a few miles north of here. In the 1890s, Newton Winchell, the state geologist, and Ulysses S. Grant II, the president's son, conducted the first survey in search of the high spot using a simple but effective ananoid barometer. Their nearly complete search led them to the edge of present day Lake Winchell, and then up the Misqauh Hills, which measure 2,230 feet. For some reason they didn't explore fur-

Eagle Mountain Trail

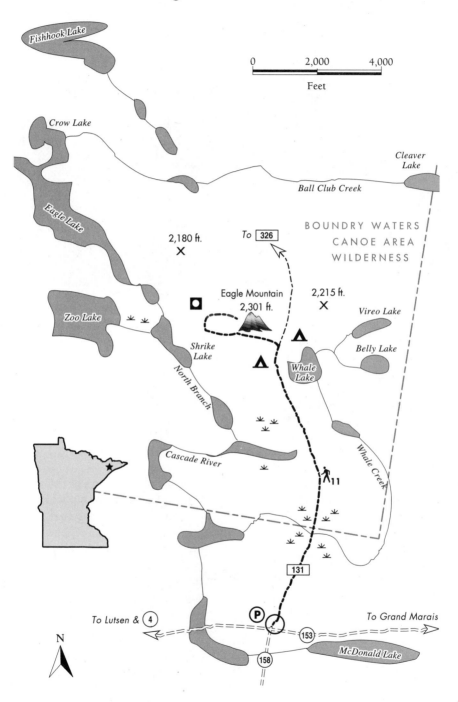

Fishhook Lake

Crow Lake

Cleaver Lake

Ball Club Creek

0   2,000   4,000
Feet

Eagle Lake

2,180 ft.
✗

To 326

BOUNDRY WATERS
CANOE AREA
WILDERNESS

Eagle Mountain
2,301 ft.

2,215 ft.
✗

Vireo Lake

Zoo Lake

Shrike Lake

Belly Lake

Whale Lake

North Branch

Cascade River

Whale Creek

11

131

To Lutsen & 4

P

To Grand Marais

153

158

McDonald Lake

N

A view of Whale Lake from the Eagle Mountain Trail.

ther, missing 2,301-foot Eagle Mountain only 6 miles to the south. Oddly enough, its height was only determined by aerial photography in the 1960s.

The hike goes into the Boundary Waters Canoe Area Wilderness (BWCAW), so a permit to camp can be obtained at a ranger station, or to day hike, a permit can be obtained at a self-registration stand at the trail head. The trail starts from the parking lot on a rolling rocky path through spruce, birch, and fir. It enters the BWCAW at the 1-mile mark. Getting to Whale Lake, the first destination, is the wettest part of the trail. It crosses three low-lying boggy areas, though boardwalks keep you from getting too wet. Arriving at the lake, right below Eagle Mountain and its sister peak, is one of the highlights of the hike. On a calm day, the mountain reflects quite nicely off the water to make a pristine scene. The whole panorama includes the steep-sided 2,220-foot sister peak that dominates the view off to the right (might be mistaken for the actual high point), and to the left, Eagle Mountain. From here, it is about 400 feet up to the top of the mountain.

One camp site, located along the southwest corner of the lake in a clearing, is on the site of a former logging camp. Along the shore the forest changes to birch, and the trail, with football-sized rocks paving the way, gets a bit more difficult. Just beyond the northwest end of the lake at the 2.5-mile mark, you come to the only trail intersection. A left starts the climb to the summit, following a gentle grade to the top. A right, going north, heads off to a campsite on the north shore of Whale Lake, and on to Brule Lake on what is an unmaintained bush trail.

To reach the actual summit, follow rock cairns to a small clearing in the thick brush. A large silver plaque mounted on a rock marks the high spot. Because of the surrounding brush the view is not the greatest here, but back on the exposed bedrock, along the western edge of the hill, are several places for a panoramic view. On a clear day, this alone makes the climb well worth it. Any of the hillside clearings make for a decent picnic area, and offer a chance to do a little surveying of the constellation of blue lakes spread out before you. The views stretch for miles, looking over green forests, light brown marshes, dark rivers, and distant hazy blue peaks. You might like to take along a large-scale topographic map to distinguishing between the far-off landmarks.

Within a mile of the overlook you spot the North Branch of the Cascade River directly below to the west. This river flows through marshes and drains Shrike Lake, Zoo Lake, and Eagle Lake. Off to the northwest is the Brule Lake Lookout Tower, and far to the north are the Misquah Hills, rising like bumps on the horizon behind a nearby hill.

12 Northern Light Lake Trail

General description:	Short hike to the top of Blueberry Hill for overlooks of Northern Light Lake and upper Brule River.
General location:	North of Grand Marais.
Length:	0.5 mile, round-trip
Difficulty:	Easy to moderate. A little scrambling is needed to get up.
Elevation gain:	About 380 feet.
Special attractions:	Overlooks, berries, and wildlife.
Maps:	USGS quad: Pine Mountain.
For more information:	Gunflint Ranger District, Superior National Forest; see Appendix B.
GPS:	47 54.259N 90 15.451W.

BLUEBERRY HILL OVERLOOK

2000
1900
1800
1700
1600
FT.
MILES   1

Finding the trailhead: From Grand Marais, it is about 13 miles north on County Road 12 (the Gunflint Trail). Park alongside the road near a small sign that indicates the trail turnoff. As you drive from the south on the Gunflint Trail, after going alongside the Brule River and coming around a sharp curve, Blueberry Hill is easy to spot as it towers over the road. There is a nearby campsite on Forest Road 140 on Kimball Lake.

The hike: Blueberry Hill on the Northern Light Lake Trail really does live up to its name, with bunches of blueberries growing on the upper slopes. If you hike during blueberry season in summer, you probably will not be alone in your grazing, as the neighboring region is know for its rich wildlife diver-

Northern Light Lake Trail

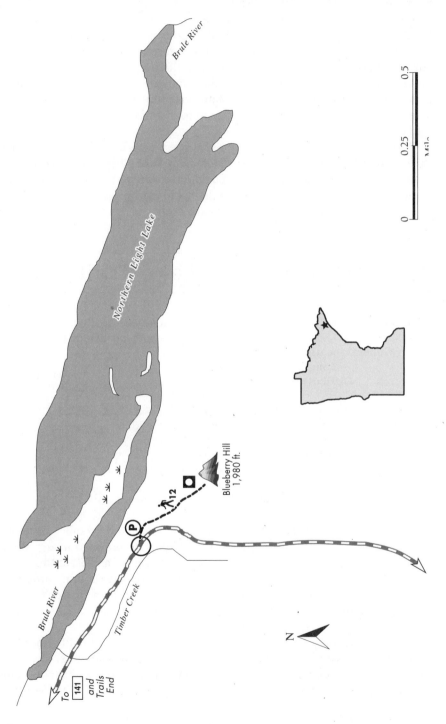

Brule River

Northern Light Lake

Brule River

Timber Creek

To 141 and Trails End

Blueberry Hill
1,980 ft.

P

12

N

0   0.25   0.5
Mile

sity. The blueberries, no doubt, draw in a few animals; as does the shoreline of Northern Light Lake, especially the marshy west side, which looks to be prime moose habitat.

This trail is a short, brisk climb leading to the top of Blueberry Hill. The path starts by veering to the south and entering a dense forest. Trees thin a bit as the trail climbs and winds its way toward the top of the hill. Getting to the lake's overlook near the top takes some scrambling up a small ledge, which opens up on a clearing that runs along a ridge paralleling the lake.

The overlooks are on lichen-covered bedrock with a few trees stunted due to the Krummholz effect—a stunting of trees caused by exposure to strong, cold winds, especially cedars, which take on a bonsai-like appearance. The panoramic vista covers the length of the Northern Light Lake, which almost seems to have a river-like appearance. The lake lies in a valley stretching out between the hills, with the Brule River entering the lake from the west and exiting to the east. To the west, sight lines look down the Gunflint Trail as it winds north to further adventures within the Boundary Waters Canoe Area Wilderness.

13 Lake Superior Pebble Beach

General description:	A hike for the whole family that follows a long and wide stretch of Lake Superior shoreline.
General location:	Northeast of Grand Marais.
Length:	3 miles, round-trip.
Difficulty:	Easy, hiking on level beach.
Elevation gain:	Nominal.
Special attractions:	The wind and waves of Lake Superior, beach-combing, and skipping stones.
Maps:	Superior Hiking Trail maps; USGS quads: Kadunce River and Marr Island.
For more information:	The Superior Hiking Trail Association guidebook covers this section.
GPS:	47 47.611N 90 09.184W.

Finding the trailhead: Drive 12 miles northeast of Grand Marais on Minnesota Highway 61, just past Kadunce River Wayside. Park off the highway along a short dirt path indicated by a Superior Hiking Trail sign. Numerous other turnoffs and hike-access points are possible along the highway. You can start this hike from either end of the beach or from a point in the middle because of the many access points.

The hike: The Pebble Beach Hike, also called the Lake Walk, follows the Superior Hiking Trail for what must be its easiest and gentlest section; the shoreline trail follows the points and crescent-shaped bays of the lake. The

Lake Superior Pebble Beach

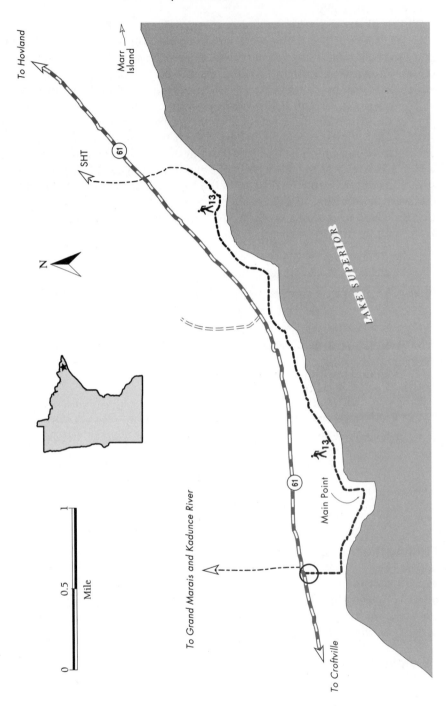

To Hovland

Marr Island →

SHT

61

13

LAKE SUPERIOR

N

13

Main Point

To Grand Marais and Kadunce River

0   0.5   1
Mile

61

To Croftville

Long shadows in the late afternoon at Lake Superior's Pebble Beach.

beach at Park Point in Duluth has ample sand; this beach has plenty of flat pebbles. One of the most popular sports among the Pebble Beach hikers is the fine art of skipping stones. The flatter stones here are certainly capable of a dozen skips. For amateur mineralogists or those who just want to know what they are throwing, the assortment of rocks includes red felsite, gray basalt, granite, jasper, and the occasional agate that got washed in from Isle Royale or Canada.

The hike can begin at either end (or for that matter in several places in the middle since there are many access drives reaching the beach along this stretch of the highway). The hike follows the water's edge the entire length, with an occasional Superior Hiking Trail sign popping up to guide your way.

Starting at the western end, head east (left), then out on the first point. Inshore from here are abandoned beaches and storm ridges. The abandoned beaches are just a few feet inland from the present day beach and are remnants of a former glacial lake of some 3,500 years ago. The ridges are left by the pounding waves, which carried the rocks to higher levels. Going around a big, jutting point, you reach a secluded cove and begin a long section of beach.

At about the 1-mile mark, the highway comes close to the trail, then passes by a few points that reach out into the water. At the 1.5-mile mark the trail veers out to the road. Farther down the beach are some houses. Off the point lies the small Marr Island, and around the point is Paradise Beach. If at this point you have done enough beach walking you can walk alongside the road on the way back. If you return the same way, you can skip some more stones.

Note: The Superior Hiking Trail continues on to Kadunce River (also spelled Kodonce River) to the west, where parking is also available at the Kodonce River Wayside. This short, 0.5-mile-long trail follows the river's amazing deep gorge up to a Superior Hiking Trail bridge. A visit here contrasts nicely with the gentle beach walk.

14 Judge C.R. Magney State Park

General description:	A hike along another one of the North Shore's classic streams, the Brule River. This hike extends a couple of miles upriver to a scenic overlook of the river's gorge and waterfalls.
General location:	Southwest of Grand Portage.
Length:	About 2.5 miles, round-trip. 7-mile trail network in the park.
Difficulty:	Moderate, steep climb and rough trail in sections.
Elevation gain:	About 200 feet.
Special attractions:	Devil's Kettle, where half the river disappears down a hole in the rocks and cascades into the Brule River.
Camping:	33 drive-in and 1 hike-in site.
Maps:	State park trail map; USGS quad: Marr Island.
For more information:	DNR Information Center; see Appendix B.
GPS:	47 49.169N 90 03.211 W.

Finding the trailhead: About 14 miles northeast of Grand Marais and 5 miles southeast of Hovland on Minnesota Highway 61. Watch for the state park signs; parking is available in the park.

The hike: This park's name honors fisherman and outdoorsman Judge Clarence R. Magney. Besides being a judge, he also sat on the state supreme court, was mayor of Duluth, and helped establish many of the state parks along the North Shore. This river was one of his favorites. Farther upstream, the state has stocked the river with trout. The adventurous can hike up unmaintained trails to the upper reaches and tributaries for some remote fishing opportunities.

Native Americans called this river *Wisacode zibi* or "half-burnt wood river," which was translated by the French-Canadian Voyageurs into the roughly-equivalent Brule River. Of all the North Shore streams, this is the third largest and has one of the most consistent water-flow rates. The Brule River cuts through red rhyolite, forming a gorge that stretches for 1.5 miles and drops 70 feet in a series of cascades. A rolling, rough trail runs alongside this gorge, dropping down twice to provide a close look at the turbulent water and falls.

The hike starts at either of the state park's visitor lots or at the campground, where you can cross the footbridge over the river to the trailhead.

Judge C.R. Magney State Park

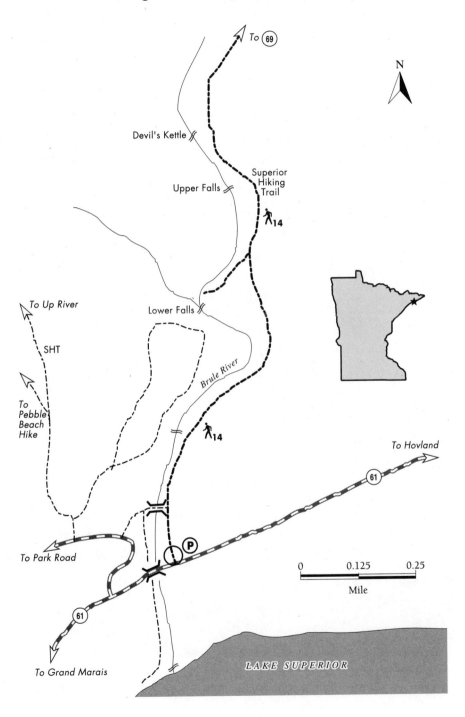

To 69

N

Devil's Kettle

Superior Hiking Trail

Upper Falls

14

Lower Falls

To Up River

SHT

To Pebble Beach Hike

Brule River

14

To Hovland

61

To Park Road

P

To Grand Marais

61

LAKE SUPERIOR

0   0.125   0.25
Mile

The Devil's Kettle.

The main trail leads upstream, climbing the upper part of the valley alongside the river. At about the 0.75-mile mark a spur turns hard left, heading back down a narrow, root-covered ridge leading to the 15-foot drop of the Brule River's Lower Falls. This cascade, while a decent drop, gives only a hint of what is upriver. Another 0.5 mile brings you to the steps leading down to the base of the Upper Falls and the first view of Devil's Kettle. A large, protruding rock divides the river, sending one side down a 50-foot falls into a pool below, while the other diverts into a large, seemingly bottomless pothole. No one knows where this water actually exits the pool, although the most likely theory is that it eventually drains into Lake Superior. Climb the trail back up the valley to view the river dropping and disappearing into the kettle.

Note: The Superior Hiking Trail (SHT) continues north of the falls heading up to County Road 69. The park is also connected by way of the SHT to the Pebble Beach hike, which is about 3 miles to the west.

15 Grand Portage National Monument

General description:	Mount Rose Trail is a short hike up to a scenic spot overlooking the fort, Grand Portage Bay, and Lake Superior. The portage itself is a long hike over a gently rolling forest trail to Pigeon River.
General location:	Tip of the Arrowhead.
Length:	A 1-mile round trip for Mount Rose.
Difficulty:	Easy. The climb is all on a paved, yet steep, trail.
Elevation gain:	300-foot elevation gain.
Special attractions:	Grand Portage Fort, Grand Portage Trail, and overlooks of Lake Superior.
Maps:	Park service map; USGS quad: Grand Portage.
Camping:	Backcountry sites at Fort Charlotte.
For more information:	Grand Portage National Monument, PO Box 668, Grand Marais, MN 55604; Web Site: http://www.nps.gov/grpo/
GPS:	47 57.797N 89 41.056W.

MT. ROSE

900
800
700
600
FT.
MILES   1

Finding the trailhead: Just off Minnesota Highway 61 about 15 miles northeast of Hovland. Follow the Grand Portage National Monument signs, turning east (toward the lake) onto County Road 17.

The hike: After exploring the Grand Portage Fort and the historic garden, you have a couple of hiking options within the national monument. One follows the park's namesake trail up to Pigeon River, the other, the shorter

Grand Portage National Monument • Mount Josephine

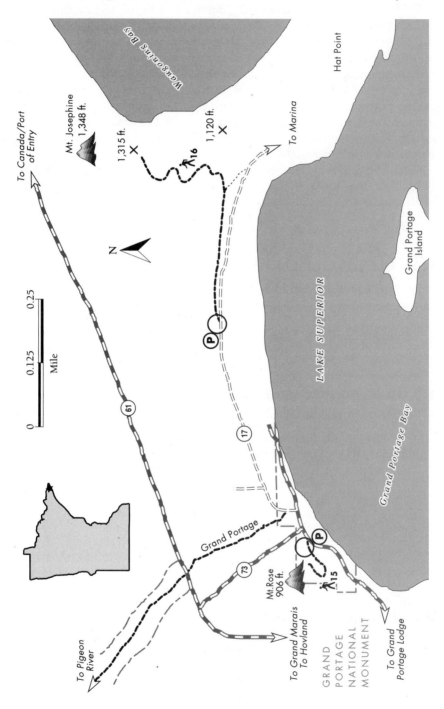

To Canada/Port of Entry

Wauswaugoning Bay

Mt. Josephine 1,348 ft.

Hat Point

1,315 ft. X

1,120 ft. X

16

To Marina

Grand Portage Island

N

0.25

0.125

Mile

0

61

LAKE SUPERIOR

P

17

Grand Portage

Grand Portage Bay

73

Mt. Rose 906 ft.

P

15

To Grand Marais
To Hovland

GRAND PORTAGE NATIONAL MONUMENT

To Grand Portage Lodge

To Pigeon River

The view from Mount Rose: the fort, Grand Portage Island, and Hat Point.

and more scenic Mount Rose Trail, is described here.

If you want to try the portage, check in with a ranger for registration. The only camping at the monument is located on the Portage Trail, at the old site of Fort Charlotte on the Pigeon River. Fort Charlotte is only a memory here, but the campsites still provide close access to an easy-flowing section of the river. The portage trail, providing both natural and historical sights, can be done as a true canoe portage for the full effect. The portage, known by the Ojibwa as *Kitchi Onigum,* or translated directly as "great carrying place," has been used for hundreds of years. Packing a canoe would give an ambitious hiker the chance to further explore the rapids on the river. Otherwise, for an easier path, take the Mount Rose trail—for what I feel might be the more scenic of the hikes.

The Mount Rose Trail starts across the road from the Fort (remember to first pick up an interpretive brochure for the nature markers along the way). The paved trail goes up a series of catwalks and steps to reach the overlook. Here the panorama looks down on the fort and out and over the Grand Portage Bay. Toward the east is the long peninsula of Hat Point; Grand Portage Island is right off the peninsula, and if the day is clear enough you can see Isle Royale more than 20 miles away. If it is hazy, this vantage point still makes a great place to watch the ferries going back and forth to Michigan's Isle Royale National Park. Back to the west you can make out the gap in the hills through which the Grand Portage Trail goes on its way to the Pigeon River.

Note: Since Isle Royale National Park is in Michigan, it is not included in this book, but it is a premier hiking and backpacking wilderness. More information on getting to the island (ferry schedules) can be obtained from Grand Portage National Monument.

16 Mount Josephine

See Map on Page 60

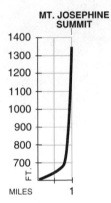

MT. JOSEPHINE SUMMIT

General description:	A steep, strenuous hike up the mountain, which is at the base of Hat Point, leading to a panorama of Lake Superior and the islands off Pigeon Point.
General location:	Tip of the Arrowhead near Grand Portage.
Length:	2 miles, round-trip.
Difficulty:	Moderate to difficult. Caution, steep cliffs on top.
Elevation gain:	About 700 feet.
Special attractions:	Big view of Lake Superior and islands off the coast.
Maps:	USGS quad: Grand Portage.
For more information:	Grand Portage Lodge and Casino; see Appendix B.
GPS:	47 58.261 89 40.057W.

Finding the trailhead: Just off Minnesota Highway 61 about 15 miles northeast of Hovland. Follow the Grand Portage National Monument signs, turning east (toward the lake) at County Road 17. Follow CR 17 east, past the fort and the town for about 1.5 miles. There is a small sign reading 'Mount Josephine' on the right (north) side for the small parking area.

The hike: This rugged, somewhat obscure climb up Mount Josephine, lies within the Grand Portage Indian Reservation. Perhaps, it's overshadowed by either the nearby national monument or the notoriety of the Witch Tree (which is now closed to visitors). Nevertheless, Mount Josephine offers vistas like nowhere else along the North Shore, with the view down the narrow peninsula of Hat Point and the chain of islands lying off Pigeon Point. Mount Josephine is named after Josephine Godfrey, who climbed the peak in the summer of 1853 in what must have been at that time a true expedition to the remote outreaches of Minnesota.

From the parking area, the trail begins on a wide doubletrack that runs parallel to the road. After about 0.25 mile, a narrow footpath on the left takes off into the deep woods, while the access trail continues on to a quarry. The path follows one of the better climbs along the North Shore (as well as in the state), as it rises 675 feet in elevation from the road to the site of the former fire tower. After the catwalks and near the top, a forest clearing gives a view straight down to the peninsula of Hat Point. Geologists de-

View of Pigeon Point and outlying islands.

scribe the peninsula as a classic example of a diabase dike—an erosion resistant rock cutting against softer bedrock. Whatever the source, it makes for one of Minnesota's more unique spots.

The top is shared with the remains of a watch tower and, according to the topo map, the actual summit, some 33 feet higher, is north of here, closer to MN 61. I didn't try to explore any farther though, as one can be more than satisfied with this view. Here the overlook is almost fjord-like and drops almost straight down to the water. The view takes in Grand Portage Bay, Wauswaugoning Bay, and out to Pigeon Point with its archipelago. The visible Lake Superior Islands include Susie Island (at one time containing a copper mine), Lucille Island, and much farther out, Isle Royale National Park in Michigan, 22 miles away.

Border Lakes

The Border Lakes runs along the northeastern edge of the state, which covers Voyageurs National Park and most of Superior National Forest. This national forest, which stretches from the Gunflint Trail over to Ely and on to Buyck, also encompasses the Boundary Waters Canoe Area Wilderness (BWCAW). Since the region features two of the nation's premier lake-oriented areas with Voyageurs and the BWCAW, it is probably known more as a canoeing paradise than for its hiking. But there are also a few lesser known places catering to those on foot. Some of these are only accessible to hikers, while others go along canoeing paths. The trails range from sections along the Border Route (which parallels the age-old canoe route), to rugged smaller lakes in the interior and up to Voyageurs where the trail is reachable only by boat.

Sigurd Olson called this land of northern Minnesota the singing wilderness for the beauty of the northern lights, the cry of loons, and the age-old connection to the past. This region includes some of our most remote and wildest land located deep in a boreal forest where lichen and mosses grow on top of 3-billion-year-old bedrock. The boreal forest, which takes its name from Boreas—the Greek god of the north wind—covers the harshest, coldest land and is composed of hardy trees of fir and spruce. Occasionally, you will find towering stands of pines that remain from the previous century. The bedrocks are a mix of precambrian granites and sedimentary rocks that were swept clean and left exposed, or deeply gouged to form lakes by the glaciers 10,000 years ago.

This part of Minnesota also has wildlife, including the most eastern extension of the timber wolves in the United States, bears, moose, and eagles.

Many of the trail are in the BWCAW and therefore you need permits for either a day hike, which you can usually get at the trailhead, or overnight camping, obtainable from a ranger station. Check with the Superior National Forest for the latest regulations.

17 Honeymoon Bluff Trail

General description:	A short trail that gives an eagle's-eye view 200 feet above Hungry Jack Lake.
General location:	East end of Hungry Jack Lake.
Length:	0.5 mile loop.
Difficulty:	Easy. Long stairway climb up to the overlook loop. Caution, steep cliff.
Elevation gain:	128 feet up to the plateau.
Special attractions:	A terrific sunset—the overlook faces west above the lake.
Maps:	Superior National Forest map; USGS quad: Hungry Jack Lake.
Camping:	State forest campground nearby at the Flour Lake.
For more informaton:	Gunflint Ranger District, Superior National Forest; see Appendix B.
GPS:	48 03.359N 90 24.699W.

Finding the trailhead: From Grand Marais, follow County Road 12 (Gunflint Trail) for 27 miles north to County Road 66. Turn east (right) and travel 2 miles to the small parking lot. Parking is 0.25 mile past the Flour Lake Campground and is located between Wampus Lake and Hungry Jack Lake.

Looking down on Hungry Jack Lake.

Honeymoon Bluff Trail

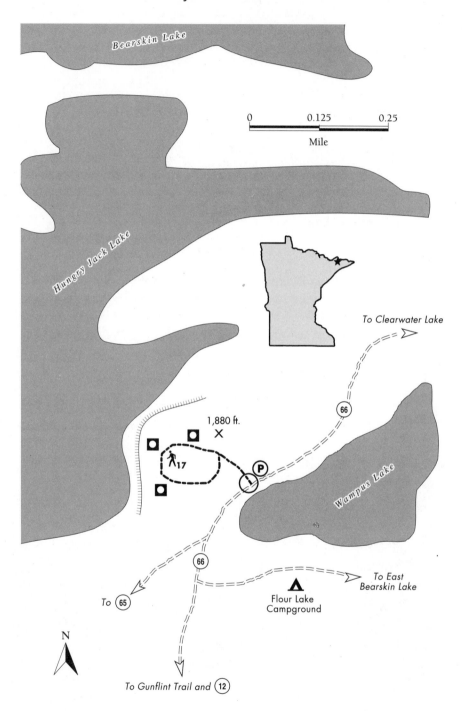

Bearskin Lake

0   0.125   0.25

Mile

Hungry Jack Lake

To Clearwater Lake

1,880 ft.

17

P

66

Wampus Lake

66

To 65

To East
Bearskin Lake

Flour Lake
Campground

N

To Gunflint Trail and 12

The hike: If you are on your way to another spot along the Gunflint Trail, this hike is well worth a quick stop. Here you get a tremendous view of this elongated lake—with only a little bit of climbing required.

Seemingly one of the most popular overlooks along the Gunflint Trail, Honeymoon Bluff draws quite a few people from both nearby cabins and the neighboring Flour Lake campground. Visit the bluff in the evening hours for a spectacular sunset view.

The trail starts from the parking lot with a climb up a staircase of a hundred or so steps. The last step intersects with the short loop, which features three overlooks of the lake. The 200-foot bluff has guard fences, but care should be exercised (especially with small children). The overlooks wrap around a small comfortable rocky point that almost hangs over Hungry Jack Lake. Positioned on the southeastern end, the panoramic view west takes in the lake with all of its numerous bays and inlets. To the north, just a sliver of Bearskin Lake can be seen.

18 Caribou Rock Trail (Border Route Trail)

General description:	A scenic and strenuous day hike going to the overlook of Rose Lake or a short trip to the first overlook at Bearskin Lake 0.25 mile up the trail.
General location:	West end of Hungry Jack Lake.
Length:	About 7 miles, round-trip.
Difficulty:	Difficult. Rough trail and many steep hills.
Elevation gain:	About 480 feet up to the Rose Lake overlook, but the cumulative gain is much greater.
Special attractions:	Many overlooks, including an amazing view of the cliffs on the Canadian side of Rose Lake, the waterfall at Stairway Portage, and chances to see wildlife.
Maps:	Superior National Forest map, USGS quads: Hungry Jack Lake, Border Route Trail map, and both Fischer and McKenzie maps.
For more informaton:	Gunflint Ranger District, Superior National Forest; see Appendix B.
GPS:	48 03.705N 90 27.365W.

Finding the trailhead: From Grand Marais, take County Road 12 (Gunflint Trail) for 28 miles to the intersection of County Road 65. Take a right (north) for 2 miles for the trailhead sign. A small parking area is on the shoulder;

Caribou Rock Trail (Border Route Trail)

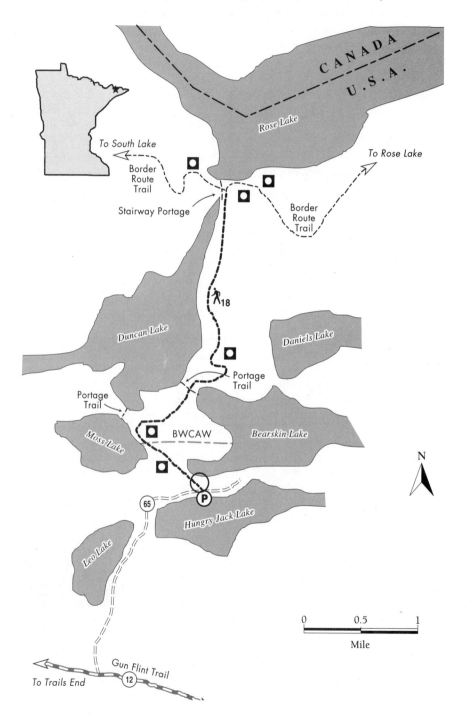

the trail starts on the other side of the road. If you plan to do any overnight camping in the Boundary Waters Canoe Area Wilderness you'll need a permit for either Entry Point 59 in the west for the South Lake Trail (2.5 miles west on CR 12), or Entry Point 82 to the east (2.5 miles to the east off CR 12 on CR 66) for the access along Daniels Lake.

The hike: The Caribou Rock Trail is one of those hikes where every time you look up from the trail you are greeted with another amazing panoramic view. The rugged Caribou Rock Trail alternates between running along the bluff above the three lakes that lead up to Rose Lake and dipping down into a number of steep creek valleys. This trail could very well be an overnight trail, but from this starting point it is designated as a day hike only. For camping, go through one of the nearby entry points that lead up to the Border Route Trail (entry points 59 or 82). A loop is possible by using either of these entry points, though a gap remains on the loop and a two-car shuttle will be needed, unless you hike along the Gunflint Trail to close the loop.

Caribou Rock is named for the first overlook on Bearskin Lake. This overlook alone could make a quick trip for those looking for a less strenuous trail. At only 0.25 mile in and on a smooth trail, it provides a perfect picnic spot with an unmatched view along the length of Bearskin Lake. For those wishing to continue, another 0.25 mile brings you to the border of the BWCAW and views of Moss Lake off to the west.

The trail then follows the ridge along Bearskin Lake, almost all the way to the portage that connects Moss Lake and Duncan Lake. At the end of the

Rose Lake overlook.

pine-forested ridge, instead of descending into the valley between these two lakes, turn sharply right. (Some maps have the portage and the hiking trail running together; however, they are actually connected only by a short trail going down the ridge.) Remain on the main path as it makes a nearly 180-degree turn and follow the ridge's other side. The trail then drops into the valley and crosses an 80-rod (0.25 mile) portage between Bearskin and Duncan Lake. Then it climbs some 200 feet to the top of a hill, only to drop back down, then to climb back up for the length of Duncan Lake. The lake slowly narrows into a creek as it heads to the Stairway Portage on the far northern end. There is no lake access until almost the end, near the portage, where the trail approaches the same elevation as the lake. (Not so many years ago, the lake water was clean enough to drink directly. Now, to be on the safe side it is better first to boil or filter it.)

At the popular Stairway Portage, you find yourself in a pleasant situation—deciding whether to explore the waterfall and portage first or just sit down and take in the overlook. Relaxation is tempting, with plenty of space to stretch out on the exposed bedrock along the bluff. The stunning vista from the nearly vertical cliff takes in Canada far on the opposite side of Rose Lake, where several more 300-foot-plus shear rock cliffs stand on the lake's edge.

The stream connecting Duncan Lake to Rose Lake drops 138 feet in a series of cascades and a spectacular waterfall during the 0.25-mile portage. Cross the bridge to look down the falls from where the water takes its initial plunge, then take the stairs for a closer view. Alongside the ninety-one steps of the stairway portage, a couple of viewing platforms provide resting spots along the waterfalls in mid-descent. On a hot summer day this is a good place for a cool refreshing blast of spray. Back on top, a short hike in either direction along the Border Route Trail leads to several more overlooks.

19 Magnetic Rock Trail

General description:	The trail goes through a burn area over exposed bedrock, then to deep woods and a strange looking monolithic rock with magnetic properties.
General location:	West end of Gunflint Lake.
Length:	2.5 miles to the rock and back.
Difficulty:	Easy to moderate. Rocky trail.
Elevation gain:	200 feet.
Special attractions:	The rock (bring a compass to test out its magnetic properties) and wildlife.
Maps:	USGS quad: Long Island Lake.
For more informaton:	Gunflint Ranger District, Superior National Forest; see Appendix B.
GPS:	48 05.291N 90 48.061.

Finding the trailhead: The trail parking is 45 miles from Grand Marais on County Road 12 (the Gunflint Trail) in a lot off the road's east side. The Kekekabic Trail's eastern terminus is just 0.25 mile before the parking lot. The Magnetic Rock Trail starts northwest, 500 feet down the road.

The hike: Under normal circumstances, a glacial erratic (a boulder dropped from a glacial ice sheet) wouldn't get much attention in Minnesota. They are, after all, just big rocks that you can find almost everywhere, including in people's front yards. But this one is special, not just for its magnetic properties, but also for its appearance. The rock's dimensions are 10 by 20 by 30 feet and it is shaped like a big monument that seems to have dropped out of the sky. Multi-colored lichens cover the rock's surface giving it various shades of yellow and orange. Its magnetism comes from the mineral magnetite, common to the underlying bedrock of the Gunflint Iron Formation.

After walking along County Road 12 (Gunflint Trail) about 500 feet northwest, turn right (east) to start the main trail, which also happens to be the start of the Border Route Trail. Go under a powerline as the trail parallels a boggy area, crossing over Larch Creek at the 0.25-mile mark. Fortunately the trail stays dry, riding high on exposed bedrock.

This interesting place is named the Magnetic Burn Area. The result of a 1974 fire, it is basically a treeless and harsh looking spot where the creek flows through a bedrock valley. This sunny spot is an ideal location for picking blueberries late in summer and fall. After the burn area, the trail continues on and enters a forest of spruce and fir with a low-lying area off to the right.

At the 1.25-mile mark, a small Forest Service sign marks the short spur trail leading to the Magnetic Rock. The Border Route Trail continues to the right to Gunflint Lake. A left turn leads to the rock, which is in a heavily

Magnetic Rock Trail

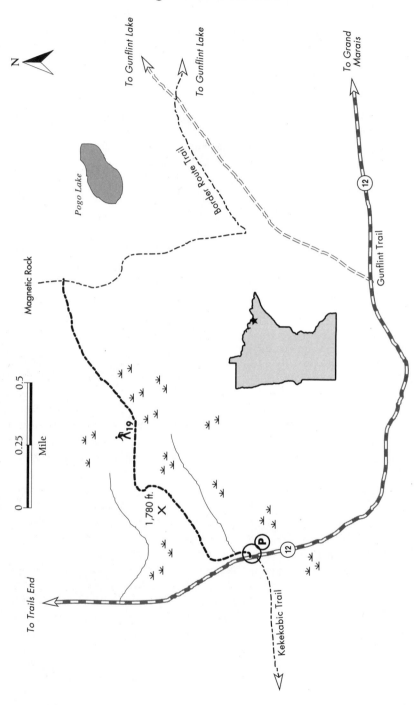

The magnetic rock.

wooded area. You may feel a little cramped as you ponder the rock's balancing act and notice all the other rocks strewn about.

Test out the rock's magnetism with a compass. As you move a compass along the face of the rock, in certain spots the polarity switches back and forth between north and south.

20 Hogback Trail

General description:	A loop along high rugged ridges that run along and between a group of lakes.
General location:	East of Isabella in the Superior National Forest.
Length:	About 4 miles.
Difficulty:	Moderate. A rocky trail in places and hilly.
Elevation gain:	About 70 feet.
Special attractions:	Hogbacks and overlooks.
Maps:	Superior National Forest map; USGS quads: Wilson Lake and Silver Island Lake.
Camping:	4 hike-in sites. Nearest campground at Divide Lake.
For more informaton:	Isabella Ranger District, Superior National Forest; see Appendix B.
GPS:	47 38.6N 91 08.2W.

Finding the trailhead: From Illgen City and Minnesota Highway 61 take Minnesota Highway 1 north to Isabella. Turn east on Forest Road 172 and drive about 12 miles to the parking area along Hogback Lake. A wayside picnic and recreational area, complete with a boat launch and a fishing dock, are on this designated trout lake.

The hike: A hogback is a ridge of hard, erosion-resistent bedrock. Hogbacks occur along fault lines where the bedrock slants up to make a ridge with a steep escarpment on one side. Along the Hogback Trail, the escarpments are up to 70-feet-high along the shoreline, yielding panoramic views of the lakes. Exploring this area makes for a decent day hike for those staying at one of the nearby Forest Service campgrounds (Ninemile Lake or Divide Lake). Backcountry campsites are also found along the shore of Scarp Lake for backcountry camping.

The trailhead is at the picnic grounds near the fishing dock, next to a big map of the trail system. Begin by going to the southeast (left) end of the Hogback Lake, toward the boat launch and crossing over a stone rock casement. At 0.25-mile it connects with the main loop, which encircles Scarp Lake. For a clockwise tour, head to the east and follow the hogback along the northern edge of Scarp Lake, where you can find a campsite at about the 0.5 mile mark. Stay on this high ridge until Mound Lake, where you drop down to cross a small creek between the two lakes. After the two lakes, you

Hogback Trail

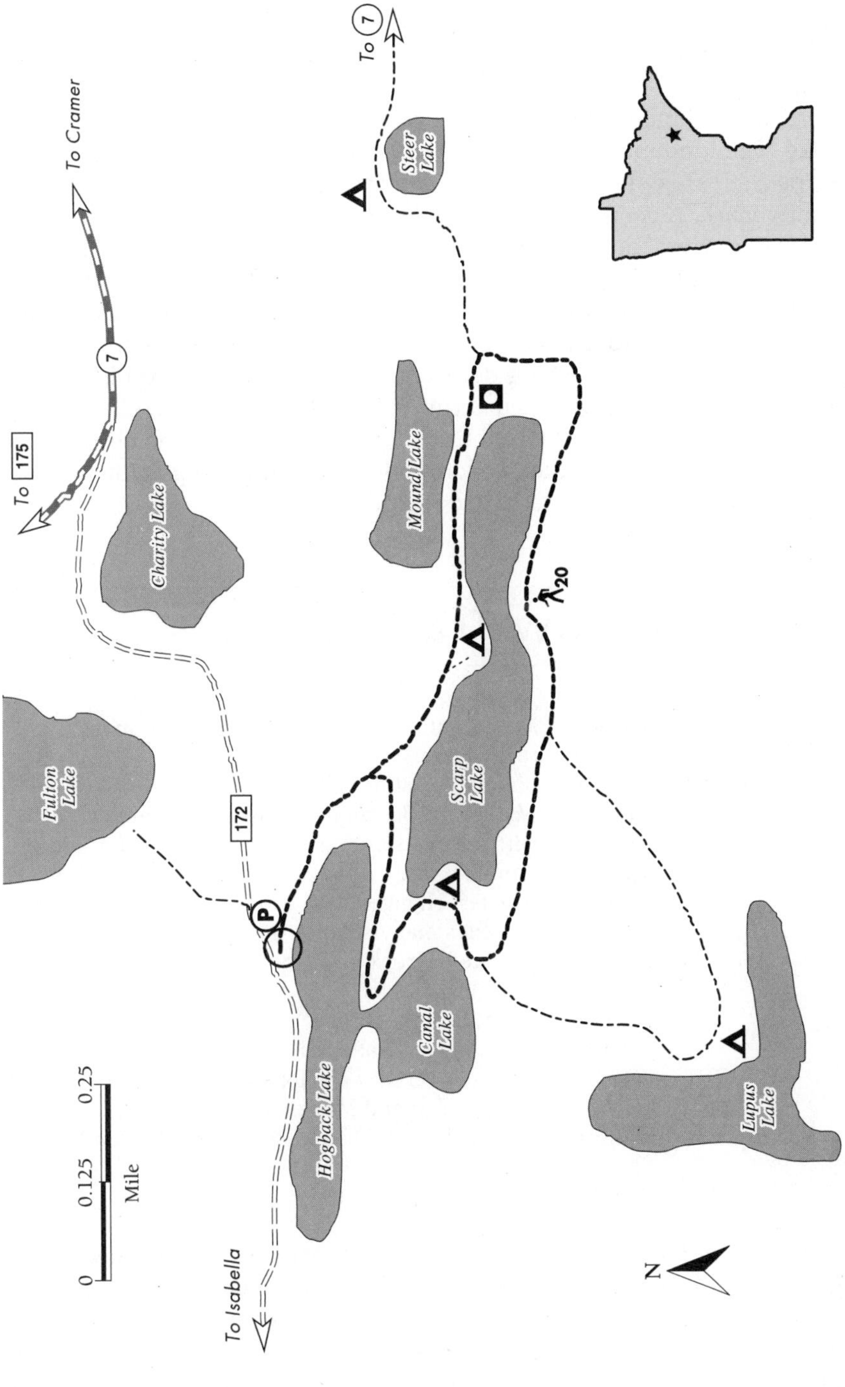

To 7

Steer Lake

To Cramer

7

To 175

Charity Lake

Mound Lake

Fulton Lake

172

Scarp Lake

P

Hogback Lake

Canal Lake

Lupus Lake

To Isabella

N

Mile
0   0.125   0.25

λ_{20}

climb an 80-foot-high hill, where at the top a trail intersection branches off to Steer Lake. Another 0.25 mile away is a campsite. Heading south (right) takes you to the southern edge of Scarp Lake. The trail enters a swampy spot, then climbs back up for an overlook that is about 100 feet above the lake. Continue to follow this trail as it hugs the cliffs on this long, rolling ridge.

At the 1.5-mile mark, an overgrown trail loops down south to Lupus Lake. The topo map marks this as the main trail, while the Forest Service maps don't show it at all. On the main trail, this loop hooks up again at the 2-mile mark. A campsite is on the western edge of Scarp Lake at the end of peninsula. Here you come to a 250-foot portage between Scarp and Canal lakes. The trail follows a peninsula, which almost touches the other side of the lake. At one time there was a railroad trestle here, as well as a dam and a sluiceway, used to transfer logs through the narrows. Looking across the lake you can see the fishing dock and the trailhead. The trail goes to the very tip of the peninsula, then abruptly turns back almost a full 180 degrees to follow the shoreline of Canal Lake. Continue to follow the northeast edge until the now familiar intersection, then turn right and go along the south side of Hogback Lake to return to the picnic area.

21 Pow Wow Trail

General description:	A long multi-day wilderness hike to remote rocky lakes.
General location:	Just northeast of Isabella.
Length:	About 26 miles total—2-plus days of hiking.
Difficulty:	Difficult. Western side composed of rough and tumble trails.
Elevation gain:	Greatest change about 100 feet. The trail climbs and descends many smaller ridges and hills.
Special attractions:	Remote bedrock lakes, beaver dams, and cascading creeks.
Camping:	8 hike-in sites.
Maps:	USGS quads: Isabella Lake, Quadga Lake, Snowbank Lake and Perent Lake for the east part; also maps by Fischer: F-4; and McKenzie: number 19.
For more informaton:	Isabella Ranger District, Superior National Forest; see Appendix B.
GPS:	47 47.67N 91 18.44W.

Finding the trailhead: From Illgen City on Minnesota Highway 61, travel north on Minnesota Highway 1 to the Isabella Ranger Station, where you can get Boundary Waters Canoe Area Wilderness camping permits. To reach the trailhead, continue on MN 1 about 4 miles north of the Ranger Station to Forest Road 177. Turn north onto a winding road that runs directly into

Pow Wow Trail

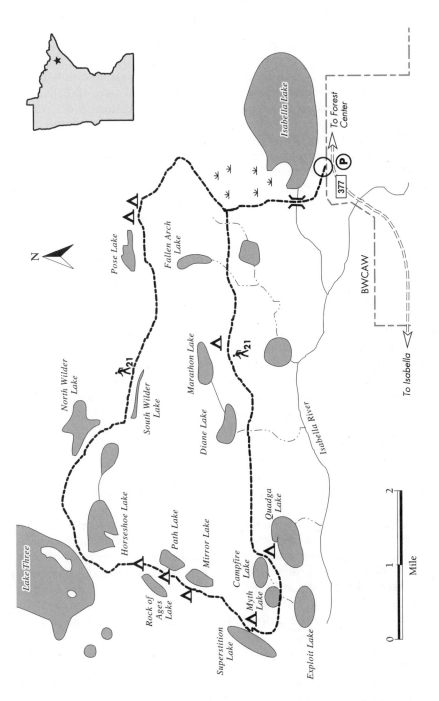

Forest Road 173 (Tomahawk Road) after about 7.5 miles. Turn right on FR 173. At about 4 miles it intersects with FR 377, which you follow northeast for about 5.5 miles to Forest Center near Lake Isabella. Parking is after the bridge crossing and near the Isabella River.

At the parking lot entrance a Forest Service sign reads Pow Wow hiking trail. This trail can also be reached from FR 173, which intersects MN 1, 16 miles northwest of Isabella for a straight shot east to parking. Another twisting route is from Forest Road 176, just a couple miles west of Isabella, up to Kelly Landing and Forest Road 369, and then to Forest Road 373.

The hike: Hiking here is like going back in time to the stone age—at least that is the feeling I got hiking among the harsh bedrock lakes with intriguing names like Superstition and Rock of Ages. The Pow Wow Trail is a multiday hike that reaches truly isolated lakes away from even the canoe routes. The trail is difficult; it requires scrambling around rocks in places or traversing miles of soggy trails, across beaver dams and through thick alder groves. But if you go, you will be treated to special lakes that you have nearly all to yourself.

Tomahawk Lumber Company logged parts of this land during the 1960s using the town of Forest Center as its base. In 1977 development of the hiking trails was started by the Youth Conservation Corps, who followed meandering logging roads through the marshes east of Forest Center and near Pow Wow Lake. These soggy trails were later abandoned, and the whole trail system moved to the more scenic, and for the most part, drier western half. In 1995 the Kekekabic Hiking Club did some maintenance and blazed the route with flags, though the trail still has plenty of downed trees to block your path, and enough deep backwoods sections to make you wonder about the path. You may have to use your orienteering skills on this hike.

The first mile leads up to Isabella bridge, which might make a nice, short stroll for someone coming back from a canoe trip. A picnic area is by the stream that empties Lake Isabella by way of a gentle cascade. Check out the huge boulder sitting right in the middle of the stream. This first part of the trail, especially the sections on the former logging roads, are the most heavily choked by alder.

At 2.6 miles you come to the intersection with the main loop, where you take a left (west) for a clockwise loop. Here the trail might actually be below water level as it goes along a beaver dam trail. The trail transforms into a footpath leading you through the boreal forest of spruce and passing by Fallen Arch Lake. Marathon Lake, at 3.9 miles, has a high and dry campsite on an exposed bedrock, a short distance from the lake. The next campsite, at about 7 miles, is near Campfire Lake. After the camp you come to a deep ravine below Diana Lake.

Shortly the hike turns north, leaving behind the alder and birch, and heads onto a friendly moss-covered trail. Along Superstition Lake the rolling trail leads to a splendid lakeshore campsite on the end of a peninsula. You are treated to water reflections of the hill and boulder of the opposing shore. For the next 4.6 miles, hiking takes you over boulders and roots, at times challenging you to keep your balance as you scramble around the obstacles, and slowing you down. Mirror Lake comes up next, where you will see a small island with the seemingly misplaced huge round rock sitting on the small chunk of land. The campsite here is a bit above the water.

The path continues to skirt the lake's western edge, then follows the shore of Path Lake.

On the north end of this lake lies an impressive campsite surrounded by a big jumble of boulders that extend into the water and invite the climber to get a better view of the lake. A large pine tree makes a tenuous stand near the shoreline, spreading its roots out over the exposed bedrock. The next campsite is just another 0.5 mile north along Rock of Ages Lake. Here the camp sits high, overlooking the lake in a canyon-like setting with views of its islands. Hang out in this fine breezy place on a hot summer night.

A few cairns and blazes mark the path as it makes its way up steep, moss-covered hills to Lake Three and Horseshoe Lake at 13.4 miles. Here you leave the relative isolation of the previous lakes to greet bigger lakes more often visited by canoe paddlers. The trail can be confusing in this area, especially with the canoe portages cutting across the trail. Note that the hiking trails are usually the less-worn paths and are marked by blazes at the portage intersections.

At 15.5 miles, situated atop a rocky ledge shared with a big boulder you come upon the campsite for North Wilder Lake. The trail turns eastward, leaves the shoreline behind, and travels through a grove of cedar trees and a stand of big white pines. It continues on a wide arc around Horseshoe Lake where you cross a creek, find another campsite, and meet up with more portages connecting this chain of lakes.

Continuing along the north shore of South Wilder Lake, you will pass by another campsite situated above the lake. Before Pose Lake, the trail passes by an overlook situated above a marsh ideal for wildlife viewing. Near the 20-mile mark, a spur goes off to Pose Lake and a campsite, though I didn't check it out. From here on to the parking lot and past Isabella Lake, the easy hiking goes along a former forest road that can, in wet weather, get mucky.

22 Secret, Blackstone, and Ennis Lakes Trail

General description:	Short loop around Blackstone Lake and a spur trail to the 100-foot scenic cliffs over Ennis Lake.
General location:	Near the end of Fernberg Trail, east of Ely.
Length:	About 4 miles, including the 1-mile loop around Blackstone Lake.
Difficulty:	Moderate.
Elevation gain:	About 100 feet.
Special attractions:	Overlooks and rock climbing.
Maps:	Fischer maps and McKenzie maps for Snowbank Lake, USGS quad: Snowbank Lake.
Camping:	1 hike-in site.
For more informaton:	Kawashiwi Ranger District, Superior National Forest; see Appendix B.
GPS:	47 59.13N 91 29.85W.

Finding the trailhead: From Ely, go 16.5 miles down Minnesota Highway 169, which turns into County Road 18 (Fernberg Road). Turn onto Forest Road 438 (Moose Lake Road) for 1.5 miles to the small parking lot on the right side for the start of the trail.

Ennis Lake overlook.

Secret, Blackstone, and Ennis Lakes Trail

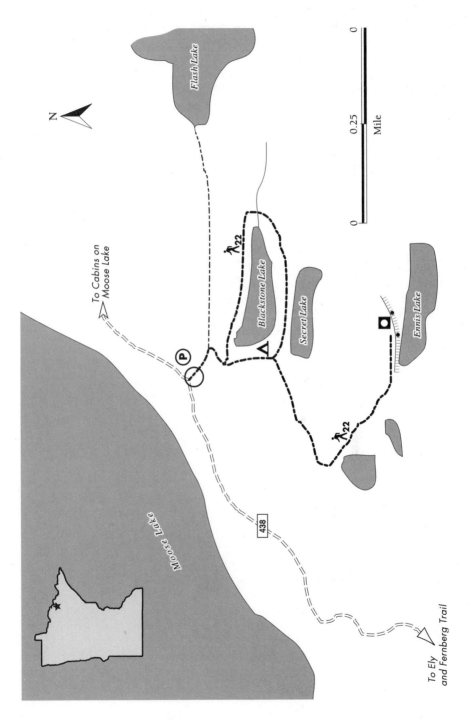

The hike: Except for the rock climbers who ply their trade on the high bluff along Ennis Lake, this hike seems to be ignored by nearly everyone. Still, this is a decent place for a warm-up hike before hiking around neighboring Snowbank Lake, or just a good place to spend an afternoon on a high overlook. The trail was originally built in 1981 by the Youth Conservation Corps.

From the trailhead on the left, about 0.1 mile into the hike, you come to an intersection with a trail leading up to the Flash Lake Portage. At 0.25 mile you come to the 1-mile loop around Blackstone Lake. The trail around the northern half of this lake is a fine path as it passes through a red pine forest.

You may have to go across a beaver dam, which may or may not be possible to cross without getting your feet wet. (This may depend on your jumping ability.) The southern section of the loop cuts between Blackstone and Secret lakes. The loop finishes off at the northwest corner of Secret Lake, where a trail leads off for the best part of the trail system—the scenic overlooks.

The trail first leads to a vantage point above a small pond, drops down to the shore, then passes a couple more small lakes. It ends on the overlook on the high ledge above Ennis Lake. If it is a warm summer day, a few rock climbers will probably be hanging off the edge here.

When I visited, a couple of ropes were going over the edge, but I did not stick my head over to check. Instead, I was more than satisfied with the view of the shimmering lake below and the forested hills beyond.

23 Snowbank–Old Pines–Kekekabic Trail

See Map on Page 86

General description:	Long, multi-day hike going from the rolling Kekekabic Trail to the rugged trail over Disappointment Mountain and back along the northern shore of Snowbank Lake.
General location:	East of Ely at the end of Fernberg Trail; in the Boundary Waters Canoe Area Wilderness (BWCAW).
Length:	A little more than 27 miles for the big loop; shorter and longer loops also possible.
Difficulty:	Difficult. Southern half follows a smooth and fairly straight path; the rest of the loop is a rugged and twisting trail.
Elevation gain:	About 300 feet from Disappointment Mountain to Snowbank Lake.
Special attractions:	Old-growth pines, overlooks of Snowbank Lake, and wildlife.
Camping:	16 hike-in sites.
Maps:	USGS quads: Snowbank Lake, Lake Insula, and Ensign Lake East and Ensign Lake West; The trail is also on maps by Fischer: F-31 and McKenzie: number 9.
For more informaton:	Kawishiwi Ranger District, Superior National Forest; see Appendix B.
GPS:	47 56.799N 91 28.071W, Kekekabic starting point.

See Elevation Chart on Pages 84–85

Finding the trailhead: The trailhead is 22 miles east of Ely. Travel past Winton on Minnesota Highway 169 to County Road 18 (Fernberg Road), which you follow almost to the end of the road. The large parking lot is located on the north (left) side. This is the western start of the Kekekabic Trail.

The hike: This hike is actually a combination of three trails: Snowbank Lake—around Snowbank Lake; Old Pines Trail—around Disappointment Lake and Moiyaka Lake to the east, and Kekekabic—which shares the southern halves of the other two trails before continuing to the east. While shorter out-and-back hikes could be attempted along the north shore of Snowbank, or maybe you could even boat to the eastern side of Snowbank Lake, this area is really made for long-distance hiking. You can hike for more than 40 miles, with loops that go around a couple of larger lakes and many smaller lakes. Additionally, there are several decent side loops and many miles of the rugged Kekekabic Trail. A backpacker could spend a week exploring just half of it.

The loop here follows the Kekekabic Trail along the south shore of Snowbank and Disappointment lakes. At the far end of the latter, it intersects with the start of the rugged Old Pines Trail. This path follows the western and northern sides of Disappointment Lake, while climbing Disappointment Mountain in the process. The trail finishes on the Snowbank Trail, running along a high ridge above its namesake lake.

Go to the north end of the parking lot to start the hike just behind the large Kekekabic Trail map. The first section is not yet in the BWCAW. Initially, the trail passes through some active logging areas, making it a bit confusing, with the footpath barely visible under the cut branches. At about 1 mile you come to an open marshy area. If you don't want to wade across, a short detour looping southward around the marsh will bring you back to the trail where it reenters the woods. This area may flood if beavers build another dam in this spot, but then the dam will make a decent bridge.

The first part of the Kekekabic Trail goes along a wide and fairly easy path, which was once considered and then dropped as a potential railroad line. During the 1930s, this trail was a firetower access trail for the Forest Service, until planes took over the fire watching duty. Following this trail you reach the BWCAW border at the 3.5-mile mark. The trail climbs a steep hill and passes by a trail intersection leading to Pickerel Bay on Snowbank Lake.

Another 0.5 mile, at the 4-mile mark, brings you to the beginning of the scenic Becoosin Loop, with four remote campsites along a couple of scenic bedrock lakes. This trail crosses a beaver dam, which spans a sculptured narrow gorge carved out of the bedrock.

The main corridor of the Kekekabic Trail offers plenty of nature watching but few major views. This main trail continues straight, coming up to a three-way intersection. A left at this intersection will make a shorter loop, running between the east side of Parent Lake and the west side of Disappointment Lake. Instead of taking the loop, continue straight ahead and pass to the other side of the Becoosin Loop, which enters on the right.

At 7.5 miles another cairn marks an intersection where a left heads north up the east side of Disappointment Lake; the Old Pines Loop continues straight ahead. A short distance from this intersection, you will run across a huge, old rusty saw blade that marks the spur to a campsite on Drumstick Lake. Next is the intersection for the Old Pines Loop, which features, logically enough, an old-growth stand of pines. A left (east) continues to follow

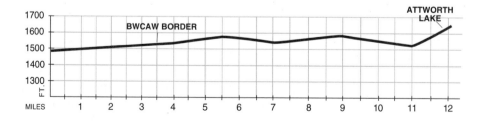

the Kekekabic Trail for what is a shorter route to Medas Lake, and a right starts the Old Pines Loop.

The Old Pines and Kekekabic meet up again at the halfway point, with their paths intersecting at right angles. The Kekekabic Trail takes off into the woods on a narrow path to complete the journey to the Gunflint Trail, while the Old Pines Loop, continuing on its journey around Disappointment Lake, seems to be the most heavily traveled. To complete this long loop, follow the Old Pines, which heads straight for the lake and then takes a right as the path ambles along under a few towering pine trees. Follow the cairns to the next attraction at the 12-mile mark, which is the frothy rapids coming off of Altworth Lake. Look for the remnants of a sluiceway, which at one time might have put some order into the log jam here.

The trail takes on a slightly different attitude from here on out, with a much rockier and hillier course. The first challenge is Disappointment Mountain. The only disappointment is that it lacks a big panoramic view, though it does offer some beautiful ravines and plenty of strenuous hiking. During the next 2 miles, the trail climbs a couple of hundred feet, drops back down into a valley, and then climbs up Disappointment proper, though not to the actual summit. On the other side it follows a ravine along its contours back down to the intersection with the Disappointment Lake Trail at 17 miles. A nice campsite lies along the north end of Disappointment Lake. Continuing on the ridge, after crossing a portage between Boot Lake and Snowbank Lake, you come to overlooks of the expansive Snowbank Lake with all of its islands. There is also a scenic view across small Grub Lake.

The trail continues to alternate between overlooks and campsites back along the northern edge of the lake, with a detour at 23 miles around Wooden Leg Lake. Near the end, only 1 mile from the road, lies one more portage, leading to Flash Lake. The trail pops out onto the dirt road, which leads to another trail (marked with blue diamonds) on the other side of the road. This trail ends at the Snowbank Trail parking. To get back to the Kekekabic trailhead, you can follow the road back to Fernberg Trail and on down the road to the other parking spot.

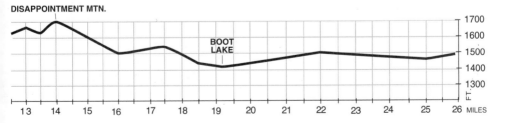

Snowbank–Old Pines–Kekekabic Trail

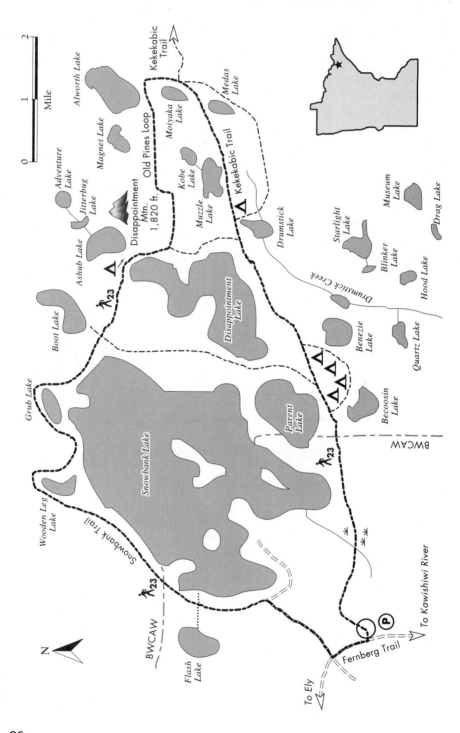

24 Bass Lake Trail

General description:	A hike around Bass Lake, which goes from a high overlook above the lake to lakeshore, and to a quaint cascade.
General location:	North of Ely on Echo Trail.
Length:	About 5 miles
Difficulty:	Moderate.
Elevation gain:	About 100 feet from the water to the overlooks.
Special attractions:	Dry Falls (it does have water), overlooks, and interesting geology.
Maps:	Superior National Forest maps, USGS quad: Ely.
Camping:	1 hike-in site.
For more informaton:	Kawishiwi Ranger District, Superior National Forest; see Appendix B.
GPS:	47 57.025N 91 52.555.

Finding the trailhead: From Ely, take Minnesota Highway 169 east to County Road 88. Travel about 2.5 miles to County Road 116 (Echo Trail) and turn right then drive another 2.5 miles. Posted trailhead parking is on the right.

The hike: What does a lake look like when the water drains out of it? Well you can find out on this hike, because it happened to Bass Lake in 1925. It seems that a glacier-formed gravel barrier, which formerly separated Bass Lake from neighboring Low Lake, gave way. The cause of this cataclysmic event was traced to an old abandoned sluiceway that was built through the dam in order to move logs between the two lakes. Eventually, after the area was logged out and abandoned, this sluiceway crumbled and gave the water an opening to tear a 250-foot valley between the lakes. In ten hours, Bass lake dropped fifty-five feet and thereby exposed 250 acres of land, not to mention lots of fish. That is about 18 million gallons of water, which drained from the lake at 30,000 gallons per minute. Three new lakes, Little Dry Lake, Dry Lake, and Bass Lake, as well as a small cascading river between the latter two lakes, resulted from the draining.

Start from the parking area and hike for 0.1 mile to the loop intersection. A left goes immediately to Dry Falls, while a right leads to the overlooks above Bass Lake. Take a right for a counterclockwise tour of the lake and you will go under a powerline at 0.75 mile, then come to the first overlook. This rocky ledge sits about 100 feet off the water surface, presenting panoramic views spanning both ends of this long narrow lake. Farther down at the 2-mile mark, there is another scenic view looking off another high cliff. Then the trail drops down to the sandy washout area and crosses a bridge. This area, before the bursting of the dam, would have been one of the deepest spots of the lake at 55 feet under water.

Bass Lake Trail

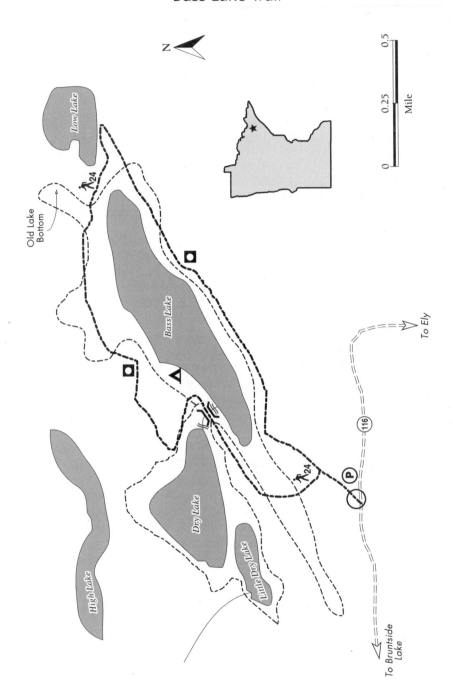

Bass Lake overlook.

Going around the corner, you come to a nice sand bar, where canoeists often set up camp. The trail continues on this side, following cairns while traveling on exposed bedrock. You get another vista from this side of the lake before threading your way through the forest to Dry Falls (which was also created by the lowering of the lake). A footbridge crosses right above the quaint falls, adding to the garden-like landscape. Rivulets of water flow over the bedrock, cascading into small pools then dropping below into Bass Lake. It is a short hike back to the start from here.

25 Angleworm Lake Trail

General description:	Hiking on high ridges that border a long narrow lake.
General location:	North of Ely on Echo Trail.
Length:	About 13 miles.
Difficulty:	Moderate to difficult on a rugged rolling trail.
Elevation gain:	About 200 feet.
Special attractions:	Scenic overlooks on high bedrock ridges and big red and white pine old-growth forests.
Maps:	USGS quads: Angleworm and Fourtown topos; Fischer: F-9.
Camping:	6 hike-in sites and a few canoe-in sites.
For more informaton:	Kawishiwi Ranger District, Superior National Forest; see Appendix B.
GPS:	48 03.714N 91 55.664W.

Finding the trailhead: From Ely, take Minnesota Highway 169 east to County Road 88. Travel about 2.5 miles on CR 88 to County Road 116 (Echo Trail) and turn right. Continue about 13 miles north. The parking lot is just off the road and has a Forest Service sign.

The hike: The loop around Angleworm Lake has everything you would expect a Boundary Waters Canoe Area Wilderness trail to have: a beautiful lake, a forest full of big, old trees, and a rugged path with many wildlife viewing opportunities. Angleworm Lake is shaped more like a river than a lake, with the water filling up a narrow gorge between two high ridges, where in the middle it is quite literally just a stone's throw across to the other side. The trail runs along both sides of the lake, passes by beaver dams, and through large stands of old-growth forests. This hike could be managed as a day hike, though it is a better bet to take some time and enjoy it fully by camping at any of the sites along the rocky shore.

From the trailhead at the parking lot, follow what was once a Forest Service road. Today, this road doubles as a canoe portage to Angleworm Lake and as the access trail to the loop around the lake. This is the straightest and smoothest section of the trail, as it descends into the Spring Creek ravine. At the bottom you enter the BWCAW. Ascending out of the valley at the 0.75-mile mark, you get the first taste of the big pines, which are more profuse later on down the trail. The trail goes around a small marshy area, then comes to a four-way intersection with a hard right (south), that heads down to Trease Lake (where apparently you can view pictured rocks—maybe an exploration for another day). The other two trails are the endpoints of the loop.

The left-most trail brings you immediately to campsites only a short 0.25 mile away, while the middle trail travels along the eastern side of the lake before coming back to these lakeshore campsites. Taking the eastern side,

Angleworm Lake Trail

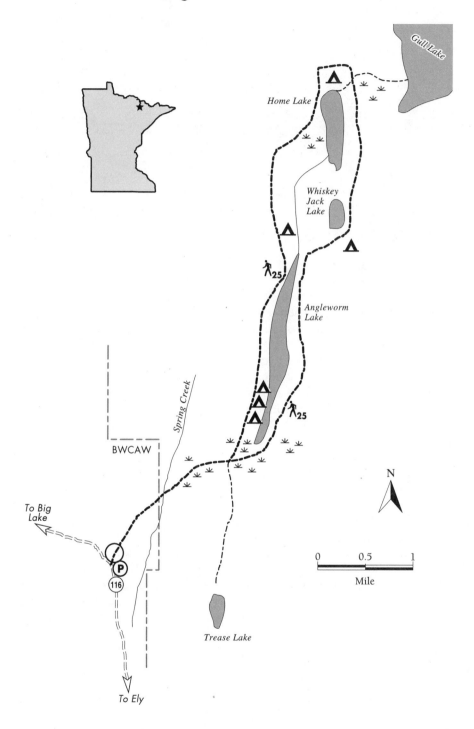

Gull Lake

Home Lake

Whiskey
Jack
Lake

Angleworm
Lake

25

25

Spring Creek

BWCAW

To Big
Lake

P

116

To Ely

Trease Lake

N

0   0.5   1
Mile

Alongside Angleworm Lake.

after crossing a low-lying area, you come to the first scenic view of Angleworm Lake, at 1.5 miles. Then the trail drops into a valley, where a beaver dam provides a bridge across the pond. At 2.5 miles another vantage point presents itself on a ridge, supplying views of a marsh nestled in a deep valley. A few spurs lead down to campsites on this side of the lake. They are tempting to hikers, but they are designated for canoe camping only. At about 4 miles, a hike-in campsite, as marked on the maps, on Whiskey Jack Lake, is where the trail veers away from Angleworm Lake to start a big loop around Whiskey Jack and Home lakes. The first part of the loop passes by some big pines and climbs more ridges for elevated views of the beaver ponds and marshes below.

At about 6 miles, a portage between Gull Lake and Home Lake marks the half-way point. After the portage you cross a creek, leave sight of the lake, and come upon a fine old-growth grove of red and white pines on the hillside. This might be one of the best stands in the state. The trail continues on, climbing ridges then veering back near the Angleworm Lake for views of the bedrock cliffs on the opposite shore. At about 8 miles, a nestled campsite appears along the narrow sliver of the lake. The trail stays a little closer to the lake the rest of the way south and passes by the site of a former fire tower. Near the end of the loop, several spur trails lead to campsites along the water's bedrock edge. The trail then goes back to the familiar intersection and the wide path that leads back to the trailhead.

26 Devil's Cascade Trail

General description:	A wilderness hike past a waterfall to the deep granite gorge of Devil's Cascade.
General location:	East of Lake Jeanette on Echo Trail.
Length:	11-miles, round-trip.
Difficulty:	Difficult. Stream crossing and rugged trail.
Elevation gain:	240 feet; rolling trail.
Special attractions:	Wildlife, waterfall on the Little Indian Sioux River, overlook on Pauness Lake, and the cascades.
Maps:	USGS quad: Shell Lake; also Fischer Map: F-16.
For more informaton:	LaCroix Ranger District, Superior National Forest; see Appendix B.
GPS:	48 08.310N 92 13.818W (Devil's Cascade parking lot).

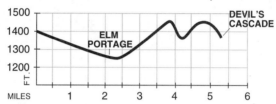

Finding the trailhead: Coming from the west at Buyck, go north on County Road 24 for 4 miles to County Road 116 (Echo Trail). Turn right (east) and travel 17 miles to the small turn-off for Devil's Cascade Trail parking. Watch for a Forest Service sign.

An alternative trailhead and additional parking are about 2 more miles east on an old woods road; this is also the start of the Sioux-Hustler Trail. These trailheads are just a few miles east of Lake Jeanette campground and about 32 miles from Ely on the Echo Trail.

The hike: Devil's Cascade Trail is a short section of the much longer 26-mile Sioux–Hustler Loop (which is a multi-day backpacking trip). Whether you plan to do the longer hike or just the all-day hike mapped out here, it can make a great late summer or fall trip, when bugs should be less of a problem. According to the hiker's log at the beginning of the Sioux-Hustler Trail, it looks like more than a few summertime hikers met their match with the mighty mosquito.

This hike extends to Devil's Cascade, which is the Little Indian Sioux River coming off Lower Pauness Lake by way of a rocky gorge. To get to this scenic attraction, the trail crosses marshes, fords the river next to a small waterfall, and follows it downstream to the cascade. From the Devil's Cascade trailhead, the route goes almost directly north, passing under a scattering of big pines. The remains of a boardwalk guide you over a marshy area, and at 1.5 miles you enter the Boundary Waters Canoe Area Wilderness (BWCAW).

Little Indian Sioux crossing.

Devil's Cascade Trail

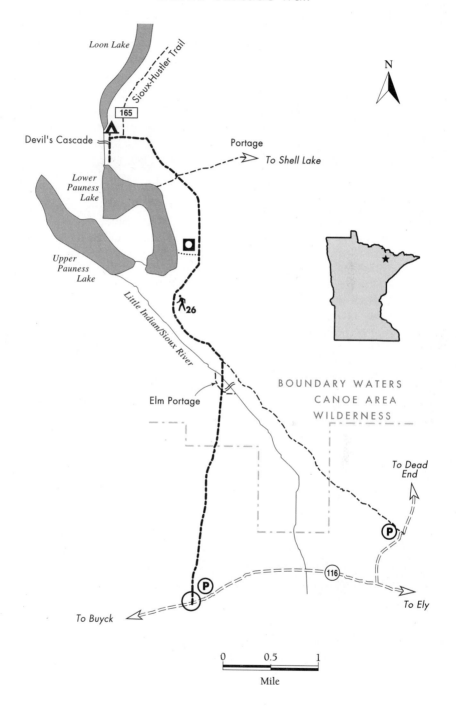

Loon Lake

Sioux-Hustler Trail

165

Devil's Cascade

Portage

To Shell Lake

Lower Pauness Lake

Upper Pauness Lake

Little Indian/Sioux River

🚶26

N

Elm Portage

BOUNDARY WATERS CANOE AREA WILDERNESS

To Dead End

Ⓟ

116

Ⓟ

To Buyck

To Ely

0   0.5   1
Mile

After a little more than 2 miles you come to the Elm Portage, which bypasses some rapids and a small waterfall. This is the spot for the hiker's river crossing. The portage runs parallel to the river's west side, while the hiking path continues on the stream's east side heading downstream. A good place to cross is downstream of the waterfall, which leaps off its rocky ledge's lip to offer just a taste of what the cascade has to offer downstream. In the fall I was able to cross over without filling up my boots by jumping from rock to rock. When the water is a little higher, you might want to take along a cheap pair of sneakers for the crossing, just in case you have to wade across.

The trail from here to the cascades is dry. Until the 3-mile mark the trail parallels the river, going through a cedar grove and providing a few glimpses of the water; then the trail veers away from the river to climb up the ridge alongside Lower Pauness Lake.

At 3.8 miles, a side trail goes to the left for a vista of the lake from a rocky ridge where in season, you might also find a few blueberries. Back on the trail, another 0.5 mile down, you cross a portage between Shell and Lower Pauness lakes. Go another mile to the portage at Devil's Cascade. The hiking trail runs perpendicularly into this 160-rod (0.5-mile) portage. The water falls a total of 75 feet from Lower Pauness Lake into the Little Indian Sioux River. Taking a left on the portage brings you to the upper portion of the cascades, a jumble of huge rocks situated in a tall granite canyon. This is another good place for the cheap sneakers, since wading around the boulders and exploring the walls is half the fun here.

27 Astrid Lake Trail

General description:	A vigorous looping trail that goes through a spruce bog (you won't get your feet wet), and then alongside three scenic lakes.
General location:	Next to Lake Jeanette along Echo Trail.
Length:	About 6 miles, round-trip.
Difficulty:	Moderate on rocky trail.
Elevation gain:	170 feet on a rolling course.
Special attractions:	Bog, some of biggest erratics in the area, and overlooks.
Maps:	Forest Service hiking map; USGS quads: Astrid Lake, Lake Jeannette; Fischer: F-8, F-15.
Camping:	3 hike-in sites. Campground at Lake Jeannette.
For more informaton:	LaCroix Ranger District, Superior National Forest; see Appendix B.
GPS:	48 07.890N 92 17.724W.

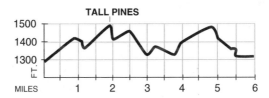

Finding the trailhead: Park at the Lake Jeanette campground. The lakeside campground is located along County Road 116 (Echo Trail), a long and winding 37 miles from Ely. Or coming from the other direction, from the city of Orr (off of U.S. Highway 53), take County Road 23 for 17 miles east to Buyck where it turns into County Road 24. Travel 4 miles north to the western terminus of CR 116 and drive east on CR 116 for about 15 miles to Lake Jeanette campground. Parking is also available on the other side of the trail system along the side of Forest Road 200, 2.5 miles south of Echo Trail.

The hike: Astrid Lake Trail is located outside the Boundary Waters Canoe Area Wilderness, so no special permits are needed for hiking or camping at backcountry sites. This pleasant little hike is ideal for anyone staying at the nearby Lake Jeanette campground. Though it doesn't have tall peaks or the most scenic of overlooks, it does offer enough, in a humble way, to make an enjoyable hike. The trail goes from a black spruce bog to quiet lakes, big trees, and big boulders.

Starting from the parking lot in the campground, follow a side trail that leads you past the walk-in campsites toward the boat launch. At the paved boat launch, head down the road about a 100 feet to the spot where the southernmost part of the lake goes near the road. On the other side of CR 116 is the true start of the trail. This first part doubles as a canoe portage

Astrid Lake Trail

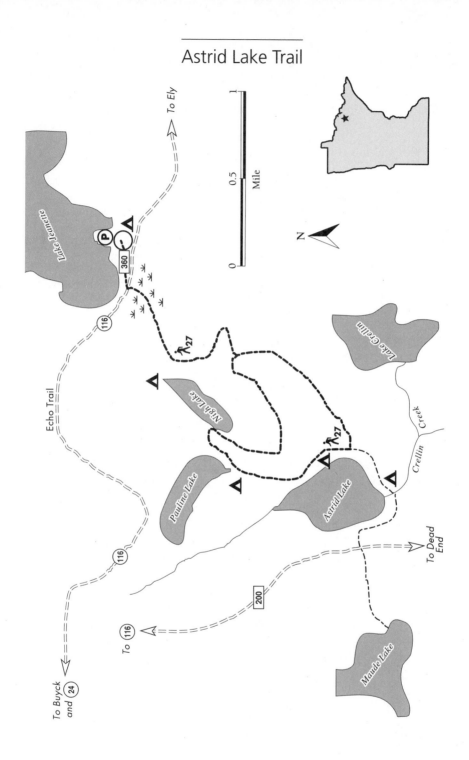

between Lake Jeanette and Nigh Lake. The trail then enters a scraggly black spruce bog. Places like this normally mean getting your feet wet or walking on a boardwalk, but here the trail stays dry.

Keep your eyes open for carnivorous bog plants, such as the pitcher plant. Soon the path leads to bedrock, begins a climb up a small hill, and you arrive at Nigh Lake. You then descend into another low-lying area, then climb up the major hill, at 1,500 feet elevation, to find a stand of big pines. The loop's main intersection is at the top; go left here, following the cairns for the trail.

The trail drops down again and continues along a hilly path until it comes to Astrid Lake and the Maude Lake Trail intersection. Going north you pass by a campsite with a sandy beach, then 0.25 mile beyond you will find one of the big glacier rocks. At about 4 miles the trail connects with the Pauline and Nigh Lake loop. This loop is a hiking-only trail with a shortcut for cross-country skiing, which cuts about 1 mile off the hike. If you take the shortcut you will miss a high overlook above the lake and some nice hilly terrain. The return path leads past more huge boulders over which to marvel.

28 Herriman Lake Trail

General description:	Actually a network of trails that go off in nearly all directions. This hike just follows the path along the Echo River, which leads to an overlook on a large bedrock knob covered with oaks, maples, and lichens.
General location:	North of Buyck near Crane Lake.
Length:	7.4 miles, round-trip; about a 15-mile network of trails branching out to the surrounding lakes.
Difficulty:	Moderate. Most of the trails are on a wide grassy path with a few spots on a rough trail.
Elevation gain:	About 230 feet to the overlook above the river.
Special attractions:	Scenic overlooks and wildlife.
Maps:	Forest Service trail map; USGS quad: Crane Lake.
Camping:	3 hike-in sites.
For more informaton:	LaCroix Ranger District, Superior National Forest; see Appendix B.
GPS:	48 15.055N 92 27.570W.

HIGH POINT

1400
1300
1200
1100

FT.

MILES   1   2   3

Finding the trailhead: From Orr and U.S. Highway 53, take County Road 23 for 16 miles to Buyck and County Road 24. Travel 9 miles north on CR 24 to County Road 424, where you turn right and go 2 more miles to a parking turnoff on the left side of the road. This is just a couple of miles before the end of this road on Crane Lake. The trail starts on the other side of the road.

The hike: Herriman Lake Trail is actually a network of trails located in the northwestern corner of the Boundary Waters Canoe Area Wilderness (BWCAW). Resorts start popping up to the west of here and Voyageurs National Park borders farther to the north, but the trails still seem out of the way and offer some remote hiking to unique spots.

There are three main loops that lead off in three cardinal directions: to Dovre Lake, Little Vermillion Lake, and down to Herriman Lake and Echo River. Most of the system is manageable in a day, though there are some backcountry campsites available for those wishing to camp and spend a night on Little Vermillion Lake, with its sandy beach, or along the shores of Knute Lake. The Dovre Lake Trail is a 4-mile loop that leads to an overlook of the lake and forests beyond. All but the Herriman Lake Trail are dual purpose cross-country and hiking trails, so the paths are wide and fairly smooth going. The exception, which leads to Herriman Lake, is a rugged footpath with several switchbacks leading to overlooks of the lake and connecting with the Echo River Trail. This hike negotiates a rolling riverside ridge which ends on a large bedrock knoll, covered with lichens and mosses and a sparse grove of stunted oak and maples.

The trail starts across the road from the parking lot and goes 0.25 mile straight to the picnic area and the bridge over Echo River. This bridge crosses a set of rapids and, no doubt, at least a few people make this impressive spot their destination. After crossing the river, take a right to follow the river south. The trail runs through a rolling course of mostly birch and aspen forest parallel to the river, which is not always within sight.

At the 0.75-mile mark, the trail intersects with the Herriman Lake Trail, which comes in from the east. Turn here on the way back to extend the trip to Herriman Lake. Next up at 1 mile is a beaver dam, which adds a bit of flavor to the landscape.

At 1.75 miles the trail passes by big rock outcroppings, then in another mile the trail splits at a large rock cairn to begin the loop on the smooth convex-shaped knoll.

Cairns are the major trail markers here, these rock piles appear about every 50 yards or so. Still they might be hidden behind shrubs or a tree, so it might take a little guesswork to find and stay on the trail. If you find yourself walking on lichen you are probably off the trail, so head back to the last cairn to find the proper path again. The knoll's bare rock features a profusion of subtly colored lichen and scrub oak forest that should provide vivid colors in the fall. The knoll itself does not have the sharp cliffs of some places; instead, it gently slopes down to the valley below. While you are hopping from cairn to cairn do not miss the overlooks that present views of the wide Echo River valley and surrounding forests.

Herriman Lake Trail

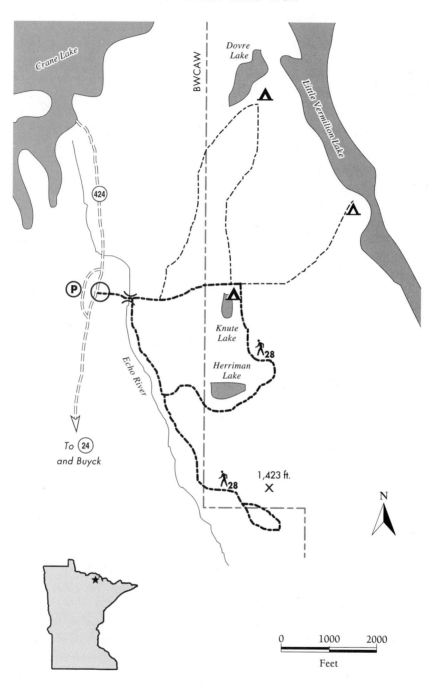

Crane Lake

Dovre Lake

BWCAW

Little Vermilion Lake

424

P

Echo River

Knute Lake

Herriman Lake

28

To 24 and Buyck

28

1,423 ft.
X

N

0   1000   2000
Feet

29 Vermilion Gorge Trail

General description:	A hike paralleling the Vermilion River gorge as it makes it way into Crane Lake.
General location:	Next to Crane Lake, north of Orr.
Length:	3 miles, round-trip.
Difficulty:	Moderate, on a gravel trail most of the way. Steep cliffs—exercise caution.
Elevation gain:	About 60 feet.
Special attractions:	Overlooks of the gorge and interpretive signs.
Maps:	Superior National Forest Trail map; USGS quads: Crane Lake and Johnson Lake.
For more informaton:	LaCroix Ranger District, Superior National Forest; see Appendix B.
GPS:	48 16.200N 92 29.446W.

Finding the trailhead: From Buyck, travel north on County Route 24 to Crane Lake. In the town of Crane Lake, stay left on Gold Coast Road for parking, which is about 0.1 mile past the U.S. Customs and the Voyageurs National Park Service offices.

The hike: Voyageurs used the Vermilion River as a trade route, to connect Lake Superior, by way of the Saint Louis River, with the far north. Today, the Vermilion River is still one of the state's outstanding canoeing rivers, with a mix of slow and fast moving sections that pass through wild rice beds, fast rapids, waterfalls, and the Vermilion gorge. The gorge is 1 mile from the mouth of the Vermilion River, which drains a sizeable watershed of more than 1,000 square miles out of the surrounding landscape. Carved out of granite along the Canadian Shield's western edge, the gorge is surrounded by 60-foot sheer cliffs.

Except for boaters entering Voyageurs National Park from the southern access point on Crane Lake, few people probably know or visit this out-of-the-way hike. From the trailhead, the trail follows a maintained gravel trail. After about 0.25 mile, near the top of a hill, the Voyageurs Snowmobile Trail veers off to the left. Boardwalks cross over the wetter spots of the trail, which passes through an aspen and birch forest.

As it nears the river, the trail takes a sharp turn south to follow the Vermilion upstream. Here the gravel trail narrows down and ends. Start a steep climb to an overlook where the dense understory gives way to an open, park-like grove of red pine on top of a knoll. From the knoll you can see the Vermilion River complete its 38-mile journey from Lake Vermilion to Crane Lake.

As you descend from the red pine knoll, you will approach the river and the mouth of the gorge. The trail has interpretive signs along the way detailing the history of logging, mineral prospecting, and the voyageurs.

Vermilion Gorge Trail

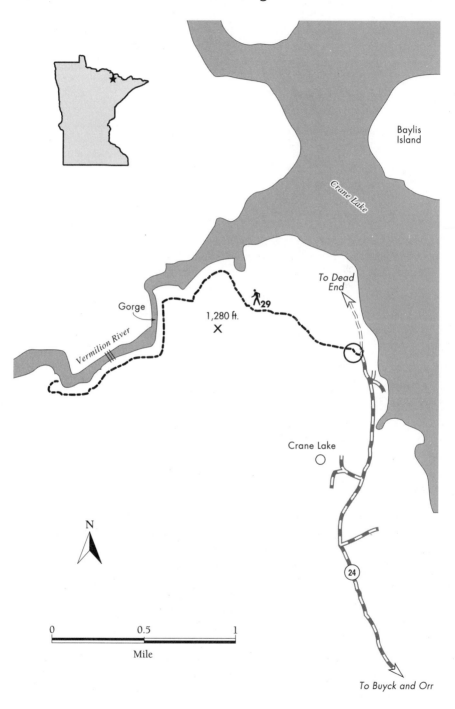

Baylis Island

Crane Lake

Gorge

1,280 ft.
X

Vermilion River

To Dead End

Crane Lake

24

N

0   0.5   1

Mile

To Buyck and Orr

Note: The Vermilion Falls Trail is another nearby trail farther upstream. It is accessible off of Forest Road 491. This is a short 0.25-mile trail that leads to a narrow 10-foot wide gap where the river rockets through a cataract.

---

30 Cruiser Lake Trail

General description:	A trail accessible only by boat. The rough trail runs upon bedrock, by beaver dams and up to a high ridge above Cruiser Lake.
General location:	On the Kabetogama Peninsula in Voyageurs National Park.
Length:	About a 7.5 mile round trip.
Difficulty:	Moderate to difficult. Trail, by turns, is both mucky and rocky.
Elevation gain:	About 200 feet on a rolling course.
Special attractions:	Canoes at Cruiser Lake (canoe reservations can be made at the ranger station), scenic views, numerous beaver ponds, and a waterfall.
Maps:	National Park Service map, USGS quad: Ash River NE.
Camping:	2 hike-in sites.
For more informaton:	Voyageurs National Park; see Appendix B.
GPS:	48 27.919N 92 49.230W at the trailhead.

Finding the trailhead: The park has four entry points off of U.S. Highway 53, which are all marked with Park Service signs. Any of the entry points can get you to the hike, though Ash River, which is about 10 miles east of US 53 on County Route 129 (Ash River Trail) is probably the closest. Another popular entrance is at the Kabetogama Visitors Center 1 mile north on County Route 122. This hike is at the end of Lost Bay, accessible only by boat in the summer. Boat rentals or boat taxis are available at nearby resorts if you do not bring your own.

The hike: Voyageurs National Park's thrity lakes occupy some 38 percent of the park's 217,892 acres. This is a lake-based park where long stretches of water serve as the main paths leading to many small islands, inlets, and the Kabetogama Peninsula. This large (26 by 7.5 miles) peninsula, has the majority of the park's hikes, including this one, which leads up to Cruiser Lake. Another trail, called Locator Lake Trail, is found farther west on the peninsula, and hooks up with a chain of lakes that are ideal to explore by canoe. By hiking in the park, one joins a long history of exploration in this region, beginning with the French-Canadian voyageurs who paddled this water highway in search of pelts, then miners who looked for gold (they extracted $5,000 in ore), followed by lumberjacks who took their share of

Cruiser Lake Trail

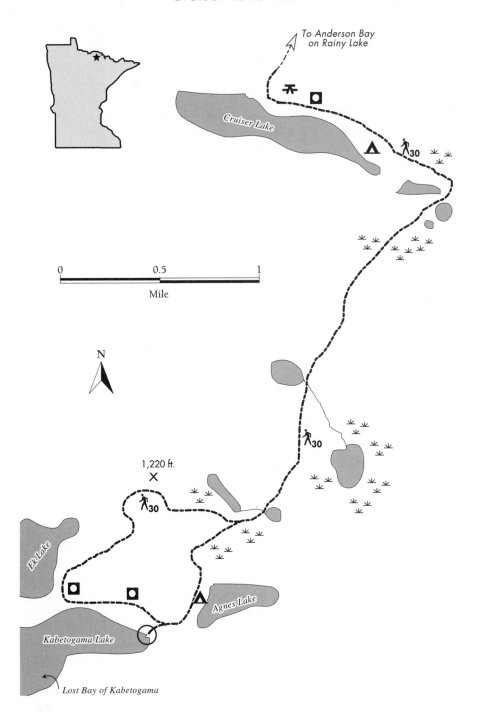

To Anderson Bay
on Rainy Lake

Cruiser Lake

30

0   0.5   1
Mile

N

1,220 ft.
X

30

30

Elk Lake

Agnes Lake

Kabetogama Lake

Lost Bay of Kabetogama

The boardwalk to the campsite on Cruiser Lake.

the trees. Then, fishermen harvested lake sturgeon from its waters, and the land even saw a small blueberry-picking industry spring up among its numerous patches. Today, it has reverted back to a wilderness where wolves roam unbothered by civilization.

Take a boat to the eastern end of Lost Bay. At the end of the bay is a hiking sign posted on the shoreline, clearly visible as you arrive by water. Land at the boat dock and scramble up the hill to the Voyageurs National Park trail map posted under the trees; this is the start of trail system. About 500 feet down the trail, stay to the right at the first three-way intersection as you head to Cruiser Lake. At a little less than 0.5 mile, a spur goes off to the right for a camping spot on Agnes Lake. Continue on skirting a scenic marsh, which drains into Agnes Lake on your right.

Next you come to an intersection with the upper half of the Ek Lake Trail, which explores deeper woods and leads to overlooks of Ek Lake and Lost Bay. For your return trip, this is a good trail to take. The path follows the boardwalk, which passes by and nearly under the huge beaver dam. On the other side, enter into a young mixed forest with excellent views of a large marsh and small pond. At about 2.25 miles you pass by another beaver pond (where an old overlook trail previously veered off to the left of the pond). The trail to Cruiser Lake continues straight ahead on rolling terrain and some exposed lichen-covered bedrock, where small rock cairns lead the way.

The 3-mile mark brings the trail to a surprising find: a cool, small creek and its 10-foot waterfall. Continuing on, the trail goes around the bend, then comes to an intersection with the campsite spur. A left heads down to this campsite, out in the lake on an island. A sturdy boardwalk connects the site to land, where you will find an elevated tent pad, picnic table, and canoes. If you remembered to sign up for a canoe at the ranger station and received a key to unlock a canoe, you can do some paddling on this remote lake. More scenic views can be found above the lake farther down the trail. On the northeast side of the lake is the turn-around point for this day hike. Plan to set up a picnic spot near the water before heading back.

For a longer trip the trail continues on up to Brown Lake and over to Anderson Bay. There is also discussion of putting in a new trail along the north side of Beast Lake, which leads down to Mica Bay. Either of these would make a great trip. Both could be done by arranging a vehicle shuttle on the far side for a one-way hike with no backtracking.

North Country

When the last glaciers receded ten thousand years ago, they left behind moraines covering most of this region with a thick glacial till. The terrain reflects its origins with a landscape dotted with innumerable lakes and rolling hills. More than 150 years ago this land was still a wilderness, when two discoveries were made in the area—iron ore and the wealth of the pine forests. The iron ore deposits were the richest finds in the world, while logging turned into a major industry for the state. The original habitat consisted of a mixed forest of aspen and pines; a few places still retain their native character. Today, the forest is mostly covered in secondary growth, which still makes for a good habitat for wildlife watching. Big bogs, swamps, and peatlands also cover large sections of this part of the state. These are actually some of the most pristine places in Minnesota, but they are also the most inaccessible and inhospitable.

At the center of Minnesota's North Country area is the Chippewa National Forest. The forest spans between Bemidji and Grand Rapids, covers more than 1,000 square miles, and encompasses countless lakes, including three major ones: Cass Lake, Leech Lake, and Lake Winnibigoshish. While Minnesota's other national forest might have more designated wilderness areas, this one offers easier access and several interesting hikes. In the northern part of the area, a short hike passes through a stand of towering pines hundreds of years old at Lost Forty. On the southern edge of the forest, a couple of sections of the North Country Trail thread their way through many woods and lakes.

Other hikes in this section feature assorted unique attractions. Near Park Rapids, hike to the source of the Mississippi at Itasca State Park. You can finds lots of rolling glacial terrain near Brainerd in Pillsbury State Forest. At Scenic State Park, a mile-long esker zigzags its way out into a lake for one of the most unusual and scenic trails in the state. And finally, there is a tour of wetlands on a boardwalk that visits marsh, lake, and a bog.

31 Bog Walk

General description:	A short hike on a floating boardwalk passing through a wide variety of wetlands.
General location:	City of Orr.
Difficulty:	Easy, all on a boardwalk. Handicapped accessible.
Elevation gain:	Nominal. Flat course.
Special attractions:	Wildflowers and carnivorous plants, as well as birds and other wildlife.
Maps:	Available at the trailhead. USGS quad: Orr.
For more information:	Orr Tourist Information Center; see Appendix B.
GPS:	48 02.863N 92 49.912W.

Finding the trailhead: Alongside U.S. Highway 53 at the visitors center just south (about 1 mile) of Orr. Park behind the information building.

The hike: The Bog Walk might be one of the easiest hikes in this book, yet it is diverse and interesting. The hike, all on a wide floating boardwalk, goes through six different wetland environments, all in a short 0.5-mile loop. It passes by a black ash swamp, tamarack forest, alder thicket, cattail marsh, lake, and black spruce bog. Probably the most popular section is the bog, where one can find carnivorous vegetation including the native pitcher plants.

From the back of the parking lot go to the National Park Service information signs, behind which the trail enters the black ash swamp, which leads to the main loop. In this first section, you can seasonally find the big flowers of marsh marigolds, irises, and orchids. At the start of the loop, a right leads to the tamarack swamp.

The tamarack is Minnesota's only coniferous tree to lose all of its leaves every year, which it does in a grand fashion, flashing brilliant yellows and golds. On the forest floor is a soft layer of sphagnum moss and clintonia (sometimes called the bluebead lily). Farther on in the walk the forest turns into an alder swamp, which then opens up near a beaver lodge nestled among the cattails.

At the point where Pelican River winds it way into Orr Bay (a part of Pelican Lake), you will find a couple of benches for relaxing along the water's edge—a perfect spot to watch for birds. The last wetland, the black spruce bog, gives you a chance to search for carnivorous pitcher plants or other bog

Bog Walk

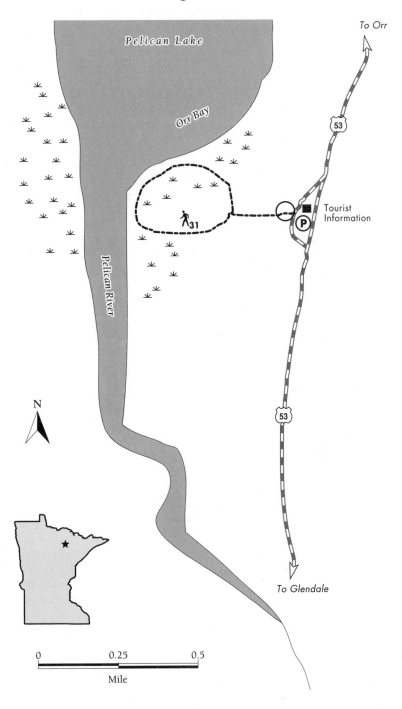

plants like Labrador tea (the plant with the fuzzy leaves on the underside), bog rosemary, and laurel.

Note: This hike is on the way to Voyageurs National Park and makes for an ideal leg stretcher on the journey north.

32 Scenic State Park

General description:	A hike along a high narrow forested ridge that partially divides 2 lakes.
General location:	East of Bigfork.
Length:	1.6 miles, round-trip. 14-mile trail network in the park.
Difficulty:	Easy, follows wide path to tip of the point. Benches along the way.
Elevation gain:	Ridge is about 70 feet off of the waters edge.
Special attractions:	The esker, an observation tower—guided tours July through August, beach and wildflowers.
Maps:	State park trail map; USGS quad: Coon Lake.
Camping:	117 drive-in and 6 hike-in sites.
For more information:	Department of Natural Resources Information Center; see Appendix B.
GPS:	47 42 739N 93 34.196W at the campground.

Finding the trailhead: From Grand Rapids go north on Minnesota Highway 38 to Bigfork. Turn east on County Road 7 and travel 7 miles to the park's entrance on the left side (north). Park at either the picnic area and beach or right at the start of the trail about 0.3 mile into the park at a small turnoff.

The hike: When the state established this park in 1921, they appropriately named it Scenic. Fortunately, the place still lives up to its title. The park offers pine trees, pleasant trails around the lake, and panoramic views from the Chase Point Trail. The trail actually follows the upper ridge of an esker, which is one of those things that gets mentioned in geology books, but seldom elsewhere.

Eskers are elevated, high ridges winding like snakes on the ground. They came about when glaciers covered the ground with a couple of hundred feet deep of ice. As the climate warmed, the glacier melted and created huge internal rivers, which also carried whatever rock or gravel that happened to be in the ice. At the mouth of these rivers, the gravel dropped out in piles as the glacier receded. The piles were dumped one right after another, incrementally growing in length to form an esker. (If only one pile is left, its called a kame, which is a cone-shaped hill). A ranger at the park can go into more detail about these unusual formations.

The Chase Point Trail starts about 500 feet up from the parking spot.

Scenic State Park

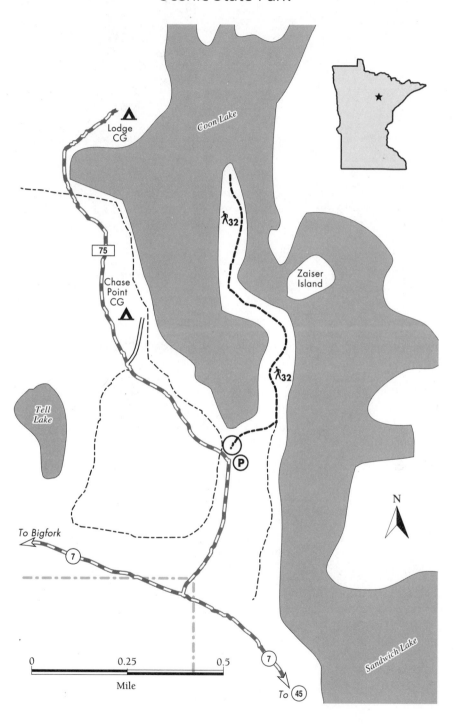

Coon Lake

Lodge
CG

75

Chase
Point
CG

Tell
Lake

Zaiser
Island

32

32

P

Sandwich Lake

To Bigfork

7

7

To 45

N

0   0.25   0.5
Mile

The esker on Chase Point Trail.

Another trail comes in from the lake's south side on the right, but our trail heads to the north (left) going onto the peninsula.

From this point on, the trail may be one of the easiest in this book, since you simply follow the gently undulating ridge surrounded by water. As you walk along, keep an eye out for the trail's interpretive signs. These point out the different habitats. On the thin sinuous ridge, you will travel through groves of white-cedar, spruce, and red pine (where the ground is a carpet of pine needles). At about 0.25 mile at a sharp curve in the esker, you come to a plaque that commemorates Zaiser Island, located just offshore from this spot. Along the path the trail offers a few benches to stop and sit and admire the water shimmering through the trees about fifty feet below. At the end of this ridge trail the peninsula's tip features an overlook deck with stairs leading down to the water's edge. No doubt this is a popular picnic and sunbathing spot. Located in the middle of the water, the point gives excellent views of Coon Lake looking back across Sandwich Lake, which is connected to Coon Lake by a narrow channel of water.

33 Lost Forty Trail

General description:	A short hike through an old-growth forest of big pines, with a spur to Moose Brook.
General location:	North of Dora Lake and near Noma Lake campground.
Length:	1 mile, round-trip.
Difficulty:	Easy.
Elevation gain:	Nominal, about 25 feet down to the brook.
Special attractions:	Big old-growth red and white pines.
Maps:	Interpretive trail map from Chippewa National Forest; USGS quad: Coddington Lake.
Camping:	Forest Service nearby campground at Noma Lake.
For more information:	Blackduck Ranger District, Chippewa National Forest; see Appendix B.
GPS:	47 45.969N 94 05.047W.

Finding the trailhead: Starting from Blackduck and U.S. Highway 71, take Beltrami County Road 30, which changes into Itasca County Road 13, for 13 miles east to Alvwood. From here go north on Minnesota Highway 46 for 0.5 mile and then turn right onto Itasca County Road 29. Travel about 2 more miles until, on the left, you find Forest Road 2240. About 1.5 miles down this dirt road you arrive at the sign for Lost Forty where there is parking off to the left. The trail starts on the north (right) side.

The hike: Driving to this spot, it is hard to believe that a stand of old-growth trees awaits you. All that is noticeable along the road are miles of scraggly, black spruce swamps and lakes. Maybe it's understandable that back in 1882 the only thing the surveying team mapped out was a large lake at the site of the Lost Forty. They extended an already surveyed lake, named Coddington Lake, 0.5 mile to the northwest, thereby putting a good chunk of forested land underwater, at least on the map. By doing this they also kept a sizeable tract of virgin pines hidden from the logging companies. Their mistake is our gain of the Lost Forty.

For hikers, it provides a beautiful stand of trees and a previously unsurveyed lake—Dishpan Lake. At the trailhead is a copy of the original plat showing the mistake as well as the correction. The area recovered from the mapping error is actually 144 acres. I guess Lost 144 does not have the same ring to it.

The forest contains 28 acres of old-growth red pines and a few white pines. The trail covers the northern half of the mistake by making a loop, and rests upon a low esker between two swampy areas. An interpretive guide is available for the twelve nature stations along the way.

From the parking lot the trailhead is on the other side of the road. The hike is basically a simple stroll through a majestic forest full of old pines. Here you can come up close to these old trees and see the sap running down

Lost Forty Trail

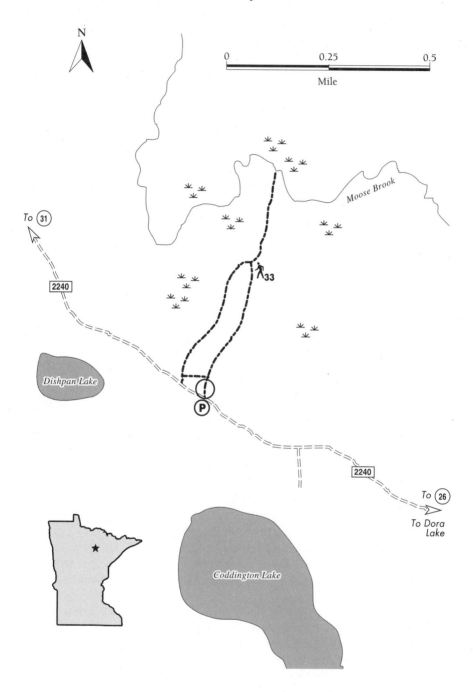

the bark, which also fills the air with pine scent. Some of the trees 350 years old and 150 inches in circumference. Another indicate forest is untouched is the number of snags and fallen giants ly... ground. At about 0.3 mile you come to the spur, continuing on another u.z mile to Moose Brook. The trail gently descends to this meandering shrub-lined brook, which winds its way to Big Fork River.

Note: The Lost Forty also is a Scientific and Natural Area of the Department of Natural Resources.

34 Suomi Hills Trail

General description:	A rolling course through a mixed hardwood forest weaving around eight lakes and ponds.
General location:	South of Marcell.
Length:	About 4.5 miles, round-trip.
Difficulty:	Moderate. Take bug repellent.
Elevation gain:	50 feet. A lot of hills.
Special attractions:	Fall colors, blueberries, mushrooms, and wildlife. Also a popular fishing spot for bass and panfish.
Maps:	Forest Service trail map. USGS quad: Little Bowstring Lake.
Camping:	2 hike-in sites.
For more information:	Marcell Ranger District, Chippewa National Forest; see Appendix B.
GPS:	47 28.574N 93 38.659W.

Finding the trailhead: The recreational area has northern and southern parking lots. For this hike, go to the northern one. To get there, follow Minnesota Highway 38 about 21 miles north of Grand Rapids, or go 10 miles south of Marcell to the parking area on the west side of the road. In this lot a rutted dirt road leads to the boat launch on Adele Lake.

The hike: Finns pronounce *Suomi* as "Soo-o-mi," which means "Finland." This region with its rolling hills, thick forests, and numerous lakes probably has more in common with Finland than just its name. For five years starting in 1905, loggers, many Finnish, worked to clear the area, taking the virgin pines out on tote roads using horses and steam-powered cables. In the 1930s, a Civilian Conservation Corps camp, which was established near the north parking lot, served as a center for trail building, fighting fires, and planting pines. Only in the 1970s did the area go non-motorized and now has more than 20 miles of trails. Many of the trails with smooth rolling hills are ideal for cross-country skiing, but they are also decent enough for a little summertime exploration. Note that during the summer months the area can be buggy, so remember your insect spray.

The selected hiking loop goes down along the shores of Spruce Island

Suomi Hills Trail

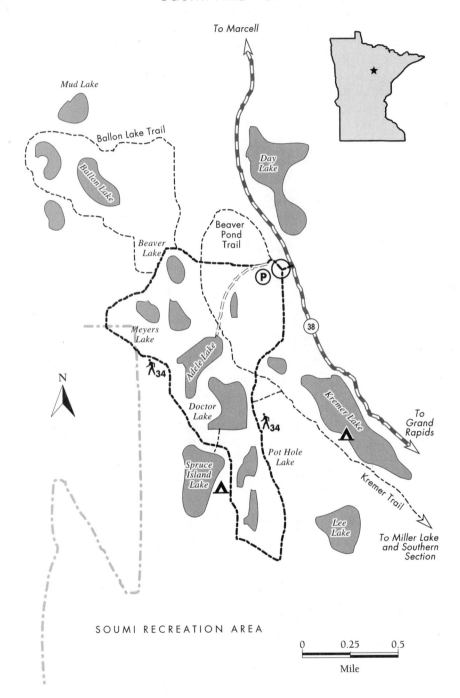

To Marcell

Mud Lake

Ballon Lake Trail

Day Lake

Ballon Lake

Beaver Pond Trail

Beaver Lake

P

38

Meyers Lake

Adele Lake

34

Kremer Lake

To Grand Rapids

Doctor Lake

34

Pot Hole Lake

Spruce Island Lake

Kremer Trail

Lee Lake

To Miller Lake and Southern Section

N

SOUMI RECREATION AREA

0   0.25   0.5

Mile

Lake and up around Beaver Lake. Trails also extend to Barney, B⸍ Mud lakes farther to the north. The southern section of Suomⁱ takes in several lakes, including Miller Lake, which would make ⸜ ⸜ trip. In 1982, this lake's impoundment broke open, creating a 40-foot ⸜⸜ in the lake's side, effectively draining it in dramatic fashion.

Start south from the main parking lot. At about 0.6 mile, the trail comes to a 4-way intersection with a converted forest road (Kremer Trail), which accesses the southern half of the recreational area and another fork, which leads to a bluff alongside Doctor Lake. Take the middle fork here and climb the hill, on top of which is another shortcut over to the Kremer Trail. Continue on and you will pay Doctor Lake a call. Along the way, be sure to check out small Pothole Lake (named for its glacier ice block origin). Skirt around a couple of marshy spots and a small unnamed lake, then turn back north to the campsite on Spruce Island Lake, a couple of miles in.

This is one of the two hiker-only campsites. The campsite is located on the end of a peninsula, and includes a fire grate and a lakeside view that looks out across Spruce Island Lake to a small island with (surprise) some spruce trees on it. The trail continues on, crossing a portage that connects Doctor Lake with Spruce Island Lake. After the lake, the trail climbs a hill on the north side of Spruce Island Lake and starts a hillier section. You will pass by Myers Lake at the top of the loop and then Beaver Lake. At the forest road it is another 0.75 mile back to the parking. Before you reach the lot, a side loop veers off from the lake access road to form the Beaver Pond Loop.

35 Simpson Creek Trail

General description:	A hike along a high serpentine ridge (an esker) that parallels Simpson Creek.
General location:	Northwest of Grand Rapids. On the northeast end of Cut Foot Sioux Lake.
Length:	5 miles, round-trip.
Difficulty:	Easy. Trails follow converted forest roads.
Elevation gain:	About 50 feet.
Special attractions:	Esker and wildlife.
Maps:	Forest Service trail map, USGS quad: Max.
Camping:	East Seelye Bay and O-ne-gum-e Forest Service campgrounds are nearby.
For more information:	Deer River Ranger District, Chippewa National Forest; see Appendix B.
GPS:	47 31.10N 94 02.783W.

Finding the trailhead: From U.S. Highway 2 and the city of Deer River, travel northwest on Minnesota 46 for about 17 miles for the center. Parking is at the Cut Foot Sioux Visitor Center on MN 46.

Simpson Creek Trail

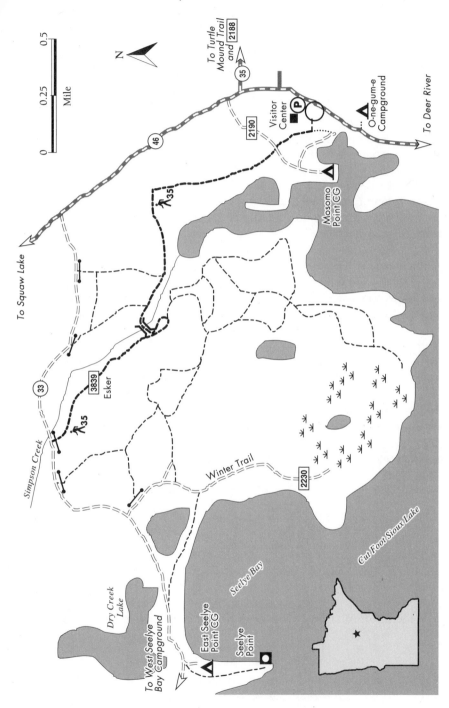

The hike: This recreation area is named for Sam Simpson, who in 1908 began logging the area and built a network of forest roads in the process. Since much of the area is swampy, he probably did much of the cutting in the winter over the frozen ground. Today, many of the trails are also set up for winter-only use and they are allowed to become overgrown during the summer. Most intersections in the network are labeled with letters, which helps out greatly in what can be a confusing trail system. I found the most interesting path to be the fairly easy path along the esker. This follows Simpson Creek for about 1 mile, crossing the river, then running for a stretch on the esker's ridge.

Another short trail nearby is the Seelye Point picnic area, which extends to an overlook in the middle of Cut Foot Sioux Lake. Circling this area is the Cut Foot Sioux Trail system, a large loop connecting miles of Forest Roads through pine and hardwood forests. Most of these trails, however, are horse trails, where hiking is only a secondary activity.

The Simpson Creek Trail starts on the left side of the visitors center, beginning on a paved path under the big pines. This path eventually leads to a boat launch, so at about 100 feet, take the small footpath on the right leading to the esker. The hiking trail passes over Forest Road 2190, which also leads down to the boat landing and to the mouth of Simpson Creek. After the marker labeled with a T, cross the creek and go up to marker M. Take a right turn here to get on top of the narrow esker ridge, which is also labeled Forest Road 3837 on the topo maps.

This ridge runs parallel to the creek on the right and has a swampy area to the left. It is covered with a thick forest and similar to Chase Point at Scenic State Park, with its high, steep sides. This ridge-top trail extends for another mile up to County Road 33 (FR 2198). At the road, you can either retrace your steps, go down the road in either direction to hook up with any other trail and do a loop, or follow the road down to Seelye Point for an overlook of the lake.

36 North Country National Trail

General description:	A rolling trail that passes by (though not always alongside) many secluded lakes in the Chippewa National Forest.
General location:	South of Walker.
Length:	About 14 miles, round-trip.
Difficulty:	Moderate. Easy-to-follow path on rolling course.
Elevation gain:	About 100-feet on many hills.
Special attractions:	Wildlife and fishing on out-of-the-way lakes.
Maps:	North Country Trail Map. USGS quads: Jack Lake, Webb Lake, and Hackensack (The topo maps show the trail and are more detailed than the handout map).
Camping:	4 hike-in sites.
For more information:	Walker Ranger District, Chippewa National Forest; see Appendix B.
GPS:	47 00.084N 94 30.890W.

Finding the trailhead: From Walker and Minnesota Highway 371, travel south for about 2 miles on MN 371 to Forest Road 2107 (Woodtick Trail) where you turn east. Another mile brings you to a small turn off at Woodtick Fields and the start of this section of the trail.

The hike: Of the nation's planned long-distance interstate trails, the North Country National Trail (NCT) will be the longest. The route will eventually reach across the country, connecting New York, Pennsylvania, Ohio, Michigan, Wisconsin, Minnesota, and North Dakota. Much of the trail is still in the planning stages, but when completed, the final distance will cover about 3,200 miles. Here, within the Chippewa National Forest, the route runs for 68 miles, and of that, this hike covers only a short scenic portion.

Chippewa National Forest is Minnesota's first national forest and has been actively logged, though a few groves of old big pines still remain at Old Pines Trail, just north of Shingobee, and at Hazel Lake. While this hike does not pass by the old-growth forests, it does go by nearly a dozen lakes and ponds where the fishing is said to be decent and where you can literally have the lake to yourself. The trail is also on public land, so camping is allowed anywhere. However, you can take advantage of a few dispersed and improved campsites marked on the map at Woodtick, Hovde, Gut, and North Stocking lakes. Of these, Gut Lake makes the best camping spot for an overnight trip, being perfectly positioned on the shaded lake shore. The trail runs parallel to FR 2107 (Woodtick Trail) and has a few forest roads cutting across its path. A loop of nearly any distance is possible by going down one of these roads and taking the Woodtick Trail back to complete the loop.

This hike goes from Forest Road 3759 to Forest Road 2110, with parking

North Country National Trail

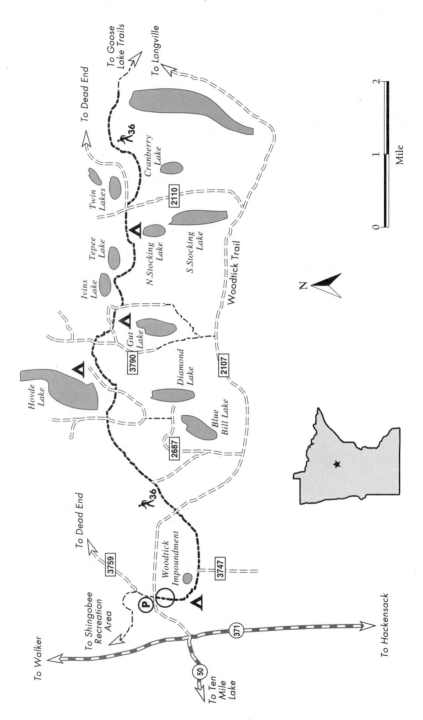

available next to the Woodtick Fields homestead. The large, open field was a pasture in the 1930s. The first section of the trail goes across the road south to the Woodtick Impoundment. This impoundment, which formed a small pond, is one of fifty that the Forest Service made in 1976 to increase the habitat for waterfowl and wildlife. In a little more than a mile, the trail swings north and cuts back over the Woodtick Trail to thread its way between a cluster of lakes. With all these lakes and marshes, bugs can be ferocious in the warm months of the year. Come prepared with bug spray and maybe even long sleeves and pants.

At 0.5 mile from the road the trail passes a couple of lakes on the left, then shortly drops down a hill about 80 feet, turning north at the bottom. At Hovde Lake, the trail passes a campsite on the hill above the lake. While the campsite is nicely sheltered, it is a little walk down a 40-foot bank to the water's edge. The trail crosses over the more substantial Forest Road 3790 in another mile.

When you come to Gut Lake, you will be pleasantly surprised to find a campsite under a nice stand of pines by the water. This makes an ideal site for an overnight stay. The spot was also quite welcoming as a bug-free zone when I visited. Another 0.5 mile to the north brings you to Ivins Lake, then the trail leads uneventfully between Tepee Lake and North Stocking Lake; the latter should have had a campsite on it, but I missed it.

Another 0.5 mile takes you to FR 2110, where you head south to get back on the Woodtick Trail. If planning a longer trip, keep going east on the Goose Lake Trail system, a couple of miles ahead. Once on the Woodtick Trail, there is not much road traffic, making for a pleasant enough walk back to the trailhead (especially if the mosquitoes are bad in the woods). This hike could also be coordinated and planned with a bike drop for the journey back to the start.

37 Shingobee Recreation Area

General description:	A roller coaster course passing next to the Shingobee River and a section of the North Country Trail.
General location:	West of Walker on the southwest side of Leech Lake.
Length:	6 miles, round-trip.
Difficulty:	Moderate.
Elevation gain:	About 100 feet. Hilly terrain.
Special attractions:	Access to the North Country Trail, overlooks, and wildlife.
Maps:	Forest Service trail map, USGS quads: Akeley and Walker.
Camping:	1 hike-in site.
For more information:	Walker Ranger District, Chippewa National Forest; see Appendix B.
GPS:	47 02.046N 94 38.599W.

Finding the trailhead: From Walker travel 6 miles south, or from Akeley go northeast 5 miles on Minnesota Highway 34. Park at either the picnic grounds or at the parking loop in front of the big sledding hill 0.5 mile down the road. Parking is also available along County Road 50 for the western end of this hike.

The hike: Shingobee Recreational Area is a multi-purpose trail system where cross-country ski trails are converted to mountain biking and hiking trails during the summer. Shingobee is located near two other trails: the Heartland Bike Trail, a converted railroad grade about 1 mile to the northeast, and the North Country Trail (NCT).

The NCT passes through the eastern half of the area heading directly east along the Shingobee River. This trail has a section to the north called the Old Pines in which the trail passes under a scattering of tall white pines. *Shingobee* means "cedar boughs" in Ojibwa and is named for the cedars growing in the low-lying areas.

Right next to the parking area a vista scans the heavily-forested river valley. This trail goes northeast (left) to parallel MN 34, as the trail follows a roller coaster course starting with a first steep descent. The trail climbs partway back to almost the road elevation, then drops again to do a series of steep hills in what is the most strenuous part of the trail. While on this section check out the views through the trees of the narrow valley below. At about 0.25 mile you come to an intersection that leads out of the recreation area; a left goes over the road to the Heartland Bike Trail, while a right leads down to the lower section of the Shingobee trail network, where there is another vista and then the NCT.

Below the Shingobee vista, you pass by a logging camp, once set up to move logs downstream to Leech Lake. After this, you start on the NCT

Shingobee Recreation Area

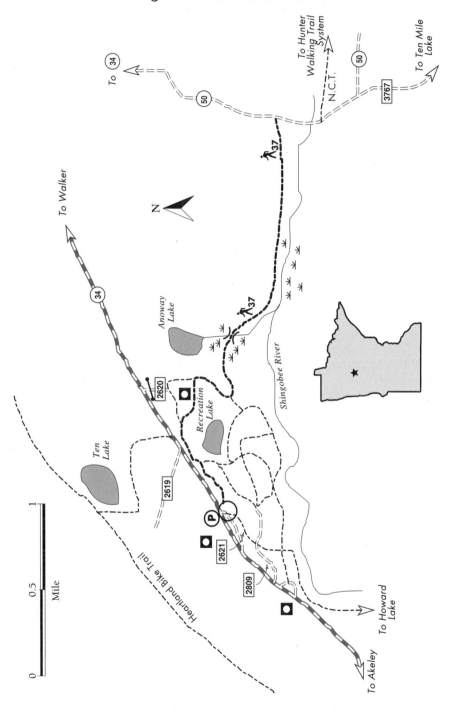

Anoway Lake.

proper. The path crosses an old cordway and then a bridge over the creek coming out of Anoway Lake. This is a prime spot for wildlife watching as the view scans the shrubby and marshy creek. From here, the trail follows a high ridge alongside the Shingobee River for what might be the most scenic section of the North Country Trail in the Chippewa National Forest. About 1.5 miles later the trail reaches County Road 50.

38 Itasca State Park

General description:	A rolling trail that goes by many small lakes, all the while under some of the biggest pines in the state.
General location:	North of Park Rapids.
Length:	7.5 miles for the loop, more than 30 miles of good hiking trails in the park.
Difficulty:	Moderate, follows wide grassy path most of the way. Easy hike at the headwaters.
Elevation gain:	About 200 feet from Lake Itasca to the base of the lookout tower.
Special attractions:	Headwaters of the Mississippi, wildlife, and big old-growth red and white pines.
Maps:	State park trail map; USGS quad: Lake Itasca.
Camping:	237 drive-in, 11 cart-in, and 11 hike-in sites.
For more information:	Department of Natural Resources Information Center; see Appendix B.
GPS:	47 11.703N 95 10.236W.

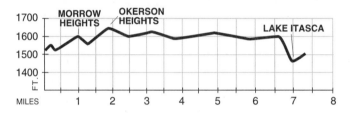

Finding the trailhead: This large state park has three entrances: north, east (the main entrance), and south. All three are connected by park roads. To enter by the north, travel 25 miles south of Bagley (9 miles on Minnesota Highway 200 and 16 miles on Minnesota Highway 92). The east entrance is 30 miles west of Walker on MN 200 or 30 miles southeast of Bemidji on U.S. Highway 71. From the southern entrance, Park Rapids is 21 miles away on US 71. Park next to the nature store and Douglas Lodge.

The hike: Itasca State Park holds the headwaters of the mighty Mississippi, which is the seventh largest river in the world and the largest river in North America. Yet, here you can walk across it on stepping stones. Some facts about the river: it runs for 2,552 miles (about one quarter of its length is in Minnesota); it drops 1,475 feet on its way to the Gulf of Mexico; and it drains thirty-one states and a couple of Canadian provinces. Its tributaries, stretching from the Rocky Mountains (with the Missouri River) to the Appalachians (with the Ohio River), create a water basin larger than the Nile. It is fitting that the Chippewa name *Mississippi* means "big river." In 1832, the headwaters were identified by Henry Rowe Schoolcraft with the help of a native guide named Ozawindib. Schoolcraft also named the headwaters Itasca, which comes from *veritas captus*, meaning "true source" in Latin.

Itasca became Minnesota's first state park in 1891, with the idea of making it into a park in the grand tradition of Yellowstone. Today, as the state's second largest state park, it has 32,000 acres which include more than 100 lakes. Within its borders lies a 2,000-acre wilderness sanctuary, a national natural landmark, and some of Minnesota's largest pines. The park has lots of other activities besides hiking, with boat and bike rentals, boat tours, interpretive centers, forestry demonstration areas, historical sites, and a swimming beach.

The park's extensive trail system has something for everybody. Trails include a short, 250-yard walk to the big pines, an easy trail to the headwaters, and an 18-mile trail network covering the park's southern half. The big trees and the headwaters of the big river are the park's main features and are easily accessible. The headwaters trail, definitely the most popular in the park is a well-maintained trail that leads to the source waters flowing out of Lake Itasca. Here stepping stones go across the narrow creek, so you can say you walked across the Mississippi. Another trail worth a visit, right by the headwaters, is the Schoolcraft Trail. This easy path goes out to Hill Point for a view of Lake Itasca and Schoolcraft Island, right offshore. The other sections of the park are not so often traveled, which means they offer more wilderness and solitude.

The longest hikes are south of Wilderness Drive (the road that circles the park) via four trails branching off from this road. This hike closes a loop on two of these trails and the Eagle Scout Trail, which act as a connector. Located here are also four backcountry camping spots, three rest huts, and the turnoff to the Aiton lookout tower.

From the trailhead, go south on the 2.5-mile Ozawindib Trail that does double duty as a small section of the North Country Trail. The grassy trail is a wide, converted forest road. A little more than 0.1 mile into the trail, you cross over Wilderness Drive (watch for traffic) and then start on the main loop. Many crossover trails enable you to make this hike as long or as short as you want. After passing by the intersection for the first crossover trail, you climb a nice hill called Morrow Heights.

At about 0.75 mile, right after the second crossover, you come to the first big section of pines. Here, a pleasant grove of red pines stands tall. A more rugged side loop called Okerson Heights Trail also turns off here, leading to a white pine grove. This side loop had some windfall with fallen giant trees that require a little climbing or ducking to get around. The trail loops back up with Ozawindib at a trail shelter.

This hillier bottom half of the Ozawindib Trail leads to Iron Corner Lake at about the 2.5-mile mark. The lake is named for an iron marker that indicates the intersection of three Minnesota counties: Hubbard, Becker, and Clearwater. Here the trail turns a 90-degree corner to go west on the Eagle Scout Trail, which connects all four north-south trails. This trail travels 1.5 miles west, passing by Gilfillan Lake, an unnamed pond, and the small Lashbrook Lake, to reach the intersection with Deer Park Trail in the heart

Itasca State Park

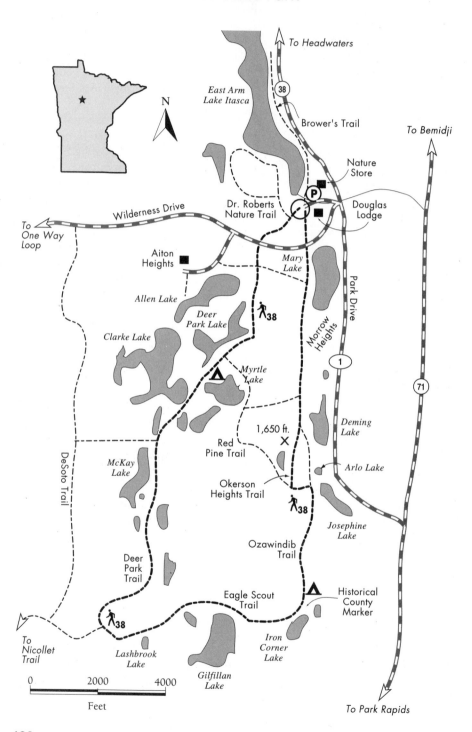

N

To Headwaters

East Arm
Lake Itasca

38

Brower's Trail

To Bemidji

Nature
Store

P

Dr. Roberts
Nature Trail

Douglas
Lodge

Wilderness Drive

To
One Way
Loop

Aiton
Heights

Mary
Lake

Park Drive

Allen Lake

Deer
Park Lake

38

Clarke Lake

Morrow
Heights

1

Deming
Lake

71

Myrtle
Lake

DeSoto Trail

1,650 ft.

X

Red
Pine Trail

McKay
Lake

Arlo Lake

Okerson
Heights Trail

38

Josephine
Lake

Ozawindib
Trail

Deer
Park
Trail

Eagle Scout
Trail

Historical
County
Marker

38

To
Nicollet
Trail

Lashbrook
Lake

Iron
Corner
Lake

0   2000   4000

Gilfillan
Lake

Feet

To Park Rapids

128

Itasca State Park

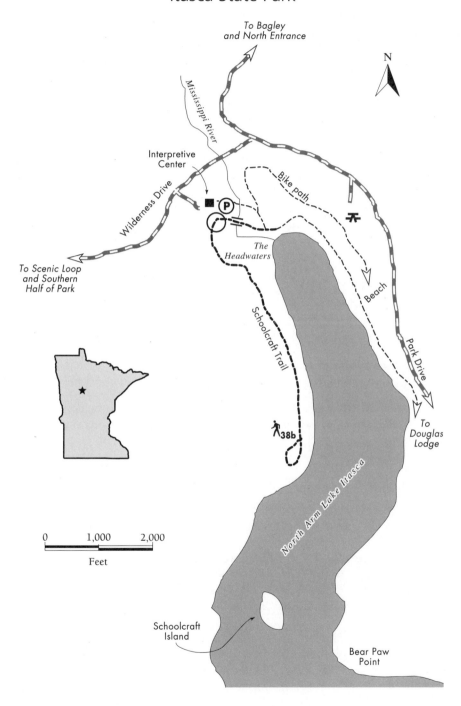

To Bagley
and North Entrance

N

Mississippi River

Interpretive
Center

Wilderness Drive

Bike path

P

The
Headwaters

To Scenic Loop
and Southern
Half of Park

Beach

Schoolcraft Trail

Park Drive

To
Douglas
Lodge

38b

0   1,000   2,000

Feet

North Arm Lake Itasca

Schoolcraft
Island

Bear Paw
Point

of one of the largest pine groves in the park.

Heading north, the trail continues rolling, climbing more hills, and overlooking small ponds. You pass by a shelter at McKay Lake and also a few more campsites situated along the lake shores. Nearing the trail's end after more than 7 miles of hiking, a spur veers west (left) to Aiton Heights and the lookout tower. This spur turns into a forest road about halfway down, leading right up to the base of the tower. By climbing it, you get a good view of the many nearby ponds and, in the fall, of the vivid colors of the surrounding maple and basswood canopy. South of the tower is also the short Allen Lake Trail.

Back on solid ground, cross over Wilderness Drive and follow where the trail drops down for the intersection with Dr. Roberts Nature Trail, and then the boat launch below Douglas Lodge. Here, Brower Trail takes off along the east shore of Lake Itasca, while the steps lead you back to the front of the lodge. There are still many more trails in the park to hike and explore; this route only touches the surface.

39 Pillsbury State Forest

General description:	A hike through a glacier-built topography of rolling hills, ravines, and pothole lakes.
General location:	Northwest of Brainerd.
Length:	About 8 miles for the loop, including 1.5 miles on forest road.
Difficulty:	Moderate, mostly a wide sandy equestrian trail.
Elevation gain:	About a 100-foot change from the ponds to the hilltops.
Special attractions:	Wildlife and ravines.
Maps:	State forest trail map; USGS quads: Wilson Bay and Pillager.
Camping:	Forest campground at Rock Lake.
For more information:	DNR Information Center; see Appendix B.
GPS:	46 22.595N 94 27.138W.

Finding the trailhead: From Brainerd go west for about 10 miles on Minnesota Highway 210 to Pillager Forest Road. Turn north (left) and continue 2.5 miles for parking at Walter E. Stark Assembly Area on the right. Pillager Forest Road continues another 2 miles down to County Road 77.

The hike: Back in the late 1800s, this rugged region of lakes and hills, filled with prime virgin pine, was a center of the logging industry. In 1900, John S. Pillsbury, a former Minnesota Governor, donated 990 acres of land to initiate this state forest and start the state's first tree nursery to replant the cut timberland. Today, the forest covers almost 15,000 acres of state, county,

Pillsbury State Forest

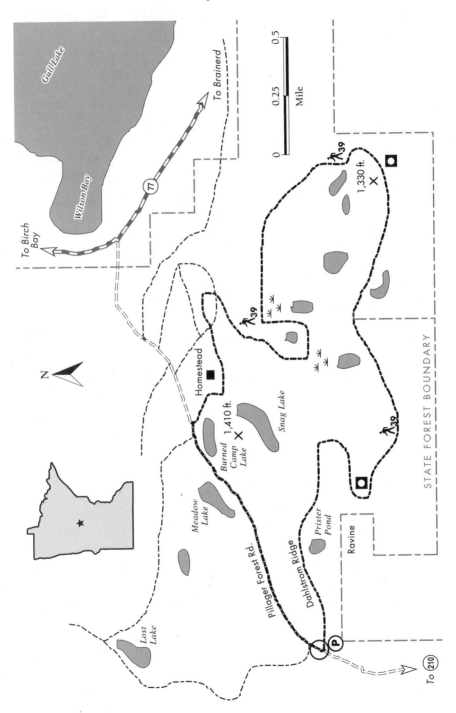

and private forest. It is interlaced with miles of multi-use and woods trails, especially popular with equestrians and mountain bikers during the summer and snowmobilers and cross-country skiers in the winter, though all trails are open for exploring on foot.

In the northern section of the forest you can find a campground and beach along Rock Lake. The mapped hike makes a twisting loop on the southern section of Pillsbury. The path overlooks some steep ravines, skirts around glacier pothole lakes, and provides some views through the trees of Sylvan Lake and big Gull Lake.

Start the hike on the east side of the shelter. The path first follows the top of Dahlstrom Ridge and then passes by Prister Pond. At 1.3 miles it climbs to the Little Devil's Ravine overlook, where land steeply drops at least 70 feet for a view of the heavily forested valley. The trail continues rolling along, passing by more small ponds and a snowmobile trail.

At 3 miles, the Sylvan Lake Overlook appears on the right. The forest map does not label it as a scenic overlook, probably because the view is obstructed by the trees, but off to the east you can see the lake about 130 feet below. The trail then turns back to the northwest, dropping down a steep hill. The route cuts between a couple of ponds where there are excellent opportunities to do some wildlife viewing. It then climbs a hill with a view through the trees to the right of Gull Lake about a mile away.

The trail from here runs alongside a few logging roads, some still in use, with the hiking trail marked by blazes. Beyond the second crossing, you come to the hardscrabble homestead site of Jacob Meier. After the logging era this land was sold cheap with the hope that farmers would move into the area; unfortunately for the buyers, the land was not suitable for agriculture. Next you will pass by the northern end of Snag Lake (Stump Lake on the USGS topographic map), a sign for Nature's Rabbit Hutch, and Burned Camp Lake. At the 7-mile mark, come back out onto Pillager Forest Road and go a little more than 1 mile back to parking lot, which is to the southwest (left).

40 Mille Lacs Kathio State Park

General description:	A short hike that goes up to an observation tower overlooking Mille Lacs Lake and the surrounding forests. There are also many more miles of rolling trails though the dense forest.
General location:	Southern edge of Mille Lacs Lake.
Length:	1 mile; 35-mile network in the park.
Difficulty:	Easy.
Elevation gain:	50 feet on land plus 100 feet up the tower.
Special attractions:	Big overlook of Mille Lacs Lake and surrounding forest, a heron rookery, and several historical sites.
Maps:	State park trail map; USGS quad: Onamia NW.
Camping:	70 drive-in sites.
For more information:	DNR Information Center; see Appendix B.
GPS:	46 07.863N 93 44.400W.

Finding the trailhead: From Onamia, go northwest about 13 miles on U.S. Highway 169 to County Road 26. Turn south (left) and drive 0.75 mile to the park entrance. Follow the signs to the park.

The hike: Along the shores of the big Mille Lacs Lake people have fished, harvested wild rice, and hunted in the surrounding forests for more than 4,000 years. Archeologists have identified copper tools and pottery from digs conducted near the interpretive center. Some of the people who inhabited this region include the Dakota, Objiwe, and Europeans, who first explored the region in the 1680s and were present much later, in the 1850s, during the height of the logging boom. While in terms of human events, the history is long, the lake itself is geologically fairly recent, forming only 10,000 years ago by glacier action. The whole south and west side of the lake is actually a moraine left by the leading edge of a glacier that now backs up the water to form the more than 200-square-mile lake.

This is the fourth largest park in the state park system, so there are bound to be a lot of hiking trails, and there are, with 35 miles of interconnected paths passing through rolling, wooded glacial land. This hike covers only a short section of this system, carving a loop through the woods to the observation tower where the view takes in Mille Lacs Lake.

The trailhead is in the northeast end of the trail center parking lot. Follow this short loop around, keeping to your left at both intersections until you reach the observation tower. On top of the 100-foot-high platform, the panorama includes Mille Lacs Lake, which spans from the north to the east. Also visible are Bass Lake to the east, Ogechie Lake to the northwest, and Rum River to the west. (The Rum River, which connects to the Mississippi River, was one of the most important during the logging era, carrying lumber to the developing Twin Cities. Some of the earliest lumber went down to

Mille Lacs Kathio State Park

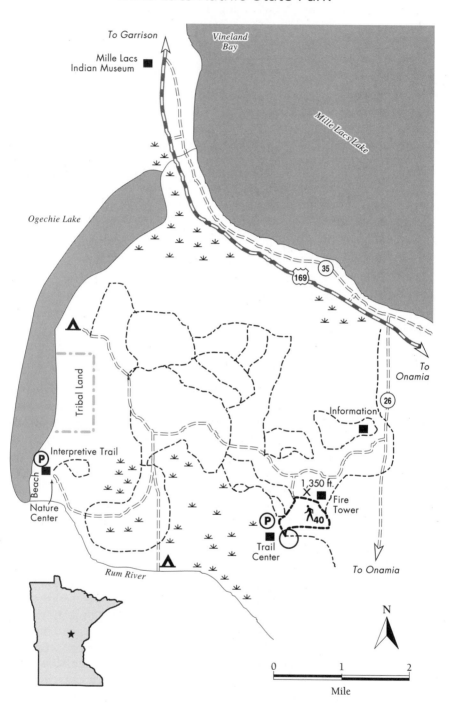

To Garrison

Vineland Bay

Mille Lacs Indian Museum

Mille Lacs Lake

Ogechie Lake

169 35

Tribal Land

To Onamia

26

Information

Interpretive Trail

P

Beach

Nature Center

1,350 ft.

Fire Tower

40

Trail Center

P

To Onamia

Rum River

N

0   1   2
Mile

the mill at Saint Anthony Falls, to help in constructing Fort Snelling). Directly to the south is a spruce–tamarack bog. A little farther are Lake Onamia and Shakopee Lake. Back on the ground, the trail continues on to the road, where another left will take you to the trail center and parking.

41 Savanna Portage State Park

General description:	A scenic trail that encircles Shumway Lake and a short section of a mucky, historically-significant portage.
General location:	North of McGregor.
Length:	5.4 miles, round-trip; 17-mile trail network in the park plus connecting trails to the Remote Lakes Trail System.
Difficulty:	Easy to moderate.
Elevation gain:	About 50 feet on a fairly level course.
Special attractions:	Lake Shumway, fishing, swimming beach, and wildlife.
Maps:	State park trail map; USGS quads: Balsam and Little Prairie Lake.
Camping:	64 drive-in, 1 cart-in, and 7 hike-in sites.
For more information:	DNR Information Center; see Appendix B.
GPS:	46 49.144N 93 10.600W, entrance.

Finding the trailhead: From McGregor and Minnesota Highway 210, take U.S. Highway 65 north for 7 miles to County Roads 14 and then County Road 36 for an additional 10 miles into the park. Park either by the turnoff for Loon Lake, just past the Historical marker, or at Lake Shumway.

The hike: Savanna Portage straddles the Continental Divide. To the west, water flows to the Gulf of Mexico by way of the Mississippi. To the east, water flows to the North Atlantic through Lake Superior and the rest of the Great Lakes. It was first used as a portage by the Native Americans, followed by the French voyageurs in the mid-1700s. Savanna Portage connects the West Savanna River, which flows south to Big Sandy Lake and on to the Mississippi, and the much-channeled and diverted East Savanna, which flows east into the Saint Louis River. The portage is a 1,650-rod (5-mile) haul, that crosses a marsh (where we now have a plank runway), travels onto a dry rolling section, and leads right into a waist-deep marsh on the far eastern side. The portage is named for this marsh and open grassland, which cover most of the portage's eastern half.

This park, at 15,000 acres, is large, and feels even larger because of its proximity to Savanna Portage State Forest. The adjacent forest has a decent trail system of its own at the Remote Lakes Solitude Area, which is accessible from Loon Lake. Hike 41 connects the drier western part of the portage with pristine Lake Shumway.

Savanna Portage State Park

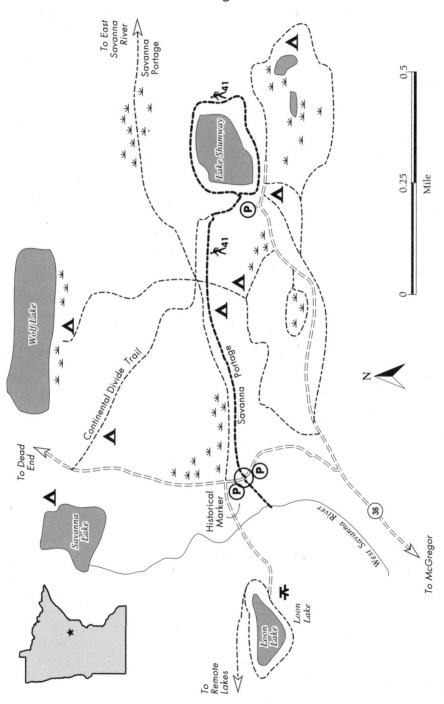

The boardwalk on Savanna Portage.

The hike, a 2-mile tour around Lake Shumway, starts at the boat launch. Take the trail in a clockwise direction for a gently rolling lakeside stroll. The trail offers plenty of views of the lake as it meanders through the woods. At 1.3 miles you can leave this dual-purpose mountain biking–hiking trail for the footpath, which hugs the lakeshore, going through the campgrounds and back to the boat launch.

The hike's next section is an out-and-back, over the portage. Take the crossover trail at intersection H, which connects to the portage and the other trails that head to Wolf Lake and the Continental Divide. Continue past intersection 10 on the left to get to intersection G, a big, five-way intersection and a crossroads for most of the park's trails. Follow the portage west to the road, crossing over boardwalks in the wetter spots. On the other side of the road, the portage's last 1,500 feet take you through a tunnel of low shrubs to reach West Savanna River. The river, as it starts its voyage south, looks to be just deep enough for a canoe.

Northwest Corner

The common perception of Minnesota as a flat place holds true in the Northwest portion of the state. Ten thousand years ago, the great, flat land of the Northwest Corner was the bottom of glacial Lake Agassiz, which was bigger than all the Great Lakes combined, covering a good portion of North Dakota and Manitoba, in addition to the northwest corner of Minnesota. The lake reached a maximum depth of 700 feet and was over 700 miles long. Today, the area contains fertile soil, the Red River of the north (which flows north to Hudson Bay), some beach ridge-lines marking the extent of the lake, and several huge shallow lakes, including Lake of the Woods.

While this corner might not have the rolling, rugged terrain found elsewhere in the state, it does have several interesting and unique features. It covers nearly one quarter of the state and encompasses many ecological zones including prairie, bogs, and boreal forest. At Buffalo State Park, hikers can wander through the heart of the prairies, which at one time covered all of the Red River Valley. Farther to the north, you can explore the aspen parklands at Lake Bronson or the coniferous forest at Hayes Lake. And along the northern edge of the state, you can stroll along sandy beaches on the large and complex Lake of the Woods.

42 Zipple Bay State Park

General description:	A beach walk along the shore of Lake of the Woods, from a picnic area to the entrance to Zipple Bay.
General location:	Northeast of Williams on the southeast side of Lake of the Woods.
Length:	1.5 miles, round-trip. Another couple of miles of beach on the other side of the Zipple Bay Channel and a 6-mile trail network in the park.
Difficulty:	Easy, along a beach.
Elevation gain:	Nominal.
Special attractions:	Bird watching and beachcombing in the black sand.
Maps:	State park trail map: USGS quad: Williams SE.
Camping:	7 drive-in sites.
For more information:	DNR Information Center; see Appendix B.
GPS:	48 52.021N 94 50.877W.

Finding the trailhead: From Baudette, take Minnesota Highway 172 along the Rainy River, NW for 10.5 miles to County Road 8. Travel 6 miles on CR 8 to the County Road 34 park road entrance. Park at either the beach or the picnic area.

Zipple Bay State Park

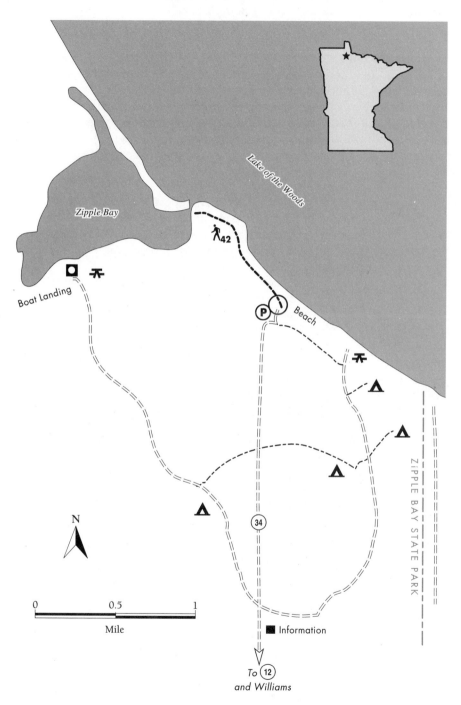

Lake of the Woods

Zipple Bay

Boat Landing

Beach

N

0   0.5   1
Mile

ZIPPLE BAY STATE PARK

■ Information

To 12
and Williams

The hike: The largest lake, excluding the Great Lakes, in the United States is not, as many would guess, the Great Salt Lake, but Minnesota's Lake of the Woods, which measures 55 by 80 miles and covers 1,485 square miles. The lake has a maximum depth of 150 feet (though an average depth of only 26 feet), 14,000 islands scattered about, 65,000 miles of shoreline (including all of those islands), and a best selling book named after it. The lake is big.

The park and the nearby bay are named for Wilhelm M. Zipple, a German immigrant and fisherman who started a town here in the 1880s. The town prospered as a fishing community, catching and selling the Lake of the Woods's plentiful lake sturgeon. These huge, long-lived fish and their roe were valuable commodities on the east coast. Today, the sturgeon are far less prevalent, and commercial and sport fishing concentrate on the more plentiful walleye, northern pike, and sauger.

Most of the park's trails wander amid jack pine and birch forests, where you can search for the four species of ladyslippers indigenous to the area. This trail starts at one of the most popular sections in the park—the fine sand beach. It takes you from the beach to the entrance to Zipple Bay, where the original fishing fleet was headquartered to protect the boats from the lake's thrashing storms.

From the beach, you can see your destination, a rock levee down to the left (west). The beach is narrower than the Lake Superior beach walk, but it does have an interesting layer of black sand formed from iron flakes. In spots, the shore is crowded by willow and alder, reaching out toward the water, which is so shallow that a few rounded boulders poke above the surface, providing perches for sea gulls. Double-crested cormorants, white pelicans, and common terns are often seen flying or wading along the shoreline. Also, out in the lake, far to the east, is the Pine and Curry Island SNA, where the endangered shore bird called the piping plover makes its home.

Almost at the levee itself, the path runs into a thicket as it leaves the shore to veer inland. It's just a short distance to view cattail-lined Zipple Bay, home to abundant bird life.

Note: If you came with a boat, there are miles of shoreline (and beaches) and thousands of islands left to explore.

43 Hayes Lake State Park

General description:	A lakeside trail that takes you from the impoundment that forms Hayes Lake to where the lake narrows to a meandering river.
General location:	Southeast of Roseau.
Length:	About 9 miles, round-trip. Part of the park's 13-mile trail network.
Difficulty:	Moderate, long hike on a wide grassy trail.
Elevation gain:	Nominal.
Special attractions:	Wildlife, big trees, old homestead site pine, and a beach.
Maps:	State park trail map USGS quads: Wannaska NE and Skime.
Camping:	35 drive-in and 2 hike-in sites.
For more information:	DNR Information Center; see Appendix B.
GPS:	48 38.311N 95 32.718W at the park entrance.

Finding the trailhead: From Roseau, travel 15 miles south on Minnesota Highway 89 (Great River Road), past Wannaska, to County Road 4. Turn left (east) and proceed 7 miles to parking, either at the beach or the picnic area.

The hike: Hayes Lake State Park is located in the heart of one of Minnesota's most overlooked wilderness regions—the hundreds of square miles of Beltrami State Forest's peatlands and forests. Just south of the park lies the so-called Big Bog, 130 square miles of peatland, considered by many to be Minnesota's most pristine place. And it will probably stay that way, since there are few hiking trails in this soggy world. Hayes Lake State Park, while not in the peatland itself, borders parts of the state forest and is easily accessible.

There is an interesting self-guided trail that passes by an original pioneer site, homesteaded in the early 1900s, which features family grave stones and scenic views of the lake. Another guided trail, the Pine Ridge Nature Trail, connects the campgrounds to the picnic grounds and allows you to tour the pine and spruce plantations. This hike takes you along Hayes Lake, created specifically for recreational use by the impoundment on the Roseau River. This trail offers many scenic views across the lake and the possibility of wildlife viewing.

From the picnic grounds and boat launch, cross over the long, earthen dam to start this hike. After about 0.5 mile you come to an intersection with the Moose Ridge Trail; take a left and follow along the shore. What might be the best views of Lake Hayes are in the first mile, where the view from the trail looks west across the twisting lake. This wide trail is fairly level and is also a dual-purpose trail, so a horse or two might pass you by. Along the way there are several big trees, a few open meadows, and at least one magnifi-

Hayes Lake State Park

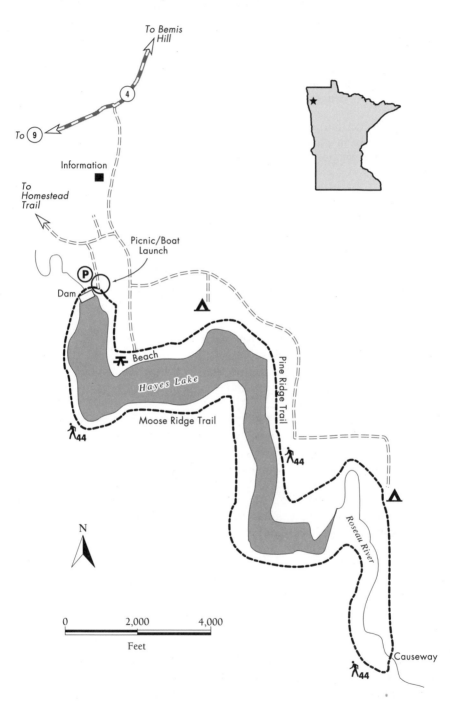

To Bemis Hill

4

To 9

Information

To Homestead Trail

Picnic/Boat Launch

P

Dam

Beach

Hayes Lake

Moose Ridge Trail

Pine Ridge Trail

44

44

Roseau River

Causeway

44

N

0   2,000   4,000
Feet

cent, tall white spruce. Toward the end, the lake begins to narrow and slowly becomes a meandering river with wetlands on the shoreline.

At the end of the Moose Ridge Trail a casement crosses the river. If the water is not running too hard, as it can be in the late summer, and you don't mind getting your feet wet, you can cross over to do a loop. This will bring you to the group camp area on the other side and onto the Pine Ridge Nature Trail. The trail on this side continues to a forest road, where you can finish the loop.

44 Lake Bronson State Park

General description:	The High Bank Interpretive Trail is a short loop through aspen, oak savanna, and prairie that takes you along the shore of Lake Bronson.
General location:	North of Karlstad.
Length:	1.5-mile loop. Part of the park's 14-mile trail network.
Difficulty:	Easy, on a well-groomed nature trail.
Elevation gain:	Nominal.
Special attractions:	Possible moose sightings, swimming beach, and prairie.
Maps:	State park trail maps; USGS quad: Halma.
Camping:	35 drive-in and 2 hike-in sites.
For more information:	DNR Information Center; see Appendix B.
GPS:	48 43.439N 96 36.101W.

Finding the trailhead: From the city of Lake Bronson and U.S. Highway 59 go 1.5 miles east on County Road 28 to the park entrance. Parking for the interpretive loop is at the end of the park road, past the camping site, near the boat landing.

The hike: Lake Bronson sits on land that used to be the shore of Glacial Lake Agassiz. It is a newer and much smaller lake, created by the impoundment of South Two Branches River in the late 1930s, that served as a reservoir for the nearby town (also named Lake Bronson) in case of drought. While constructing the dam, workers had a problem with the dam's foundation—100 feet of quick sand was part of the old glacial lake beach. One of few lakes in the region, the park has proved popular with both residents and visitors from North Dakota and Manitoba.

Although the park's focus is on water sports and activities, a surprisingly wide assortment of wildlife also find a home within the park's boundaries. An estimated two hundred bird species visit the park each year. The park also hosts more than fifty kinds of mammals, which include (and this is just in the Ms): mice, mink, moles, muskrats, and moose. Lake Bronson State Park is one of the few parks in which moose are fairly common. An easy, yet

Lake Bronson State Park

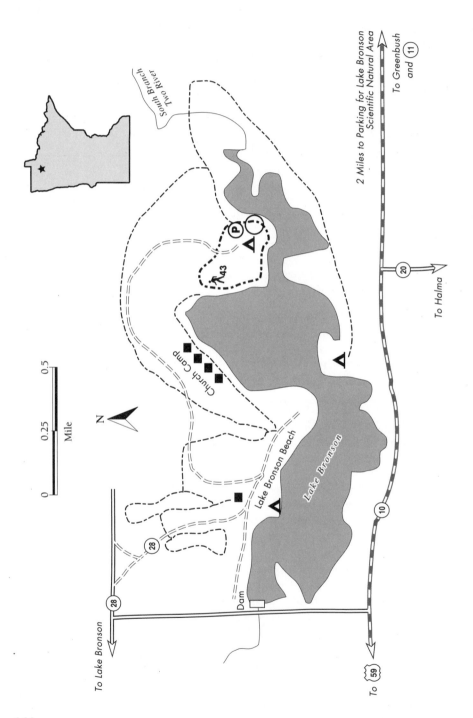

South Branch
Two River

2 Miles to Parking for Lake Bronson
Scientific Natural Area

To Greenbush
and 11

To Halma

20

Church Camp

Lake Bronson Beach

Lake Bronson

Dam

28

28

To Lake Bronson

10

To 59

N

0   0.25   0.5
Mile

P

43

scenic trail circles the campground while following the meandering bank of the lake and river. This is an excellent hike in the evening when animals are more likely to be heading down to the shore. Be sure to pick up the interpretive guide at the main office.

From the trailhead, go south along the wall of cattails lining the shores of Lake Bronson. The trail passes some bur oak trees, one of the few trees that can survive a prairie fire. Pass some side trails, which veer off to the right and lead back to the campground. At station 7, the path comes to an overlook on the still, river-like Lake Bronson and its islands. This is a great place to watch for wildlife and birds (a bald eagle was flying above the large island during my visit). The trail continues, passing by a small prairie and some aspen groves, and then heads back to the trailhead.

45 Buffalo River State Park

General description:	A hike along the meandering Buffalo River to one of the premier prairies left in Minnesota. (The Bluestem Prairie Scientific and Natural Area borders the park's southern boundary).
General location:	East of Moorhead.
Length:	About a 2-mile loop. Part of the park's 12-mile network of trails.
Difficulty:	Easy.
Elevation gain:	Nominal, on a flat prairie.
Special attractions:	Wildflowers and prairie chickens.
Maps:	State Park trail maps, USGS quad: Downer.
Camping:	44 drive-in sites.
For more information:	DNR Information Center; see Appendix B.
GPS:	46 52.294N 96 28.475W.

Finding the trailhead: From Moorhead, travel 13 miles east on U.S. Highway 10. A park sign and entrance are on the right, at the historical marker for glacial Lake Agassiz beach.

The hike: Only small sections remain of the ocean of prairie grassland that once grew over much of mid-America. In Minnesota, the prairies once covered the southern third of the state and the state's western edge along the Red River valley. Today, most of this prairie has been converted to some of the most productive and intensively-farmed land in the nation. Buffalo River State Park and the neighboring Scientific and Natural Area preserves a section of virgin prairie, which is said to be one of the nation's best remaining grasslands.

On this land, there are over 250 species of grasses and plants. For example, along the Buffalo River you may find a flood plain forest with ash,

Buffalo River State Park

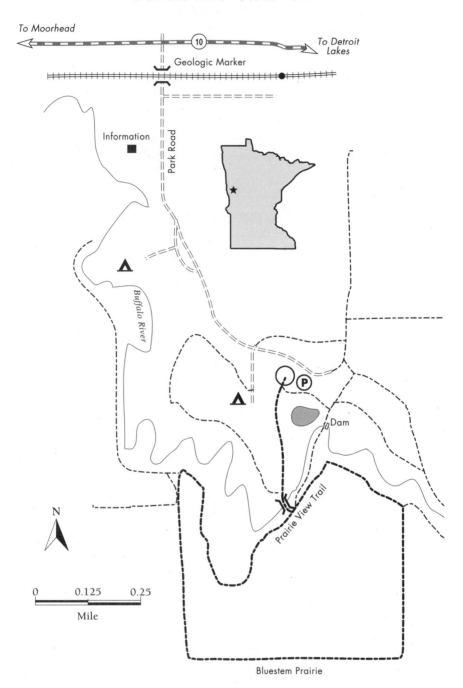

To Moorhead

To Detroit Lakes

10

Geologic Marker

Information

Park Road

Buffalo River

Dam

P

N

Prairie View Trail

0   0.125   0.25

Mile

Bluestem Prairie

cottonwood, and basswood; in low lying spots, sedge meadows take over; while the tallgrass prairies cover the majority of the land. Here, depending on the season, you may find wildflowers, such as small white lady's slipper, sunflowers, and pasque flowers. The park is also home to two hundred bird species, including the rare greater prairie chicken.

The region was covered by glacial Lake Agassiz 10,000 years ago, so the landscape is flat and easy-going. There are trails on both sides of the river and two bridge crossings: one by the picnic grounds and the other on the far-eastern end of the park, past a house located on private property. This hike closes a short loop on the Prairie View and Bluestem trails.

Start from the main parking lot and go south, past the beach picnic area to the bridge over the forested Buffalo River. Leaving the floodplain forest you come out on the edge of the expansive prairie and begin the Prairie View Trail. A right or a left takes you first along the border of the forested, meandering river, and then at about 0.25 mile to an intersection with the Bluestem Prairie. The prairie trail follows a geometric path, making 90-degree turns through the heart of the tall grasses. Miles of additional trails extend farther east and west for much more prairie viewing.

Hardwood Hills

This region is known by several nicknames, including Lake Country, Blue Hills, Vikingland, Park Land, and Moraine Terrain. Whatever it is called, the Hardwood Hills is an area of scenic countryside, with rolling hills and thousands of lakes. Early explorers commented that they half expected to see castles over the hills. (Perhaps the landscape reminded them of the Lake District of England). For the most part, the landscape took its form from the glacial action of the Alexandria Moraine and its several-hundred-foot-thick glacier drift. Hikes range from overlooks in Sibley State Park and Maplewood State Park to the rolling hills and lakes of Glacial Lakes State Park and Lake Carlos State Park.

46 Mount Tom, Sibley State Park

General description:	A climb up Mount Tom—the highest point within a 50-mile radius.
General location:	North of Willmar.
Length:	A 2.5-mile loop. Part of the park's 18-mile network of trails.
Difficulty:	Easy to moderate. A short trail that is rough in some places.
Elevation gain:	185 feet from the lake to the top of Mount Tom.
Special attractions:	Observation tower with a 360-degree view, beach on Lake Andrew.
Maps:	State park trail map; USGS quad: Mount Tom.
Camping:	138 drive-in sites.
For more information:	DNR Information Center; see Appendix B.
GPS:	45 18.798N 95 01.983W, entrance.

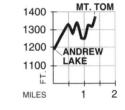

Finding the trailhead: From Willmar take U.S. Highway 71 north for 15 miles to County Road 48. Watch for the park sign and turn left (west). Park at the trail center. The interpretive center is a little more than 1 mile west.

The hike: Sibley State Park and Mount Tom are located in the northcentral part of Kandiyohi County. *Kandiyohi* is a Dakota word meaning "lakes." Needless to say, this county lives up to its name with 361 lakes, or a lake for about every 2 square miles of area. The park is named for Henry Hasting Sibley, the first governor of Minnesota. He mentioned this as his favorite hunting grounds.

A variety of hardwoods grow here, from oak and ironwood on the hills to basswood near Lake Andrew. At one time, native prairies surrounded the park and its drier upper slopes; today, the DNR is restoring a few of these through prescribed burns. Most of the park, though, is covered with a dense deciduous forest common to the Hardwood Hills.

The park has several trails and loops, including a canoe route that connects four lakes. A couple of trails that extend to the back of the park are dual-purpose horse–hiking paths and another five trails radiate from the interpretive center. The most popular hike is the one to the beach, with the hike to the top of Mount Tom (described here) running a close second. Hiking the trail, you follow in the tradition of native peoples who used it as a lookout (remnants of clay pipes have been found on top). To reach the top, you can start from either side of the hill, or if need be, you can also get there by car, since a road also climbs to the summit. This surprisingly good hiking trail goes through the woods, up and down the hills, comes out on open

Mount Tom, Sibley State Park

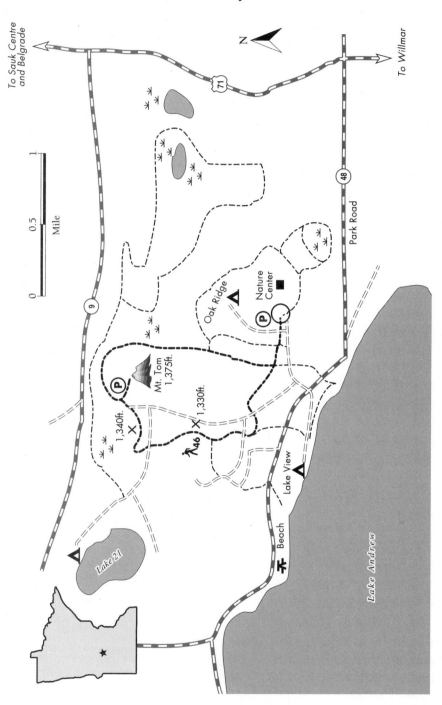

To Sauk Centre and Belgrade

To Willmar

N

71

48

Park Road

9

Mile

0.5

1

0

Oak Ridge

Nature Center

P

Mt. Tom 1,375ft.

P

1,340ft.
X

1,330ft.
X

46

Lake View

Beach

Lake 21

Lake Andrew

prairies and marshes, and of course reaches the peak and its observation tower.

Starting at the interpretive center, cross the road, pass the campsite trail, and follow trail marker 3 to the Mount Tom Trail. At 0.25 mile this trail arrives at the Oak Hills Trail (trail marker 5), which makes a decent return trail through the dense woods of the hillside, while the Mount Tom Trail veers off to the right and continues 0.75 mile to the top. Starting up the backside of the hill, you begin to climb at a little over 0.5 mile.

You travel around a ridge and pass by an upper prairie, which is burned occasionally to keep out invading species. The trail turns to a paved path and leads to the parking lot and the two-story observation tower. This is quite a structure, solidly built out of granite and large timber. The climb to the observation platform offers a 360-degree view of the surrounding lakes and forest. The whole region is covered in glacial drift, up to 450 feet thick in spots, which makes up the foundation of Mount Tom. After getting your fill of the panorama, head to the other side of the lot and take the western trail down. At the bottom, either cross back on the Oak Hills Trail or go all the way down to Lake Andrew and the Lakeview Trail, or maybe to the beach for a swim.

47 Glacial Lakes State Park

General description:	A great hike on the prairie among the glacial kettles (lakes) and kames (hills).
General location:	South of Alexandria.
Length:	2.5 miles, round-trip. Part of the park's 16-mile network of trails.
Difficulty:	Easy to moderate on rolling hills.
Elevation gain:	152 feet from Mountain Lake to the highest point in the park.
Special attractions:	Mountain Lake and wildflowers on some of the most scenic prairie in the state.
Camping:	39 drive-in and 4 hike-in sites.
Maps:	State park trail map, USGS quads: Starbuck and Lake Minnewaska.
For more information:	DNR Information Center; see Appendix B.
GPS:	45 32.440N 95 31.475W.

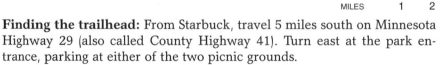

Finding the trailhead: From Starbuck, travel 5 miles south on Minnesota Highway 29 (also called County Highway 41). Turn east at the park entrance, parking at either of the two picnic grounds.

Glacial Lakes State Park

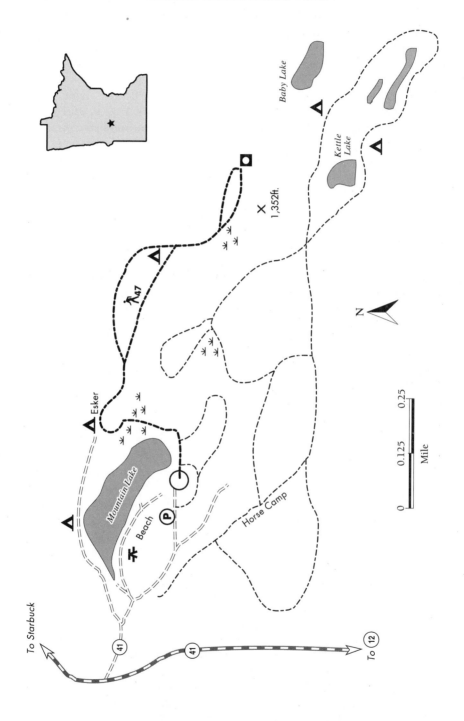

The hike: Almost any of the parks in the Hardwood Hills could have been named glacial lakes, but this park probably deserves the name most with its pristine pothole lake. Surrounding the spring-fed lake, a tallgrass prairie undulates with swells and swales—dropping down for a pond or a marsh and rising for an overlook from a knoll. Two thirds of the park's 1,880-acre park are virgin prairie, while the remaining third is a mix of oak forest and wetlands.

The prairie holds some of my favorite species of wildflowers, which range from the pasque flowers in spring to the goldenrods, asters, and purple gentians in the fall. Down in the low-lying areas you might see the red-orange flowers of the swamp milkweed or the green-headed coneflowers. In other parts, you might see sunflowers, prairie clover, blazing star, and lead-plant. Since the park has a nice transition from prairie to woods, birdlife is prevalent in all of its varied forms.

The trail system has two basic parts—the southern half consists of horse-back–hiking trails and a separate hiking-only trail is located in the north half. All the trails are wide, mowed paths and are easy to follow.

Follow the trail around the southern edge of Mountain Lake, a 56-acre, steeply-sloped, and spring-fed lake. Here the trail skirts the edge of a marshy area on a boardwalk and provides easy access to some moisture loving plants. The path climbs up to the main campground, which sits upon a wide esker. Follow the trail southeast past a couple of walk-in campsites to the highest point in the park, at 1,325 feet. The overlook provides a vista of the neighboring treeless valley and the farms farther off in the distance. If you are feeling intrepid, and are not afraid of getting wet, you may want to cross the kettle and the wet prairie to the horse–hiking trail on the other side.

48 Lake Carlos State Park

General description:	First a stroll by the lakeshore, then up to a prairie and scattered woods.
General location:	North of Alexandria.
Length:	About a 2.5-mile loop. Part of the park's 12-mile network of trails.
Difficulty:	Easy.
Elevation gain:	About 50 feet on gently rolling terrain.
Special attractions:	Grasslands and Lake Carlos—a deep clear lake with a swimming beach.
Maps:	State park trail maps; USGS topo: Lake Miltona East.
Camping:	124 drive-in and 2 walk-in sites.
For more information:	DNR Information Center; see Appendix B.
GPS:	45.59.720N 95.20.700W.

Finding the trailhead: From Alexandria, take Minnesota Highway 29, about 8 miles north, to the intersection of County Road 38 (which turns into County

Lake Carlos State Park

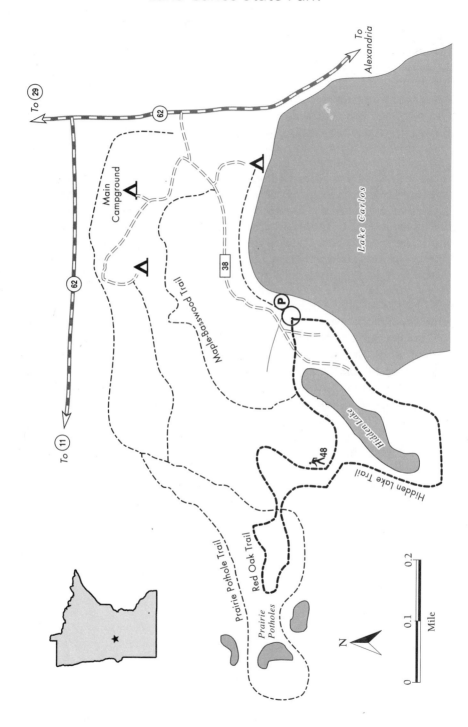

Road 62) and then 2 miles to the park entrance. Park at the beach and picnic area.

The hike: Lake Carlos State Park was established in 1936, and ever since, the main attraction has been the park's swimming beach. Lake Carlos stretches across 3,017 acres and has a maximum of depth of 163 feet, making it one of the state's deepest lakes. The lake also acts as the headwaters for Long Prairie River, a stream that served as a route for native cultures and early explorers. From here, even the Twin Cities are accessible by boat, if you are willing to travel 100 miles downriver to the Crow Wing River, and on to the Mississippi River. But the park has more than the lake to offer: prairie, maple-basswood, aspen–oak forests, and even a tamarack bog.

The park has several loops and trails, including: (1) an interpretive trail (starting from the campground leading to the beach through a section of the maple-basswood forest); (2) a couple of hiking-only trails going around Hidden Lake and on to the prairie; and (3) a long dual-purpose horse–hiking trail. The latter covers most of the park and travels through prairies and forests and alongside wetlands. The Hidden Lake Trail is a short loop and a decent tour that connects with the Red Oak Trail on the far northwest end of the park. From the Red Oak Trail you can also hook up with the horse-hiking Prairie Pothole Trail that loops and weaves around the many small kettles (ponds).

The Hidden Lake Trail starts at the beach. Pass the group center and turn the corner on the southern edge of the park boundary, where there are a few side paths coming into the trail. At about 1 mile, the intersection with the Red Oak Trail comes up right after a marsh along the shore of Hidden Lake. From here, the trail gets some roll into it, going through the red oak forest and then out to the prairie. This is one of the nicer places in the park, with the views looking across the gently rolling hills as the path loops around the small hills and depressions. On the edge of the forest, the Prairie Pothole Trail also intersects it, making for a larger loop, threading its way through the small ponds. The Red Oak trail provides a shorter loop, which returns along the northern side of Hidden Lake to the main parking area.

49 Maplewood State Park

General description:	Many hiking options: A hike up Hallaway Hill to a scenic overlook of Lake Lida, a short trail to the state's largest ironwood tree, a forest demonstration plot, and miles of trails winding around lakes, marshes, and climbing hills.
General location:	Southeast of Pelican Rapids.
Length:	0.3 mile, up to the overlook. Part of the park's 25-mile network of trails.
Difficulty:	Easy, with a short climb up a steep hill.
Elevation gain:	176 feet from the lake to the top of Hallaway Hill.
Special attractions:	Overlook of the lake; state's largest ironwood tree, and a swimming beach.
Camping:	60 drive-in and 3 hike-in sites.
Maps:	State park trail map; USGS quad: Lake Lida.
For more information:	DNR Information Center; see Appendix B.
GPS:	46 32.331N 95 59.118W.

HALLAWAY HILL

```
1500 ┬
1400 ┤
1300 ┤  LAKE LIDA
 FT. ┤     BEACH
MILES              1
```

Finding the trailhead: From Pelican Rapids and U.S. Highway 59, take Minnesota Highway 108 about 8 miles to the park entrance. Parking for Hallaway Hill overlook is at the beach.

The hike: Maplewood State Park was established in 1963 on the site of a town that had thrived there more than a hundred years ago. The town had sixty-two buildings, including a school, a town hall, and a couple of churches. Visiting this 9,000 acre park today, one would be hard pressed to imagine the old town, since most of the habitat has reverted back to its wild nature. Here, thick forests grow on the hillsides, birds chirp in the marshes, and beavers and muskrat make their homes in over forty ponds and lakes. The park is positioned at the intersection of three ecological zones—prairies, hardwoods, and coniferous forests, a combination that gives the park a great diversity of wild- and plant life.

The park's trails get most of their use from equestrians, though hikers are welcome on all of them. There are also a few hiker-only trails that lead to some of the best and favorite attractions in the park: the big ironwood tree, the Forest Interpretive Trail, and the short, brisk hike up Hallaway Hill.

A short trail, accessible from the park road, takes you to the big tree, which is actually the state's largest ironwood tree: 52-feet-tall and 76 inches in circumference. This tree isn't Bunyanesque compared to a towering white pine, but, nevertheless, it is a record breaker with plenty of character. The Forest Demonstration Area, just past the equestrian trail center, includes a short loop where nearly all of the park's different tree varieties are found and may be labeled. Here the trail passes by red oak, white oak, black ash,

Maplewood State Park

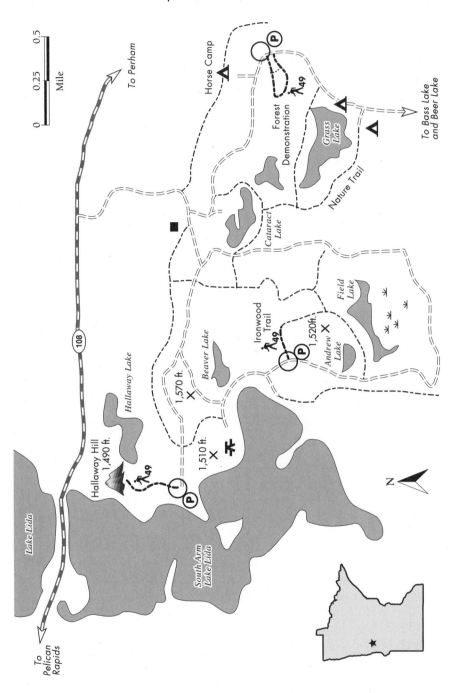

To Perham

Horse Camp

0.5
0.25
0
Mile

Forest Demonstration

Grass Lake

To Bass Lake and Beer Lake

Nature Trail

Cataract Lake

108

Hallaway Lake

Field Lake

Ironwood Trail

Beaver Lake

Andrew Lake

1,520 ft.

1,570 ft.

1,510 ft.

Hallaway Hill
1,490 ft.

N

Lake Lida

South Arm Lake Lida

To Pelican Rapids

Overlook from Hallaway Hill toward Hallaway Lake.

basswood, and sugar maple, to name just a few species.

The Hallaway Hill trail starts at the beach parking lot where there is a small sign marking the trail. This is an easygoing trail passing by open meadows and leading to a picnic area near the top. The overlook is at 1,490 feet, 176 feet above the South Arm of Lake Lida. From this vantage point you can watch the boats zipping around on the water below or the hawks doing lazy spirals in the sky. Opposite the lake, the view looks off to the park's forest, Lake Hallaway, and the rolling prairies.

Metro

The metro region includes a sizeable portion of the Big Woods, a mature maple–basswood forest. The woods once covered 2 million acres, extending through parts of Minnesota, Wisconsin, and Iowa, though, now only isolated stands remain. Within the region, at stands such as Nerstrand or Wolsfeld Woods, you can explore the marvels of the deep woods and enjoy the showy flower displays. A varied display of wildflowers first appears in the spring, when the rising sun warms up the forest floor. Later in the year, when the leaves shade the floor, other flowers bloom under the subdued light.

The parks take in a diverse selection of environments, ranging from the open prairies at Crow–Hassan Park Reserve to the coniferous forests at Sand Dunes State Forest. The region also includes the banks of the Mississippi, Minnesota, and the Saint Croix rivers, as well as the famous waterfall at Minnehaha Creek. Other hikes in the regional park system enable you to explore wetlands and marshes, such as those found at Carver Park Reserve where the trail includes a nearly 2,000-foot boardwalk over the water.

50 Lake Maria State Park

General description:	A hilly hike through the Big Woods, complete with marshes and forest ponds.
General location:	Just a few miles west of Monticello.
Length:	About a 3-mile loop. Part of the park's 14-mile network of trails.
Difficulty:	Easy to moderate, following a wide dirt trail.
Elevation gain:	80 feet on a mostly rolling course.
Special attractions:	Bird watching and spring flowers.
Maps:	State park trail map; USGS quad: Silver Creek.
Camping:	16 hike-in sites.
For more information:	DNR Information Center; see Appendix B.
GPS:	45 18.818N 93 56.356.

Finding the trailhead: From Monticello and Interstate 94 travel 8 miles on County Road 39 to County Road 111. Turn north (right) on CR 111 and travel 0.75 mile to park entrance on your left. Parking is available at the trail center.

The hike: Lake Maria is located on the Big Woods's northern edge and is really just a small remnant of what was once an expansive forest (over 3,000

Lake Maria State Park

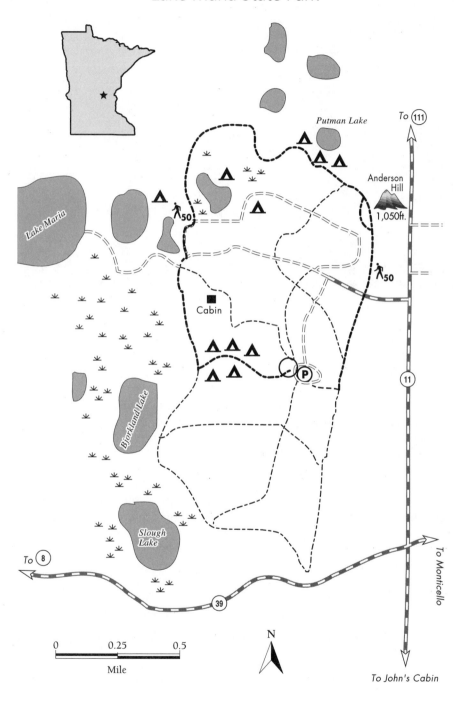

Putman Lake

To (111)

Anderson Hill
1,050ft.

Lake Maria

Cabin

Bjorkland Lake

Slough Lake

To (8)

(11)

To Monticello

(39)

To John's Cabin

0   0.25   0.5
Mile

N

The Big Woods.

square miles). The park is a wooded island in a sea of farmland. These woods are predominantly oak, not like the rest of the Big Woods, which has a higher proportion of maple and basswood. In the trail system's northern half, you will find a nice oak stand, and in the other parts you will find tree species, such as maple, basswood, and aspen. In addition to woods, the trails take you through woodland marshes, lakes, and open meadows, all the while following the undulating, short, steep hills through the park.

The park has a 14-mile network of trails packed together in the eastern half, while the western half of the park's acreage is mostly marsh. Only a few state parks cater to hike-in campers—Lake Maria is one of them. Although, any one of the seventeen campsites will give you a sense of remoteness, the true wilderness experience of the far north might not be attainable here; at the very least, you will be given a chance to camp away from civilization. The park also has a camper's cabin that can be rented out, for those seeking a little more comfort.

The trail center is more than just a starting point. Inside the building you can view several interpretive displays of local flora and fauna and pick up a birding check-list. Outside, on the elevated porch (which has bird feeders), you can overlook a small pond cum ice-skating rink. From the center, the trails radiate out in all directions, but for this hike take the one to Bjorkland Lake for a clockwise loop around the park.

The trail starts with a downhill through some young birch. After 0.5 mile you come to benches and the intersection with the Bjorkland Trail. A right leads to the majority of backcountry camping sites, which are close to the lake. A left takes you north, past hike-in campsite 7, and on to the main park road.

At the road, turn right and cross over. Then take the side road that heads up to group camp, for about 500 feet. Turn off before the camp to cross the earthern bridge by the muskrat houses. At the top of the hill you come to an intersection for Maria Lake and the picnic grounds. At this point, go the other way, where you come to some decent oak groves and vernal ponds, which fill up during the spring runoff. A view of Putman Lake pops up in the distance. Climb to the overlook at Anderson Hill, which is the park's high point and gives views of the farmland across the road and the forest in the park behind you. At the top is a bench and one scraggly tree that looks down at this popular winter sledding hill.

The trail cuts back across the road, by the information center, and then back to the parking lot at the far end. Other hiking options include the trail to Lake Maria, which passes through a prairie and alongside a farmer's field.

51 Sand Dunes State Forest

General description:	A looping trail, through a pine forest and a nearby oak–savanna prairie.
General location:	Northeast of Big Lake.
Length:	2.5 miles in a series of loops.
Difficulty:	Easy to moderate.
Elevation gain:	About 75 feet from the lake to the lookout tower.
Special attractions:	Uncas Dunes SNA and beach.
Maps:	State forest trail map; USGS quad: Orrock.
Camping:	State forest campground.
For more information:	DNR Information Center; see Appendix B.
GPS:	45 25.774N 93 41.583W.

Finding the trailhead: From Zimmerman and U.S. Highway 169, take County Road 4 west about 5.5 miles to the state forest sign at North Sand Dunes Forest Road (the first left after County Road 15). You first pass by a parking lot at the intersection of CR 4 and North Sand Dunes Road to get to the parking at Ann Lake and the parking areas at either the picnic area or the campground.

The hike: To the north of this state forest lies the Sherburne National Wildlife Refuge, which is 30,000 acres of wetlands, sloughs, and oak groves. To the south lies Uncas Dunes Scientific and Natural Area, a place noted for its sand dune habitat and a rare butterfly called the uncas skipper, which lives in only two places in Minnesota. (The caterpillar feeds off the hairy grama in spring and the adults go after the hairy puccoon in June.) This hike is

Sand Dunes State Forest

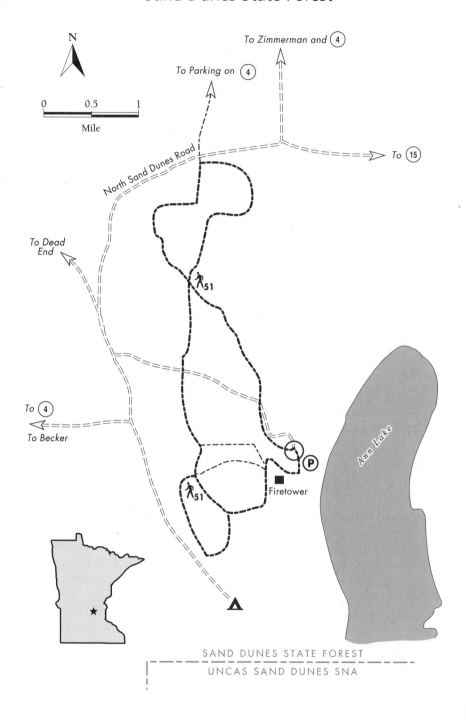

N

0   0.5   1
Mile

To Parking on ④

To Zimmerman and ④

To ⑮

North Sand Dunes Road

To Dead End

To ④
To Becker

🚶51

🚶51

Firetower

P

Ann Lake

SAND DUNES STATE FOREST
UNCAS SAND DUNES SNA

surrounded by wilderness habitat wild enough for even several bald eagles to nest.

However, on your first entry to the forest it is easy to be distracted by the uniformity of the regular rows of the pine plantation. Sand Dunes Forest was planted on farm land after a drought hit this area in the 1940s. The Department of Natural Resources's aim was to stabilize the light blowing soil. Still, sections of the original landscape remain in the state forest's nearly 10,000 acres. The refuge and the forest's acreage, together, make for the largest wild area near the Twin Cities.

The sand dunes themselves are not the towering kind you might imagine rising up in the desert, but instead, much less dramatic, low hills covered with an oak savanna. They were created from a glacial outwash of fine sand which was then blown by winds. The dunes' ridges, aligned perpendicular to the prevailing winds, run southeast to northwest.

The Ann Lake Trails, set up as a chain of hiking loops, are the main hiking paths in the forest. The intersections are numbered, making the trails easy to follow, though there is also an undesignated side trail leading up to the lookout tower.

The trails start near the campground entrance with the first loop marked by a trail post labeled 5. These first loops below the picnic area's access road explore native and untouched oak savanna–dune habitat. While hiking, keep your eyes open for several species of plants: bur oak, leadplant, prairie rose, sea-beach needlegrass, and skeleton-weed, to name a few. In late summer you can find asters and goldenrod blooming. Poison ivy is also prevalent and, luckily, marked in places by signs.

After post marker 6, keep going right, where a spur climbs a steep hill to the former lookout tower. The tower is closed to climbing, but you can still look through the trees to get a bit of a view of the lake below. After the tower, the trail leads down to the beach and picnic area, where you can follow the road up to the next intersection for trail marker 8 and two more miles of hiking on some hilly paths. At the top of the northern loop, another trail intersects with the other parking area.

52 Elm Creek Park Reserve– Eastman Nature Center

General description:	A hike along creeks, by marshes, and through some big woods.
General location:	Between Anoka and Osseo.
Length:	4.5 miles total, more options in the rest of the park.
Difficulty:	Easy, on well-groomed paths.
Elevation gain:	About 60 feet, generally flat with a few small hills and ridges.
Special attractions:	Overlooks of the creek, a big marsh, and Eastman Nature Center.
Maps:	Nature center trail map; USGS quad: Anoka.
For more information:	Hennepin Parks; see Appendix B.
GPS:	45 09.19N 93 26.71W at Eastman Nature Center.

Finding the trailhead: From Osseo, go about 3 miles northwest on County Road 81 to Territorial Road. The main turnoff for the park is just off the highway. To get to Eastman Nature Center continue 1 mile down Territorial Road to County Road 121 (Fernbrook Lane North). Turn north (right) and travel another 1 mile to the intersection with Elm Creek Road. Turn east and about 0.6 mile brings you to the nature center, which is on the right. Additional access is off the North Hennepin Bike Trail Corridor.

The hike: Elm Creek Park Reserve is the largest park in the regional park system at 5,300 acres, though it does not seem to be as appreciated as some of the smaller parks in the system. Nevertheless, the park does offer plenty of nature: three streams, five lakes, lots of marshes, restored prairies, lowland forests, and a small section of the Big Woods. All of this gives a gentle feel to the place where a short stroll through the woods, along marshes and meandering streams can turn into miles of walking before you know it.

The main park's trail system is a little like a spaghetti junction, since trails for just about every activity cross paths every which way. There are paved trails for in-line skaters and bicyclists, a dog-walking trail (converted from an old dirt road), and a grass path for mountain bikers and hikers; all making a loop around Mud Lake. Any of the paths are open to hikers. A couple of especially interesting spots include a boardwalk over a marsh and a decent overlook from the ridge on the southwestern end of Mud Lake. But I think the best hiking is at the Eastman Nature Center. Here seven trails and loops go by the heavily-forested shores of meandering creeks, through small prairies, and even to a little overlook of the Rush Creek valley.

One of the most popular routes is the 1.5-mile Meadowlark Trail, which starts on the western side of the center. The first part shares a section with the short self-guided Sumac Interpretive Trail. Pick up a leaflet at the cen-

Elm Creek Park Reserve–Eastman Nature Center

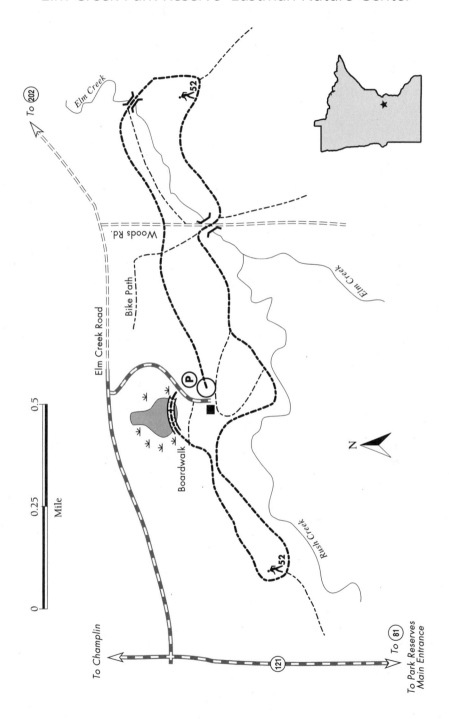

ter; there is a different one for each season, designed to provide some ecological details about these rich woods.

Off this trail, a very short side loop called the Landscape for Wildlife
Loop goes on a tour of the shrubs. After this, the loop splits in two for the
upper and lower sections. Taking the upper section, you come to a bench
and an overlook of the narrow Rush Creek valley, about halfway down, the
creek takes a meandering course in a miniature bluffland landscape. The
lower section takes a sharp turn down the bluff to return alongside the
creek.

South of the center there are two linked trails for a 0.75-mile hike: the
Heron Trail and Oxbow Loop, which loops off the Heron Trail. These both
go right into the heart of the lowland forest with the Oxbow Loop traveling
along the much winding Rush Creek and crossing over a number of small
footbridges. (The Dakota name is *Wan-ye-ca wa-kpa-dan* and means "rushes.")
Big maples and cottonwoods line the creek here, and a number of wood
duck houses are mounted in the trees. The Heron Trail is so-named for the
occasional nesting herons at the confluence of the Elm and Rush creeks.
This trail enters the middle of the Monarch Trail.

The 0.75-mile Monarch Trail and 1.25-mile Creek Trail form a figure-
eight loop for a tour of some meadows, a maple-basswood forest, and the
Elm Creek valley. The trail starts on the eastern side of the interpretive
center and is part of the Hennipen Park Autumn Hike series. The first loop
goes through a gently rolling prairie with a number of scrub oak popping up
in the fields. At the halfway point, an unmaintained road cuts across the
path. A left here brings you to a bridge that goes across Elm Creek to a
section on a ridge, overlooking the creek. Stay to your left after the bridge
for this good view. The next intersection is near a picnic area where you
take a left up into a section of the Big Woods. This beautiful hillside forest of
maple and basswood leads to the other bridge and back to the other side.
After the crossing, a large spruce sits at the intersection for the return loop
where there are parallel paths leading back to the first loop and the nature
center.

53 Crow-Hassan Park Reserve

General description:	A quiet riverside park with overlooks above the Crow River and a sizeable bluestem prairie.
General location:	Just west of Rogers.
Length:	About 5 miles.
Difficulty:	Easy; follows a grassy path on flat to gently rolling terrain.
Elevation gain:	40 feet from the river to the hilltops.
Special attractions:	Prairie, wildflowers, and the riverside.
Maps:	Park reserve trail map; USGS quad: Saint Michael.
For more information:	Hennepin Parks; see Appendix B.
GPS:	45 11.138N 93 37.741W.

Finding the trailhead: From Rogers and Interstate 94, take County Road 150 south for 1 mile to County Road 116 (Territorial Parkway); go west about 4 miles to Hassan Parkway and the park entrance. Park at the trail center.

The hike: Crow–Hassan Park Reserve sits nestled along the meandering Crow River. About a quarter of the park's 2,600 acres are comprised of rolling prairie, transitional habitat that includes the riverside banks and the high, dry slopes of forest land. The park feels bigger than some of the other parks in the state, partly because of the surrounding metro area and partly because of its continuous acreage, uninterrupted by roads. The park is named both for the Crow River, a popular canoeing river that merges with the Mississippi a short 7 miles downstream, and for the township of Hassan. The trails along the river also happen to follow the historic Ox Cart Trail, which went from Saint Paul up to Pembina on the Canadian border. In the mid-19th century, buffalo hides were hauled in ox carts (rolling on 5-foot wheels) to be exchanged for goods and merchandise with the pioneers farther north.

The parking lot is at the trail center. Hikers can start behind the posted maps (left-hand side when you drive in); the return loop comes out on the other side of the lot. The trail follows some hilly terrain, goes along the river, and then turns away from the river at the barn to return back through the prairie.

Start at the trail center and walk to a bypass loop created for cross-country skiers. A left brings you to the top of the mound, where, at about 1 mile, the view takes in the marsh and river valley below. Continuing down the mound's other side, follow the wide path as it goes toward the woods. At the western-most point of the trail are a couple of intersecting access trails; stay to your left (north) to meet up with the river. Hike beside the river bank for the next 2 miles. You pass a steep, narrow ravine that cuts through the loose glacial till and into the river. Soon enough, you come up to a rest stop

Crow-Hassan Park Reserve

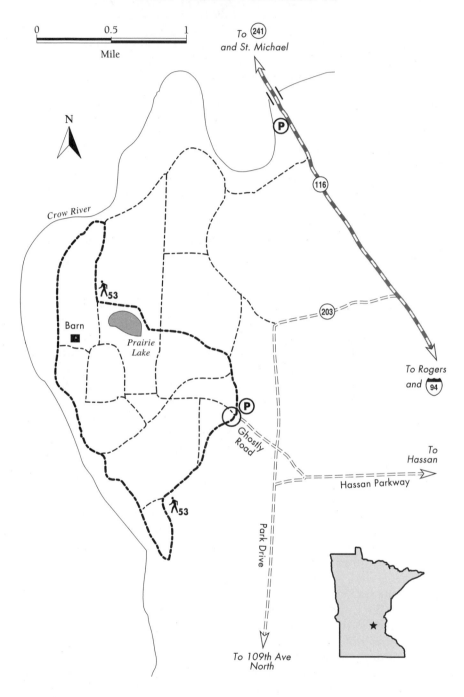

0   0.5   1

Mile

N

To (241)
and St. Michael

P

116

Crow River

53

Barn

Prairie
Lake

203

To Rogers
and (94)

P

Ghostly
Road

To
Hassan

Hassan Parkway

53

Park Drive

To 109th Ave
North

with a picnic table and an overlook of the muddy Crow River, with its steep slope leading down to the tree-lined river.

At the intersection, marked with an 8, one can turn right and take the shortcut back or continue up the river past the two group camping sites. Continue straight ahead to meet up with more rolling hills. After the second camp, veer away from the river.

The second site is called the Blue Stem Group Camp, which is easy enough to identify with its big barn, used for horses, and an enclosed shelter that looks a little like a converted chicken coop from the outside. Fortunately, the cozy shelter contains a potbellied stove and some benches for taking a break. This is a perfect spot to warm up during a late season hike, or a good place to seek shelter from a summer shower. From here, take a right before the barn or continue hiking upstream and take a right at the next intersection, followed by a turn at intersection number 13 to get to the Blue Stem Trail.

Hiking the Blue Stem Trail you can imagine what it must have been like over a hundred years ago, when the tallgrass brushed the wheels of the ox carts. Here the trail dips down to pass by small Prairie Lake. This section of prairie swells gently on the hills, where at times deer can be seen on distant ridges. This is probably one of the nicest prairies in the metro area. Looking to the north, in the center of the prairie, you view nothing but grassland stretching out as far as the eye can see. This trail continues for 1.25 miles and leads back to the visitor center

54 Wolsfeld Woods Scientific Natural Area (SNA)

General description:	A trail through a dense forest with lots of big trees.
General location:	West of Plymouth and just north of Long Lake.
Length:	3-mile loop.
Difficulty:	Easy to moderate. Wide footpaths, might be some windfall to climb over or crawl under.
Elevation gain:	About 80 feet from the lake to the top of the hill.
Special attractions:	Largest sugar maples in the state and other old-growth trees.
Maps:	Trail map posted at site; USGS quads: Hamel and Excelsior.
For more information:	Scientific Natural Area–DNR Information Center; see Appendix B.
GPS:	44 59.989N 93 34.428W.

Finding the trailhead: From U.S. Highway 12 at Long Lake, go to Brown Road and travel north 0.8 mile. At the intersection with County Road 6,

Wolsfeld Woods SNA

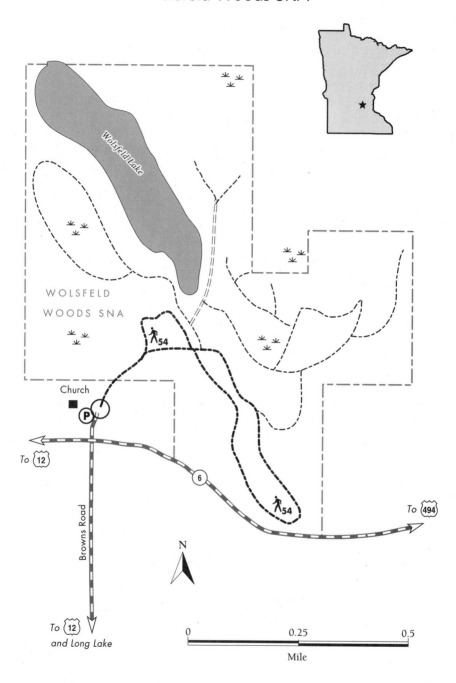

park directly across the road in the Trinity Lutheran Church lot. A small sign in the northeast corner of the lot leads to the trail.

The hike: Hike here in the spring, before the trees shade out the carpet of ephermal, blooming wildflowers; hike here in the summer to walk in the cool shade of the leaves; and hike in the fall to see the changing colors. Wolsfeld Woods is a premier example (and one of the last remnants) of the Big Woods; its old-growth trees are the highlight of this hike. The trails loop through some of the biggest sugar maples in the state and past two-hundred-year-old red oak, basswood, butternut, and ironwood trees.

The woods are named for the Wolsfeld brothers, who, in 1855, harvested tree sap from the sugar maples to process into syrup. The woods could have gone the way of so many of the woods in the metro area, and been cut down for development, but this stand was donated to the Nature Conservancy instead, who in turn gave it to the Scientific Natural Areas program of the Department of Natural Resources. The area is small (only 221 acres), but it is packed full of trails—enough to make for a decent afternoon of hiking. Some climbing might be necessary to get over the deadfall, which gives the place a more remote look and feel.

The trail starts at the northeast corner of the parking lot. About 200 yards up the trail you come to posted intersection numbered 1. Take a left for the side loop leading into a large red oak forest. On the far end of this loop, stay on the trail (which means that you do not head downhill on the unauthorized path) and continue back to the main corridor trail. This trail is a prime location for viewing flowers in the spring; keep your eyes open for trillium, hepatica, and bloodroot. Coming out of this short loop onto the larger trail system can be a little confusing. SNAs do not always have maintained trails and are kept as inconspicuous as possible. If you head down the hill, you will reach Wolsfeld Lake. The first trail to the left leads up to a glacial ridge above the lake.

55 Carver Park Reserve–Lowry Nature Center

General description:	An easy hike through open meadows, forests, and wetlands with prime wildlife and bird habitat.
General location:	Just southwest of Lake Minnetonka near Victoria.
Length:	1.2 miles.
Difficulty:	Easy.
Elevation gain:	Nominal, about 40 feet.
Special attractions:	Nature Center with many family-oriented activities.
Maps:	Nature Center trail map; USGS quads: Mound and Victoria.
For more information:	Hennipen County Parks; see Appendix B.
GPS:	44 52.906 N 93 40.945W.

Finding the trailhead: From Victoria and Minnesota Highway 5, go west 0.5 mile to County Road 11. Park at the Lowry Nature Center; the trail starts on the east side of the building.

The hike: Wetlands are some of the most productive ecosystems in the world; a cattail marsh produces more than 20,000 pounds of plant material per acre, which is twice as much as a forest's production and four times as much as a prairie's. It's been estimated that duckweed, muskrats, egrets, and about 900 other plants and animals use wetlands at some point in their life. At the Lowry Nature Center, you get a chance to be close to this wetland habitat on a 1,700-foot boardwalk that zigzags through a marsh, situated between four lakes. Naturalists have also reintroduced the world's largest aquatic bird—trumpeter swans—to the park. Find out more about these birds at the nature center.

Carver Park has miles of paved and turf trails, but some of the best footpaths are at the nature center. The center's trail also features, in addition to the boardwalk, a rolling prairie and a maple–oak forest, allowing you to visit plenty of habitats on a short and accessible trail. First, visit the trail center, where there is an interesting hands-on exhibit and a chance to pick up a trail brochure. The brochure for the Maple Trail includes ecological comments about the plant and animal life found along the path.

From the center, start on the wide grassy path that veers toward the parking lot and go straight ahead to station 1, where you will have a view of the Elbow Slough, the edge of the forest, and the grasslands. At the second intersection, a left leads to the Oak Trail loop to the north, while a right leads to the Maple Trail and the loop around the marsh. Station 5 has a view across the marsh, looking toward the boardwalk.

As you continue on and circumnavigate the marsh, you will come to a long section of boardwalk that allows you to walk across the water. The boardwalk bobs a bit as you walk on it, but takes you among the cattails and

Carver Park Reserve–Lowry Nature Center

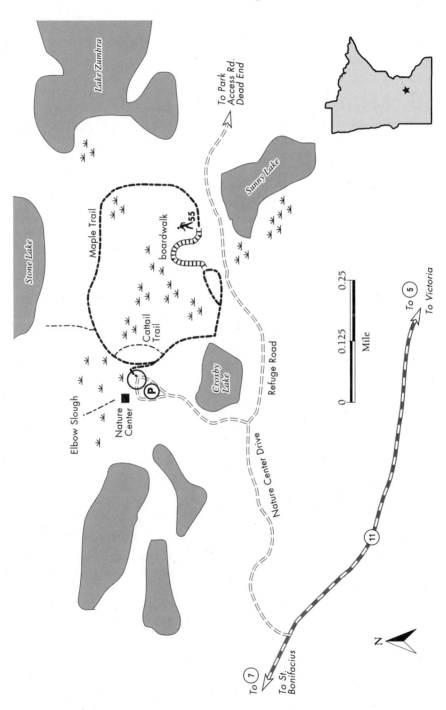

ducks. Upon leaving the water's edge, hike the side loop up the small knob for an overlook at station 9. Here, you will find a partially obstructed view of Sunny Lake, which has an osprey nesting site. The Cattail Trail follows the west edge of the marsh, allowing you, if you desire, to get more of the wetland experience before returning to the center.

56 Minnesota Valley National Wildlife Refuge–Louisville Swamp

General description:	A hike along the floodplain of the Minnesota River into cottonwood stands and past the ruins of old farms from the 1800s.
General location:	Southwest of Shakopee.
Length:	About 4.5 miles.
Difficulty:	Moderate, the trail follows a wide path that gets muddy in spots.
Elevation gain:	50 feet from high bank to the swamp.
Special attractions:	Wildlife, giant cottonwoods, birding, and historic homesteads.
Maps:	Visitors' trail guide; USGS quads: Jordan West and Jordan East.
For more information:	Minnesota Valley National Wildlife Refuge; see Appendix B.
GPS:	44 44.405N 93 35.914W.

Finding the trailhead: From the intersection of Minnesota Highway 41 and U.S. Highway 169, travel south on US 169 for 2 miles to the brown sign for Louisville Swamp at 145th Street. This is the same turnoff as the Renaissance Festival and Bryan Quarry exit. Over the railroad tracks, there is a large parking lot at the end of the road on the left.

The hike: Most people would not guess that one of the nation's largest urban wildlife refuges is just outside of Minneapolis; but it is. The MVNWR's 17,000 acres and seven management units line the Minnesota River for 34 miles from Jordan to Fort Snelling State Park. The main aim of the park is to provide a habitat for wildlife, while simultaneously allowing people to observe nature. It does both well.

Habitats range from oak savanna (where even prickly pear cactus can be found), expansive swamp, dense hardwood forests, and towering lowland forests. Wildlife residents of the refuge include mink, foxes, coyotes, and beavers. The prairies and floodplains in the valley also provide habitat for some 250 different migrating or nesting bird species, including thousands of migrating songbirds and waterfowl as well as birds-of-prey, such as bald eagles, hawks, and owls. Because of all the swamp's standing water, bugs

Minnesota Valley National Wildlife Refuge–Louisville Swamp

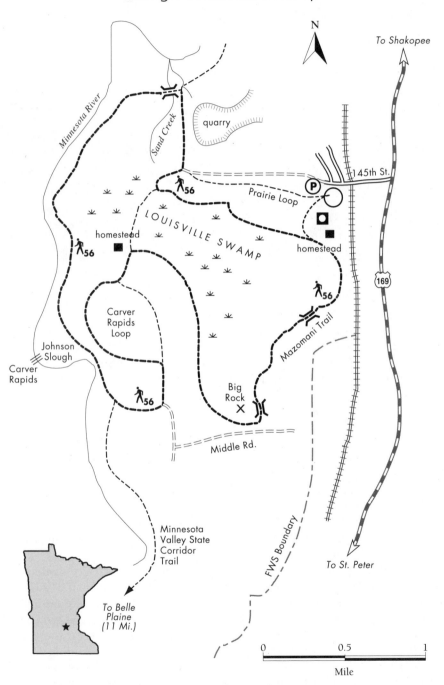

N

To Shakopee

Minnesota River

Sand Creek

quarry

145th St.

Prairie Loop

P

169

LOUISVILLE SWAMP

homestead

homestead

Carver
Rapids
Loop

Johnson
Slough

Carver
Rapids

Mazomani Trail

Big
Rock
X

Middle Rd.

FWS Boundary

Minnesota
Valley State
Corridor
Trail

To Belle
Plaine
(11 Mi.)

To St. Peter

0   0.5   1

Mile

Floodplain forest.

are fierce during the summer—take bug spray.

The four trails here allow for a full day of hiking and exploring: the State Corridor Trail (3.5 miles) runs along the river and continues out of the refuge; the Little Prairie Loop (2 miles) takes you through an oak savanna; Johnson Slough (1.5 miles) is a short loop below Jabs Farm; and the Mazomani Trail (4.5 miles), the longest loop, travels from the prairie to the floodplain.

A dirt access road at the north end of the parking lot leads directly west to the State Corridor Trail. The other trails start behind three big information signs (you can also pick up a map of the area and a birder's list here). Starting behind the signs, the Mazomani Trail passes by the Little Prairie Loop first, then turns off for an overlook above Louisville Swamp. The overlook has a west-facing bench, making it a relaxing place to take in a sunset, looking out across big sky country. Stay to the left at the next intersection, the returning half of the Mazomani loop. After about 0.5 mile, the trail passes by the remains of the Ehmiller homestead. Only a few building foundations are left standing here.

Up next, at 1.25 miles you enter the bottomland forest dominated by towering cottonwoods. During low water, the place has a spartan or austere look with no ground cover and only telephone-pole-like trees pointing in every direction. Old, big silver maples with long peeling flakes of grey bark lead up to the first bridge. Check out the high water mark on the trees, nearly at eye level, which were caused by flooding in 1993. Flooding occurs approximately three out of every five years. The next bridge looks like it was partially washed away in the flood. It gets a bit hilly with some sandstone outcroppings along the way. Take a right at the access road and follow it for 100 yards or so before taking another right at 1.5 miles. Right around the corner is a mini-bus sized glacier erratic. If you are nimble, this boulder is high enough to provide a vantage point. Otherwise it is big enough to walk around while pondering the glacial force that moved it here.

Follow the bluffline along the southern edge of the swamp to Jabs Farm at 2.5 miles, where there are two slowly decaying buildings and a chicken coop converted into a warming hut. If the swamp is not flooded, you can continue on, crossing over the rock causeway to finish the Mazomani trail. If the water impedes your passage, turn south for the DNR's Carver Rapids Unit and the Johnson Slough (backwater of the river). At the bottom of the Carver Rapids loop, you can gain access to the Minnesota Valley State Corridor Trail.

Across from Jabs farm, on the far side of the swamp (at 3 miles), you will come to the intersection of the oak savanna and the winding Little Prairie Loop. A right takes you to the upland forest, while the remaining section of the Mazomani Trail is on the left. Both head back to the parking lot; take your pick, grassland or trees.

Note: The multi-purpose Minnesota Valley State Corridor Trail also runs through the refuge along the river. This trail stretches from Shakopee to Belle Plaine, with several sections for biking. In its run through the refuge, the trail is dirt and seems to be favored mostly by equestrians, though hikers are allowed on all sections.

Wildflowers along the Prairie Loop in the Minnesota Valley NWR.

57 Hyland Lake Park Reserve–Richardson Nature Center

General description:	An easy, relaxing hike around a prairie, some woods, and ponds.
General location:	Bloomington.
Length:	2 miles.
Difficulty:	Easy, on wide mowed paths.
Elevation gain:	Nominal, about 50 feet.
Special attractions:	Nature Center programs, prairie, and wildlife watching.
Maps:	Nature Center trail map; USGS quad: Bloomington.
For more information:	Hennepin Parks; see Appendix B.
GPS:	44 50.563 N 93 22.345W.

Finding the trailhead: From Minnesota Highway 100 and Interstate 494, take County Road 34 (Normandale Boulevard) south to County Road 28 (East Bush Lake Road). Turn right and travel about 1.5 miles to the Nature Reserve sign and entrance. The entrance is on the west side of the reserve.

The hike: Hyland Park Reserve is perhaps the busiest of the metro parks, with more than 400,000 people visiting annually. Fortunately, the park's 1,000 acres are split into a couple of parts; the southern half, which offers recreational activities, and the quieter, less-visited northern part centered

The Prairie Loop.

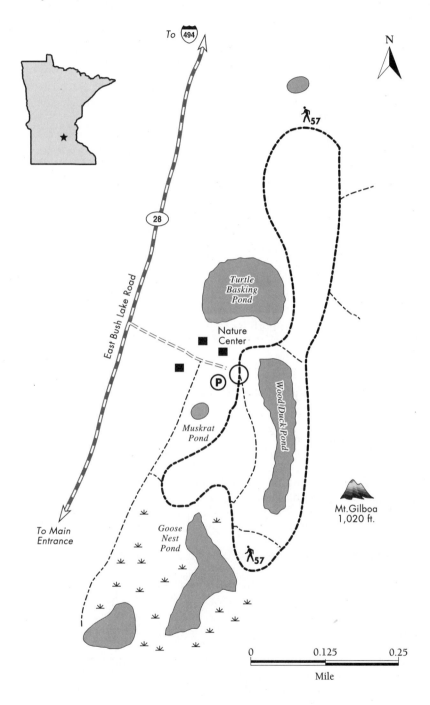

To 494

N

28

East Bush Lake Road

Turtle Basking Pond

Nature Center

P

Wood Duck Pond

Muskrat Pond

Mt. Gilboa
1,020 ft.

To Main
Entrance

Goose Nest Pond

57

57

0   0.125   0.25

Mile

around Richardson Nature Center. The southern part has paved bike trails, boat rentals, a large picnic area, and a huge children's creative play area. The northern section has a separate entrance and retains a degree of wildness within its boundaries, showcasing wetlands, prairies, and woods. Hiking the northern section's woodchip trails, it is easy to forget that the park is literally surrounded by the city of Bloomington.

The starting point, the Nature Center, has special events like bird-of-prey demonstrations or an occasional apple cider pressing. The trail leads out from the back of the center and then splits off in two directions—the Prairie Trail followed by the Aspen Trail, and the Oak Trail.

The Prairie Trail is an easy-going, clockwise, 0.75-mile loop among 40 acres of a gently sloping grassland, surrounded by woods. Formerly, this grassland was an old farm field that was purchased by the park in 1964. Here, in summer, you may find goldenrod and other prairie wildflowers in bloom. There is also a small turtle basking pond with an observation pier that makes a fine spot to do some basking in the sun yourself.

The Prairie Trail's far side connects with the 0.75-mile Oak Trail, which lives up to its name by going around and through a thick oak forest. Right before the Goose Nest Pond you'll find the best oak stand with some 100- to 150-year-old trees. From the pond's observation pier, you can check out the geese making water landings and take-offs. Heading back to the center you can either follow alongside Wood Duck Pond or head over to the Aspen Trail, where you will find another observation deck, situated above the pond.

58 Murphy Hanrahan Park Reserve

General description:	One of the least-developed regional parks, and also the most rugged, with the trail going along steep glacial hills by Hanrahan Lake.
General location:	Between Burnsville and Prior Lake.
Length:	1.5 miles; an additional 9 miles of horse trails are also available for hiking.
Difficulty:	Easy to moderate; follows a wide path on a rolling course.
Elevation gain:	About 50 feet up the steep hill from the lake to the top of the kame.
Special attractions:	Bird watching and kames (conical hills).
Maps:	Park reserve trail map; USGS quad: Orchard Lake.
For more information:	Hennepin Parks; see Appendix B.
GPS:	44 43.469N 93 20.884W.

Finding the trailhead: Near the southern confluence of Interstate 35W and Interstate 35E, take County Road 42 west for 2 miles to County Road 74 (Hanrahan Lake Boulevard). In another 2 miles, turn off at County Road 75

Murphy Hanrahan Park Reserve

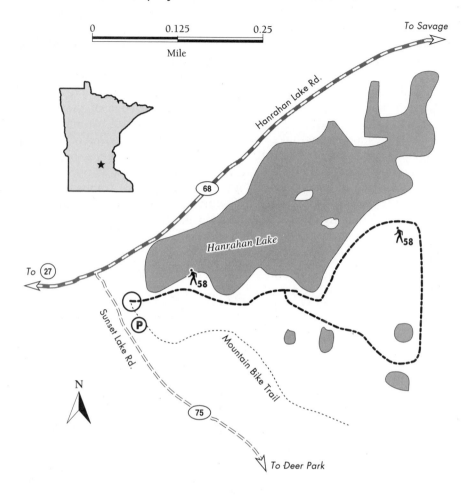

(Murphy Lake Boulevard). Park just 0.1 mile down the dirt road on the right.

The hike: Murphy Hanrahan has three lakes, a couple dozen ponds, some former farmland in varying stages of restoration to prairie, and oak-covered hills. It also offers prime wildlife habitat, including that for birds seldom seen in Minnesota: the hooded warbler, blue-winged warbler, and Acadian flycatcher. The land is some of the most rugged in the regional park system, worked into shape by glacial action. Here the hiking path climbs steep hills and descends alongside low pothole ponds to make for an invigorating, but short hike.

The park seems to be more well-known among mountain bikers and equestrians than hikers, which is surprising, since with nearly 3,000 acres it offers a myriad of hiking opportunities. The park puts the different users on separate trail loops, which alleviates a lot of potential problems. This allows bikers to zip down the hills without worrying about people or horses getting in their way, and lets the hikers not worry about getting run over. As always, hikers can also take advantage of the 9 miles of horse trails. This hike follows the short hiking-only path that goes alongside Hanrahan Lake.

From the trailhead, stay to the left at the first intersection, and look for the hiking-only trail. Coming down off the right, you might see a few ragged mountain bikers. The trail runs along the southern edge of the shallow Hanrahan Lake for about 0.3 mile on a mostly level course. At intersection marker 1, the loop begins. Take a left and you will meet the first of the steep hills (kames and eskers). The hills, formed by glacial activity about 10,000 years ago, are composed of sand and gravel and rise about 50 feet from the level of the lake to enter an oak forest. In the fall, the colors should be superb on these big trees. After following along a ridge, the path drops down to some marshy areas where boardwalks cross the wetter spots. The trail then loops its way back, winding through a few small ponds.

59 Minnehaha Falls Park

General description:	A tour around the famous falls that inspired Longfellow to write his poem "Hiawatha," and a trail down into deep Minnehaha Creek glen.
General location:	Minneapolis, at the confluence of Minnehaha Creek and the Mississippi.
Length:	A short stroll around the falls; about 3 miles to the Mississippi and back for the hike down the glen.
Difficulty:	Easy going around the falls, moderate on the, at times, mucky footpaths farther downcreek.
Elevation gain:	About 130 feet from above the falls to the Mississippi (falls are 53 feet high).
Special attractions:	The falls and a sand bar at the confluence.
Maps:	Trail maps in the information building; USGS quad: Saint Paul East.
For more information:	Minneapolis Park and Recreation Board; see Appendix B.
GPS:	44 55.043N 93 12.684W.

Finding the trailhead: From Minnesota 55 (Hiawatha Avenue), take Minnehaha Parkway east for just 0.1 mile for parking. From the other direction, the falls are right after Lock and Dam number 1 on East River Road. Park by the newly meandered road or in the lot overlooking the falls. The park is also accessible by bike path from the west on Minnehaha Creek regional trail, which connects with Minneapolis's chain of lakes; from the

Minnehaha Falls Park

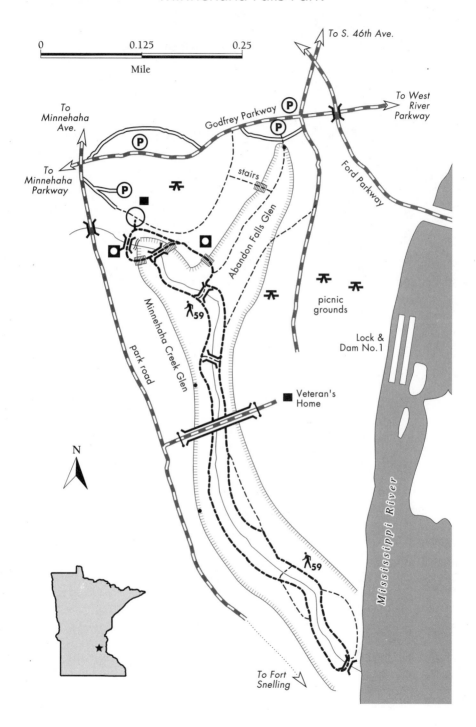

To S. 46th Ave.

To Minnehaha Ave.

Godfrey Parkway

To West River Parkway

To Minnehaha Parkway

Ford Parkway

stairs

Abandon Falls Glen

picnic grounds

Lock & Dam No.1

Minnehaha Creek Glen

park road

Veteran's Home

Mississippi River

N

To Fort Snelling

0   0.125   0.25

Mile

Minnehaha Falls.

south, the trail goes alongside the Mississippi to Fort Snelling State Park. From the north, the park is accessible from the West River road hike path.

> The Falls of Minnehaha
> Flash and glean among the oak trees
> Laugh and leap into the valley
> from the waterfall he named her
> Minnehaha Laughing Water
> —Henry Wadsworth Longfellow, *The Song of Hiawatha*

The hike: Minnehaha Falls is one of the truly unique places in the metro area. Water drops 53 feet from an overhanging layer of Platteville limestone into a perfect pool formed out of Saint Peter sandstone. This is one of the Twin Cities' most popular places and access is made easy with steps and platforms to watch the falls from every height and angle. However, this area has more to offer than just the falls. Farther down the trails, at the bottom of the falls, you can explore one of the metro area's unparalleled places. With the steep sandstone bluffs creating a secluded glen, hikers can pass by spring-fed marshes and follow along the creek as it makes its way to the Mississippi River.

Minnehaha Falls has long been noted for being special; initially by the native cultures who revered it as a sacred place, and later, though he never visited, by Longfellow, whose "Song of Hiawatha" was inspired by the falls. In 1867, it would have become our first state park, and for that matter the first state park in the nation, if the state had found the money to purchase the land. Instead, something just as good happened when the city of Minneapolis purchased the land to make it, in essence, but not in name, Minnehaha State Park.

The trailhead starts in an oak savanna, located next to the picnic area and concession stand. Behind it, the trail leads to the creek and the bridge. From the bridge, the view looks down the Minnehaha Creek valley from the point where the water tumbles off the edge of the falls. On the other side of the bridge and off to the side, there are flower gardens and John Steven's House (the first house in Minneapolis). This hike follows the steps leading to the bottom of the falls. There are a couple of platforms for viewing the falls in mid-descent. This is quite a sight in winter when the water freezes in a cascade.

At the bottom of the valley you can decide to make it as long or short of a hike as you please by crossing over any of the five footbridges. The first is located right across the creek by the falls; on the other side are two additional staircases to get back up. For a full hike you can follow either side of the creek since both sides lead to the confluence at the Mississippi River. Only 500 feet down from the falls on the north side, a wide grassy valley opens up within the Minnehaha Creek valley. This glen, called Abandoned Falls, was a meandering course of the Mississippi River that ended when Saint Anthony Falls slowly cut its way upstream. Half-way to the big river (0.75 mile), you walk under a bridge, built in 1908, that leads to the Soldiers Home. On the way to the river you also pass by a number of marshes and springs—most are marked with descriptive plaques. At the river, get out in the sunshine and find a sandy bar for a perfect place to take in some rays or go fishing. A bridge located at the mouth allows you to try hiking the other side on the way back.

60 Fort Snelling State Park

General description:	A loop around Pike Island, a flat floodplain island at the confluence of the Mississippi and Minnesota rivers.
General location:	Just east of the Minneapolis–Saint Paul International Airport.
Length:	3-mile loop. Part of the park's 18-mile network of trails (on both sides of the river).
Difficulty:	Easy, on a wide path along the rivers.
Elevation gain:	Nominal, in floodplain.
Special attractions:	Historic Fort Snelling, Interpretive Center, the two rivers.
Maps:	State Park trail map; USGS quad: Saint Paul East.
For more information:	DNR Information Center; see Appendix B.
GPS:	44 53.46N 93 10.81W.

Finding the trailhead: From Saint Paul, take Minnesota Highway 5 to Post Road. The park is 0.5 mile down the road, under the Mendota bridge. Watch for the state park sign—it comes up quickly and is easy to miss on this busy highway. It is also accessible by bike trail from the north on the Minnehaha Trail (just two miles from Minnehaha Falls).

The hike: The metro area has a wealth of regional and city parks, but few state parks, so it is fitting that this one straddles three counties and the border between the Twin Cites. The park's 3,200 acres are definitely spread out. Fort Snelling State Park starts upstream along the Mississippi, leads down around the fort, over to Pike Island, and to a long stretch following the Minnesota River. Within the park's boundaries, there is something for everyone: historic Fort Snelling, recreational grounds with volleyball nets, remote bluffs, and backwaters of the two rivers.

This hike explores Pike Island, situated where the Minnesota and the Mississippi flow together. The loop goes through a floodplain forest featuring towering cottonwood trees, which provide a shady path along the slow-moving rivers. Pike Island is named in honor of Zebulon Pike who landed here in 1805 and negotiated the ownership from the Dakota. A few years later, in 1821, the army built Fort Snelling on the bluffs. The fort soon became a regional hub of activity for what would later become the nation's thirty-second state.

The 3-mile hike starts at the bridge crossing to Pike Island. To get there from the parking lot, follow the signs to Pike Island and its Interpretive Center. Across the bridge turn left; after about 500 feet the Interpretative Center appears. All year long the center has an ongoing series of programs featuring the historical and natural features of the park. Much of the island was deforested after the fort was built, and then farmed, so the center main-

Fort Snelling State Park

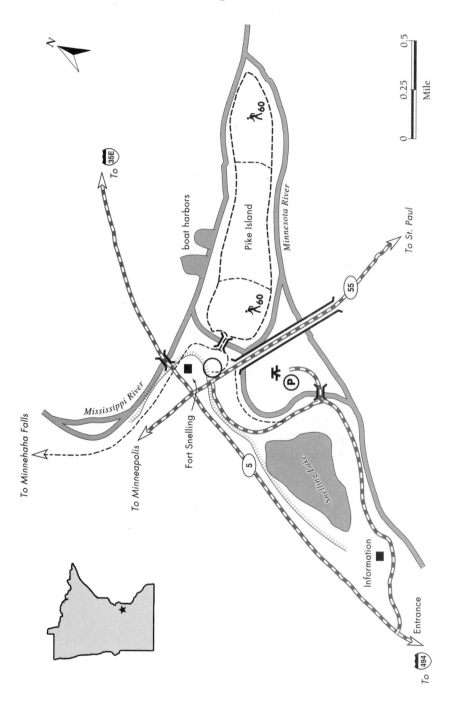

To 35E

boat harbors

Pike Island

Minnesota River

To St. Paul

55

Mississippi River

Fort Snelling

To Minnehaha Falls

To Minneapolis

P

5

Snelling Lake

Information

Entrance

To 494

N

0   0.25   0.5
Mile

Pike Island at the confluence of the Mississippi and Minnesota rivers.

tains a traditional Dakota garden, a historic fort garden, and a prairie demonstration plot. After the center, follow the north side of the island as it goes in and out of sight of the river, to the left.

About halfway down the island, large, hundred-year-old cottonwoods take over. On some of the trees, there are scars caused by the river's winter ice flows piling up on shore. At the island's tip (1.5 miles), you find a bench and a calm relaxing place to watch as the brown, muddy waters of the Minnesota slowly merge with the Mississippi's dark, deep waters.

The path turns the corner here, continuing along the southern side where the sun reflects off the water and warms the air. Along this side you might catch a glimpse of a beaver, or at least see its handiwork. Closer to the end, near the bridge, you will pass by some backwaters of the rivers where waterfowl often swim around trying to keep out of the way of barge traffic.

61 Nerstrand Woods State Park

General description:	A hike through a small remnant of the Big Woods, a heavily shaded forest of maple and basswood. The trail goes into a valley featuring a waterfall on prairie creek.
General location:	Southeast of Northfield.
Length:	About a 2.5-mile loop. Part of the park's 14-mile network of trails.
Difficulty:	Easy to moderate on well-maintained paths.
Elevation gain:	130 feet down the valley's bottom by the falls.
Special attractions:	Hidden Falls, wildflowers, and fall colors.
Maps:	State park trail map; USGS quad: Nerstrand.
Camping:	54 drive-in and 13 hike-in sites.
For more information:	DNR Information Center; see Appendix B.
GPS:	44 20.501N 93 06.284W.

Finding the trailhead: From Northfield and Minnesota Highway 3, take Minnesota Highway 246 for 12 miles south to County Road 40 and the entrance to the park. Just 2 miles west of the town of Nerstrand.

The hike: Nerstrand is one of Minnesota's best and largest examples of the Big Woods. This forest still retains much of its pre-settlement vegetation, with a rich mixture of maple, basswood, oaks, and ironwood. Nerstrand Woods is also a botanical reserve with more than forty native plant species per 60 square feet catalogued, and at least fifty varieties of wildflowers identified. On the forest floor you can find a smorgasbord of wild leek, ginseng, and the fiddleheads of ferns. Appeasing the eyes in early spring, there are blooming ephermals, including trout lilies, Dutchman's breaches, spring beauty, and false rue anemone. Later in summer, the wide leaves of shade-tolerant plants take in the diffuse sun; you will spot bloodroot, wild ginger, hepatica, and large-flowered trillium. This is definitely a good place to take along a wildflower guide.

The park is divided east to west by CR 40. The trail system to the south of the road can be a bit soggy at times in early spring, though it is passable with waterproof boots. On the north side of the road, the two trails leading up to Hidden Falls are the most popular. One starts from the campground and slowly descends into the thick woods of Prairie Creek valley. The other leaves from the picnic grounds, taking a staircase to reach the falls. Both of these trails descend into the valley through the thick woods, where you have a good chance of seeing many of the flowers listed above. Only 0.5 mile from the picnic area and right before the falls, check out the small clear-water spring that flows into the creek. Early in the season here, the bright yellow flowers of marsh marigolds bloom in profusion.

Past this spring, at the bottom of the valley, you will find a bridge over

Nerstrand Woods State Park

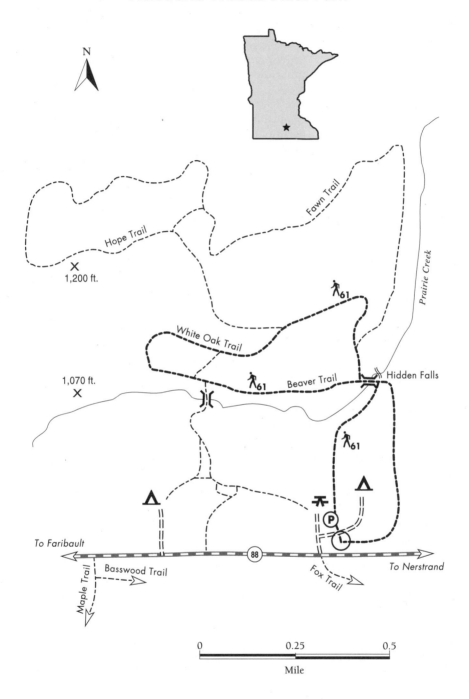

Prairie Creek and the waterfall. The falls are about 12 feet high and 90 feet long, with the water coming off in sheets from a ledge of Platteville limestone, and plunging into a pool below. Ten thousand years ago, raging glacier rivers eroded about 130 feet of glacial till down to the limestone layer to form this deep valley. Today, the creek meanders on the bottom of its oversized valley. Three more loops and some of the park's best trails are behind the falls on the valley side. A good route is the White Oak Trail, which follows a densely-forested ridge overlooking the creek valley. From this trail, you can drop down to Oak Bridge and venture back to the trailhead or go back to Hidden Falls along the flat valley bottom of the creek.

62 Afton State Park

General description:	Hike from the shore of the Saint Croix River up a densely wooded ravine to the bluff tops, for prairies and overlooks of the river valley.
General location:	Along the Saint Croix River, south of Afton. (metro).
Length:	About a 4-mile loop. Part of the park's 20-mile network of trails.
Difficulty:	Moderate. Steep climbs up and down the bluffs and ravines.
Elevation gain:	About 300 feet from the river to the top of the valley.
Special attractions:	Views of the Saint Croix, bird watching, swimming beach, and prairie.
Maps:	State park trail map; USGS quad: Prescott.
Camping:	24 hike-in sites.
For more information:	DNR Information Center; see Appendix B.
GPS:	44 51.194N 92 46.545W.

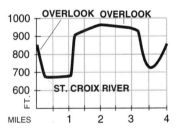

Finding the trailhead: From Interstate 494 in Saint Paul, travel east about 5 miles on Interstate 94, take Minnesota Highway 95 (County Road 15) exit south and go 7 miles to County Road 20 (70th Street South). Turn east (left) and continue 3 miles, following the downhill ski signs for Afton Alps. At the three-way intersection, right after County Road 21 (Saint Croix Trail), take a right for the park entrance. The drive into the park itself follows a steep, winding road that leads to the parking area and interpretive center.

The hike: The nearby town of Afton, and for that matter Afton State Park, comes by its name from a Robert Burns poem called "Afton Waters." In the

Afton State Park

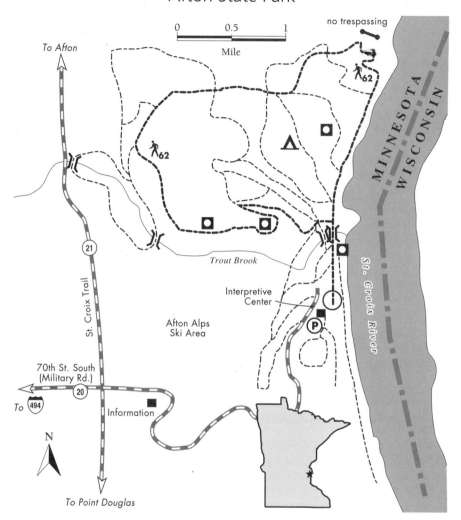

poem he mentions "neighboring hills and clear winding rills," which describes this area perfectly with its surrounding bluffs and flowing brooks. Here, miles of trails explore the rolling prairies, forested ravines, and the banks of the Saint Croix River. There is an easy loop around the edge of the prairie, with wildflowers, oak savanna, and overlooks onto the Saint Croix River and surrounding ravines. Some trails descend into the deep, secluded ravines, which offer the hiker plenty of chances for some strenuous climbing and discovery along the rambling brooks. Trails along the Saint Croix River pass by basswoods and silver maples on a converted train bed that makes for a level grade.

This particular route traverses the river's beach up the valley side into the prairie and several ravines of the park. Follow the paved path down past the picnic shelters to the footpath and an overlook of the river, a short 0.25 mile. This is one of my favorite views, looking north, upriver, with all the sand bars jutting out in the water and with large trees lining the bank. The overlook provides an almost tropical looking scene on a hot summer day.

The hiking path continues north, going across Trout Brook and on toward the beach on the paved path. At this tempting beach, a swim is always an option, or at least a beachcomb among the sand bars. Thereafter, the trail returns inland, running parallel to the river on what used to be a rail line. This trail runs for nearly 2.5 miles alongside the river on a level, wide path, passing by small creeks that drain into the river. The climb is about 200 feet to the upper plateau from the river; on top the trail then gains another 100 feet on the hills farther into the park.

The top of the plateau has rolling fields almost wholly surrounded by valleys and ravines. This was at one time agricultural land, so all the plants might not be native; still, there is enough wildlife to make the soaring hawks feel at home. One of the best loops follows the outer edge of the expansive prairie.

On the western edge, a couple of side loops descend into narrow, wooded valleys that are worth exploring as they disappear into hidden parts of the park. The loop in the southwestern side has unexpected rock outcroppings along Trout Brook. Back on top, following the plateau on the south side, you are presented with views across Trout Brook and over to the hills of Afton Alps. Just before going down the last ravine back into the Saint Croix River valley, you get another view from a point that looks south over the valley.

63 William O'Brien State Park

General description:	Gently rolling prairie along the valley basin of the river.
General location:	Just north of Marine-on-Saint Croix.
Length:	About a 7-mile loop. Part of the park's 12-mile network of trails.
Difficulty:	Moderate, on a wide grassy path. Easy trails by the river and around center.
Elevation gain:	190 feet, far western side much hillier than the middle portion.
Special attractions:	Wildflowers, birding, and a swimming beach.
Maps:	State park trail map; USGS quad: Marine-on-Saint Croix.
Camping:	125 drive-in and 2 walk-in sites.
For more information:	DNR Information Center; see Appendix B.
GPS:	45 13.486N 92 45.926W.

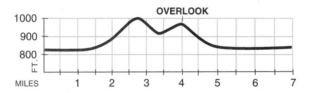

Finding the trailhead: It is along Minnesota Highway 95 (Saint Croix Road North), about 14 miles north of Stillwater or about 1 mile north of Marine-on-Saint Croix. Or from Interstate 35, take Minnesota Highway 97 east 13 miles to Minnesota Highway 95 and 2 miles south to the park entrance. Parking is available at either the beach, on the road that loops back under MN 95 or on the right, at the interpretive center.

The hike: When this park was first established in 1947, it almost instantly became a favorite destination on the Saint Croix, and its popularity hasn't diminished over the years. No doubt part of its popularity—it can be crowded in the summer—is due to its proximity to the car camping spot nearest the Twin Cities. The park doesn't have the geologic wonder or the wild charm of other Saint Croix parks, but it does offer a pleasant respite of rolling hills, marshes, and lowland forest.

The park's land is neatly divided into thirds, north to south, separated by MN 95 and railroad tracks. The eastern third, along the river, is the oldest section of the park and has a few campsites as well as some interesting ecological habitats. One of these habitats is a black ash stand just north of Lake Alice and its swimming beach. The whole of the Saint Croix River valley was heavily logged for white pine over a hundred years ago, but a few pine saplings survived that era. Today these saplings are fully grown and tower along the shore, only hinting at what the former forests must have been like. Out in the river, Greenberg Island contains a habitat of silver maple floodplain forest. In late summer you might find the pineapple-shaped blooms of cardinal flowers.

The middle third, where you enter by car or bike trail, hosts the interpretive center, the upper campground, and a mixture of open marsh and wooded hillsides. The western third, west of the railroad tracks, is my favorite part. Here the trails cut across oak-covered hills and small meadows.

From the interpretive center, go north to start the big loop around the park's western side. The trail markers are in consecutive order, one through sixteen. The first part goes by the campground, past a marsh, and after about 1 mile, under a railroad bridge. Past this large concrete arch the trail leads to a hilly section containing an old oak grove. The trails pass by a smorgasbord of pine plantations, prairies, and marshes. Several trail options and a few trail shelters along the way save you if you get caught in a downpour. The side loops usually detour into the hillier sections, and a recommended side loop, at 3.6 miles, goes between posts 9, 10, and 11 on the

William O'Brien State Park

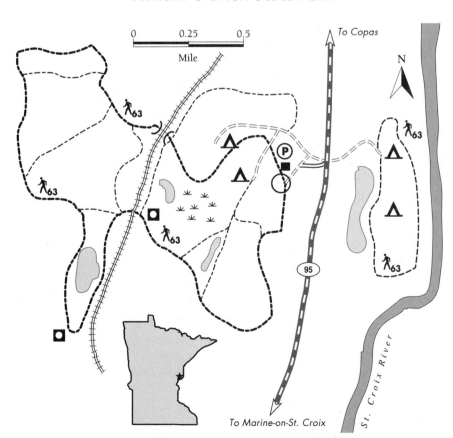

southern side before the tracks. This 1.4-mile loop goes to a high knoll to give a nearly 360-degree panoramic view of the prairie and hills. Here, you might spot deer or wild turkeys in the distance. And with a bench and a picnic table, it makes a perfect spot for a lunch.

With a couple of miles left, cross over the tracks for a curving downward trail that provides you with a scenic view of the big marsh in the center of the park. From the other side of the marsh, the tree-covered hill named Wedge Hill is actually a stranded island, carved when glacial Saint Croix River coursed its way down through the valley. On the other side of this hill, the trail points back through a meadow to the center and parking lot.

Upper Saint Croix River Valley

Few places in Minnesota are as removed from civilization as the Saint Croix River valley. Only in a few spots north of Taylors Falls do roads make inways to the river, which acts as a border for 125 miles of its 150 mile length between Minnesota and Wisconsin. In this distance, over a dozen creeks and rivers flow into the main river and six parks and state forests line the shores. In 1968, Saint Croix River was designated as a Wild and Scenic River, thereby limiting new development that might infringe on the river's beauty for visitors by boat or on foot.

The region supplies miles of hiking and many nature viewing opportunities, yet this was the first part of the state to see industrial development with logging and saw mills. Starting in the mid-1800s and continuing for the next sixty years, it was a different story here when lumberjacks worked at cutting down the scattered stands of white pine. Over this time, 11 billion board feet floated down the river, often clogging it with long rafts of logs. The cleared land proved unsuitable for agriculture. After many ill-fated farming attempts, the state ended up buying or leasing the land for the state forests and parks we have today.

The trails in this section begin at the bluffs high above the river at Interstate State Park, where there are also huge potholes large enough to swallow a truck (Minnesota is famous for its potholes, after all). They continue up to Banning on the Kettle River and by the wild rapids at Hell's Gate, and to the narrow valley of the Tamarack River in the Saint Croix State Forest. Minnesota's largest state park, Saint Croix, provides a relaxing set of trails leading to the confluence of the Kettle and Saint Croix rivers. A couple of hikes close to the Twin Cities are in the Metro Section—William O'Brien and Afton state parks (hikes 62 and 63).

64 Interstate State Park

General description: A short hike to hidden falls and a overlook of the Saint Croix River valley.

General location: Just south of Taylor's Falls on the Saint Croix.

Length: 3 miles. Part of the park's 9-mile network of trails, on the Wisconsin side of the park.

Difficulty: Easy paths around the potholes, moderate paths on the rocky riverside trail.

Elevation gain: About 250 feet from the river to the overlook at Curtain Falls.

Special attractions: Potholes, waterfall, and the dalles.

Maps: State park trail map; USGS quad: Saint Croix Dalles.

Camping: 37 drive-in sites.

For more information: DNR Information Center; see Appendix B.

GPS: 45 13.486N 92 45.929.

Finding the trailhead: The park lies on the edge of downtown Taylors Falls on U.S. Highway 8 (Minnesota Highway 95). Park at either of the two state park parking lots (at the campground or by the potholes) or you can walk in from town. You can also visit the Wisconsin side of the park, just a short hike across the bridge.

The hike: For over a century, this small park along the river has been a getaway favored for its scenic beauty and unusual geology. In fact, its worth was so apparent that it became Minnesota's second state park, after Itasca. A bit later it became the country's first interstate park, with both Minnesota and Wisconsin sharing the river's charms on both banks.

The Wisconsin side has the larger park with over 1,000 acres, featuring good trails along the Dalles of the Saint Croix. The Minnesota side also has several unique qualities: a tour of the towering 50-foot basalt bluffs on the western side, a waterfall, and an amazing collection of potholes. These potholes are located just outside of Taylors Falls alongside the river. More than eighty holes, with names like Bake Oven, Bottomless Pit, and Devil's Parlor give an idea of what the area is like. The holes formed out of the turbulent glacial river, where stones and sand swirled around, cutting and boring the holes out of hard basaltic rock; the biggest goes down 60 feet and is 10 feet across. The sand-polished rock feels smooth to the touch and has a finish that brings out the subdued colors of the rock.

The park seems to offer almost everyone a little something. The potholes fascinate kids, who play hide and seek around the rocks and in the crevices. High above on the cliffs, rock climbers play, scaling vertical sections of

Interstate State Park

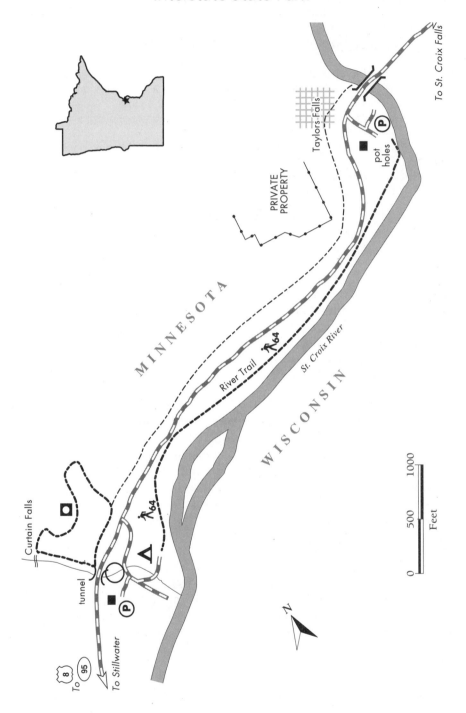

rock. The river rapids offer kayakers a ride through the remnants of Taylors Falls and several short scenic trails are available for hikers.

To get away from the crowds, hike up and out of the valley for downstream views of the river valley at Curtain Falls. There are a couple of ways to get there—a level, easy converted railroad track above the highway or the Lower River Trail. The river trail is a narrow footpath; good sturdy boots are a plus for this scramble around rock outcroppings covered with lichen and moss. The route, on its way to the campground, also goes by an overlook alongside the road that peers straight down on the spires along the bank. At the campground you can take a tunnel underneath the highway to get to Curtain Falls.

During the summer, the falls have only a trickle flowing over their ledge, yet the spectacular sandstone theater is always there. The layers of rock here have one of the most exposed, complete sequences of cambrian rock in North America. The time period covered in this 100-foot cliff of sandstone and shale is even named for this valley, the "croixan." It formed on the edge of a sea over 500 million years ago—quite a bit later than the rocks at the potholes. These cliffs have their flora habitat constantly moistened by the falling water, while just a short distance away you are surrounded by a maple-basswood forest. The trail goes up one side around the falls, then over to the high spot in the park for an overlook far down the Saint Croix River valley.

65 Wild River State Park

General description:	The trails go from a large meadow to a lowland forest on broad terraces alongside the river.
General location:	East of North Branch.
Length:	About 5 miles; 15 additional miles of trail in the lower section of the park and another 20 miles on the Sunrise Loops.
Difficulty:	Easy, though wet in places.
Elevation gain:	Over 60 feet from the river to the top of the bank.
Special attractions:	Interpretive center and wildflowers in the forest and the prairie.
Maps:	State park trail map; USGS quads: North Branch and Sunrise.
Camping:	96 drive-in, 8 cart-in, and 8 hike-in sites.
For more information:	DNR Information Center; see Appendix B.
GPS:	45 31.580N 92 44.712W, trail center.

Finding the trailhead: From Interstate 35 and North Branch, take Minnesota Highway 95 east for about 10 miles to Almelund. From there proceed on County Road 12 (Park Road) north for 4 miles to park in the state park.

Wild River State Park

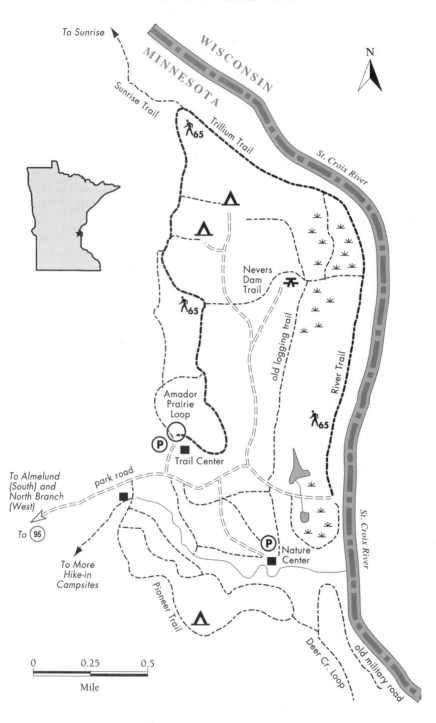

Ferns along the St. Croix River.

Or from Taylors Falls, follow MN 95 north for 8 miles to Almelund and then Park Road.

The hike: Wild River refers not to a turbulent whitewater river, but to the National Wild and Scenic Rivers Act of 1968. This act, which included the Saint Croix as one of the eight original designated rivers, protected rivers rich in ecological, scenic, recreational, geologic, historic, and cultural significance. And the Saint Croix River easily meets these criteria, with abundant animal life and lush forests.

This park follows 16 miles of river, covered with virgin forests, some secondary growth forest, and wetlands. Most of the virgin forest is in the park's northern section, which goes up to Sunrise River and beyond—the summer trails in this section are not maintained and might actually be best done by winter cross-country skiing. If you want to explore this area bring waterproof boots; the flat terrain gets soggy in places.The northern section features a wide assortment of untouched forest habitats ranging from a scattering of white pines, to oaks on the drier spots, to floodplain forest. The southern section also has a decent trail network that loops through prairies, follows old roads along the river, and ends at the interpretive center.

The trail center is on the edge of a large sandy prairie, called Amador's Prairie, which is currently being reseeded. This fairly expansive grassland has forests bordering its edges. The trail leaves from the end of the parking lot and does a clockwise loop that circles the prairie's eastern half. You pass by the Nevers Dam Trail and a couple of spurs leading to the campground on the right. The intersection for the Sunrise Trail at the northern end comes after about 1.5 miles; take a left to head north (upstream). To head to the southern section, take a right to hook up with the Trillium Trail. In mid-summer the path truly lives up to its name, with an abundance of the large white flowers covering the forest floor. This path travels past the camp-ground, after which it drops down to a lower river terrace.

Once on the terrace by the river, the trail splits in two. The River Trail closely follows the river in the midst of a floodplain forest; this also means it does get seasonally flooded. Even if it is not flooded out, the trail still passes near small backwaters, which make for a slightly mucky trail. Look for scar marks on the trees from the winter ice break-up. A higher and drier route is on the easy grade of the Old Logging Trail, which also runs parallel to the river.

Both trails lead to the Interpretive Center, which is definitely worth a visit. It often has nature programs and demonstrations, and in front the park maintains a demonstration plot of native plant gardening. Here you can also pick up trail brochures for the guided loops that begin at the center. South of the center, by Deer Creek and a large marsh, is a section on a mid-1800s military road that went from Saint Paul to Lake Superior. To return to the trail center, follow any of the numerous trails back up or go along the park road.

66 Saint Croix State Park

General description:	A short hike in this huge state park, the trail goes out on the point for the confluence of the Saint Croix and Kettle rivers.
General location:	East of Hinckley.
Length:	6 miles for this loop. Miles and miles of trails in the park.
Difficulty:	Moderate, trail gets overgrown a bit by the Saint Croix River. Other parts easy.
Elevation gain:	Nominal. About 40 feet. Trail travels alongside the rivers for most of the way.
Special attractions:	Wildlife, fishing, and lookout tower in the park.
Maps:	State park trail map; USGS quad: Lake Clayton.
Camping:	213 drive-in, 13 cart-in, and 4 walk-in sites.
For more information:	DNR Information Center; see Appendix B.
GPS:	45 54.304N 92 43.849W.

Finding the trailhead: From Hinckley and Interstate 35, take Minnesota Highway 48 east for 15 miles to the park entrance sign on County Road 22. Turn right and continue on the long park drive to the information booth.

Saint Croix State Park

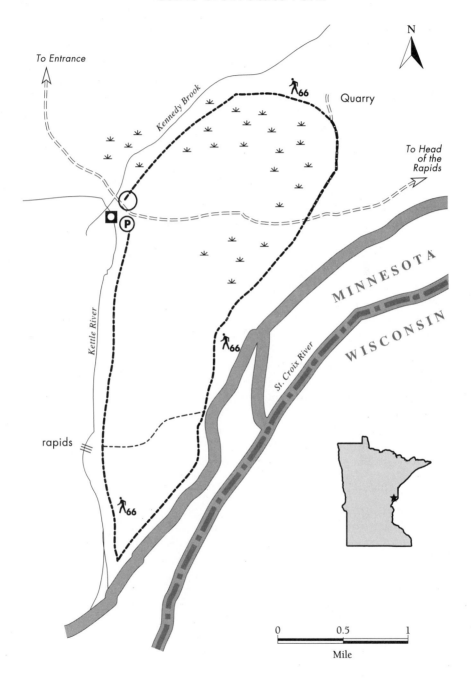

N

To Entrance

Kennedy Brook

🚶66

Quarry

To Head
of the
Rapids

Kettle River

🚶66

St. Croix River

MINNESOTA

WISCONSIN

P

rapids

🚶66

0   0.5   1

Mile

Turn right toward the Head of the Rapids for parking at the overlook near Kennedy Brook.

The hike: Saint Croix State Park, Minnesota's largest park (34,000 acres, a couple thousand more than Itasca), is also one of its most popular—as evidenced by the 500-plus camp sites. The park borders the Saint Croix River to the southeast and the Kettle River to the west, covering a vast woodland that includes many streams and marshes. The woods are mostly secondary growth, though, in spots, you can find a riverside grove of tall red and white pines. Wildlife also abounds in the park, from the occasional black bear scrambling about in the brambles to timberdoodles (American woodcock) searching the creek's shores for earthworms.

This park has the state's longest system of trails, with a listed 127 miles for hiking. This total mileage includes the Willard Munger Border Trail, a multi-use trail that connects this park with two other state forests. The best hiking is along the eastern section of the park near the Kettle River as it flows down to the Saint Croix. Except for a self-guided trail at the interpretive center, this is also where most of the hiking-only trails are in the park. For a short hike that gives a panoramic view over the forests, Kettle River, and Bear Creek, check out the observation tower. This is actually a vertical interpretive tour with informative signs posted from ground level to above the canopy of trees. Other possible trails include the Kettle River rapids trail that parallels the river to its mouth. The best trail might be the Two Rivers Trail, which makes a loop at the confluence of the Saint Croix and the Kettle rivers. This hike goes from tall red pines on the banks of the Kettle River to the larger Saint Croix River with its many islands and scattered white pines.

From the second overlook along the Kettle River, the trail starts to the southeast, just 100 feet or so down the road from the parking area. Here the trail begins a counterclockwise loop, first paralleling the Kettle on a high bank. This section might be the most scenic, going under tall stately pines, with long sight lines up and down the river and its rapids. If you want just a relaxing hike, you need not go any farther than 2 miles to the point. At the confluence there is a picnic table and a small sandy point, which reaches out dividing the two rivers.

Turning the corner, the path alongside the Saint Croix River can be a bit more overgrown and flood prone. Still, the hike along here among the basswood offers views of the river's islands and of canoeists paddling the waters. It is about 2 miles back to the road and gate 25. A couple of choices present themselves here. Either take the road back to the first overlook, or take another loop, Bear Creek Trail, through a young aspen forest for 2 miles. This loop starts across the road at gate 27, passes by a quarry and comes out on an access road near Kennedy Brook.

67 Saint Croix State Forest

General description:	A rugged horse/hiking trail that goes up and down the steep valley sides of the Lower Tamarack River.
General location:	East of Hinckley; just north of Saint Croix State Park.
Length:	About 8 miles for the loop around the river.
Difficulty:	Moderate to difficult; there is a water crossing on the southern end, and steep hills.
Elevation gain:	Over 100 feet from the bluff to the river. A hilly course.
Special attractions:	Overlooks of the river and wildlife.
Maps:	State forest trail map; USGS quad: Danbury West.
For more information:	DNR Information Center; see Appendix B.
GPS:	46 02.917N 92 25.204W at Rock Lake.

Finding the trailhead: From Hinckley and Interstate 35, take Minnesota Highway 48 east for 23.5 miles to County Road 173. Turn north (left) and go 5 miles north to Tamarack Forest Road and 6 miles east to the river. Park at the campground at Rock Lake or at the Equestrian Camp. From Sandstone, take Minnesota Highway 123, which turns into County Road 30 for 18 miles east to Duxbury and the intersection with County Road 24. Turn south and travel 2 miles to County Road 25, CR 173, and then Tamarack Forest Road. Signs lead the way.

The hike: The loop around Tamarack River is a multi-use trail, with horseback riders using it more often than hikers. The forest offers access to the Gandy Dancer Trail, which is a trail-to-rail route linking Wisconsin and Minnesota, catering to ATVers and mountain bikers. The Saint Croix State Forest's main trail goes around the Lower Tamarack River in its rugged valley. The one advantage the horseback riders have over hikers on this route is the river crossing. If on foot, crossing is probably better in late summer with the lower river level and the cool refreshing water in the heat of day.

From the Boulder Campground, pass by the boat launch on Rock Lake. The first mile of trail on its way to the main loop goes through a marshy area with boards laid over the muckier spots. Pass by the first intersection, which connects to Tamarack Road. The next intersection is with the river loop; a left (north) takes you 3 miles upstream directly to the Tamarack River Bridge, while a right (south), leads to the other river crossing another 0.5 mile down.

Going in a counterclockwise direction, head south. The path climbs, by way of switchbacks, to the top of a pine-covered steep ridge; then descends to the river's edge for the crossing. The river was about 100 feet wide at this point and only about 2 feet deep when I crossed it in mid-summer. Though the riverbed rocks are smooth enough for a barefoot crossing, cheap sneakers or sandals would come in handy.

Saint Croix State Forest

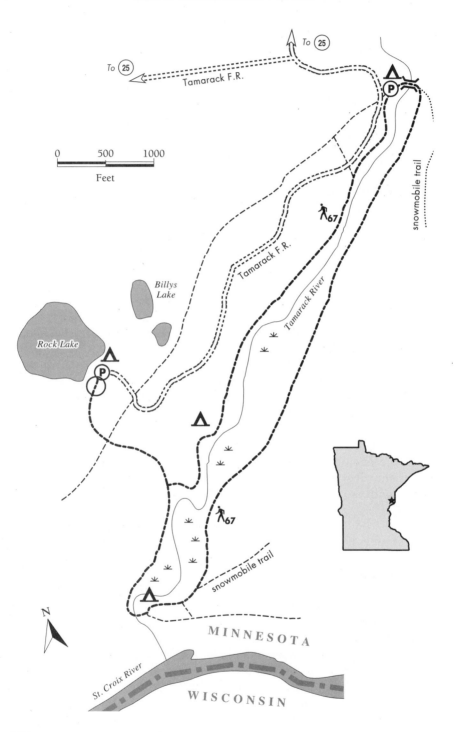

The Tamarack River.

On the river's other bank, the trail immediately reverts to switchbacks up the steep ridge to one of the high points of the route, both in elevation and for what it offers. A clearing is situated under a tall stand of pines with enough room for a decent sized campsite. This prime camping spot, except for the steep climb to the water, provides a cool breeze and views 100 feet off the river. The trail from here goes in a couple directions: east (right), which parallels the Saint Croix River for 3.5 miles to hook up with the Gandy Dancer Trail, or north (left) to along the Tamarack River upstream and up to the bridge crossing.

Taking the northern direction (left) for 1 mile, you hit the river bottom. Here the trail hugs the side of the valley, dipping down to the floodplain and then climbing the next few miles. A few more do-it-yourself river crossings and several little-used campsites are next to the floodplain. At about 2 miles past the stream crossing, climb out of the valley, through the maple trees, cross over a small creek, and then pass by a Norway spruce planting area.

Nearing the end of this side of the trail, you can see the footbridge. On the other side, the undulating trail follows closer to the river's edge, providing a number of overlooks down the twisting river. About 2 miles down from the bridge, the trail drops onto a grassy plain at a bend in the river for a picturesque scene. After this, the path ascends the valley for another overlook and then leads to the trail back to Rock Lake.

68 Banning State Park

General description:	A short hike along the cliffs overlooking the rapids of Kettle River and a tour of a remains of a century-old town and quarry.
General location:	Just north of Sandstone.
Length:	About 3 miles; part of the park's 17-mile network of trail.
Difficulty:	Easy to moderate, some scrambling needed alongside the river.
Elevation gain:	More than a 100 feet from the river up to the campground.
Special attractions:	Tour of old quarry, potholes, and overlook of rapids, including Hell's Gate.
Maps:	State park trail map; USGS quad: Sandstone North.
Camping:	34 drive-in, 4 cart-in, and 1 hike-in site.
For more information:	DNR Information Center; see Appendix B.
GPS:	46 09.900N 92 50.00W.

Finding the trailhead: From Hinckley, go north 4 miles on Interstate 35 and exit at Minnesota Highway 23 at Sandstone. Follow signs a short distance east to the park.

Banning State Park

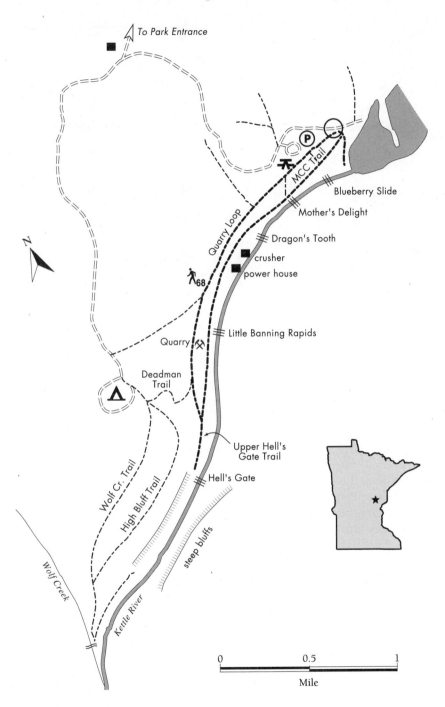

To Park Entrance

P

MCC Trail

Blueberry Slide

Mother's Delight

Quarry Loop

Dragon's Tooth

68

crusher

power house

Little Banning Rapids

Quarry

Deadman Trail

Upper Hell's Gate Trail

Wolf Cr. Trail

High Bluff Trail

Hell's Gate

steep bluffs

Wolf Creek

Kettle River

0   0.5   1
Mile

N

Trillium.

The hike: This 6,000-acre park is named for the former town of Banning, which was once located along the shores of the Kettle River. In its prime this town housed over five hundred stone cutters who drilled and pried sandstone from the bluffs for use in the streets of Minneapolis and Saint Paul. The town lasted only until 1912 when the market for the stone ended, but a number of old ruins remain in the park.

The river is named for the potholes or kettles along the river's bluffs. The holes resulted from miniature whirlpools, twirling bits of sand and stones that bore into the relatively soft sandstone. While the basalt potholes in Interstate State Park are bigger, these have a charm all their own. The smooth shapes and light colors of the sandstone almost have a feel of the canyons of the southwestern United States. A few holes going right through the bluff face are almost big enough to crawl through as they angle up toward the sky.

The river is also quite impressive as it drops a total of 500 feet in elevation, making for a popular kayak and canoe route. The trail passes by five rapids of the river, from Blueberry Slide to Hell's Gate. On shore, hikers can stay high and dry as the boaters get drenched navigating the rapids and the chutes. Other trails in the park follow converted railroad beds leading out from the town or wander though the park's forest.

The Quarry Trail is the easiest way to get acquainted with the park; but first, at the information building pick up a self-guided tour brochure that gives details of the town. To get there from this starting point at the boat landing, take the MCC Trail. The first set of rapids (Blueberry Slide) are right offshore near the trail's start. Take a short side spur along the river for a better shot upriver as the water rushes over the flat rocks. Back on the MCC Trail, pass by a vista through the pines, called Teacher's Overlook, which is right above the Mother's Delight set of rapids.

The Quarry Loop itself starts after the picnic area, where the trail splits for the upper and lower sections. The lower section goes by the few ruins, then hooks up with the riverside Hell's Gate Trail. The Hell's Gate Trail spur stops at a dead-end against the high bluffs, right at the entrance of the gate, a narrow canyon with a steep-sided bluff that constricts the river down to what must be half its width, creating what kayakers attest is a thrilling boat ride. On the shore, one could spend a good part of a day bouldering around the rocks and exploring the kettles and rock formations. For an easy return trip, go back on the upper section of the Quarry Trail, which follows along an old level railroad grade. If you want to explore farther downriver, take the turn at the steep hill for the Deadman Trail, which connects with the High Bluff trail that leads to the waterfall at Wolf Creek and the Lower Hell's Gate Trail.

Blufflands

The Blufflands are one of the more unique regions in Minnesota and not what most people expect the state to look like. Typically, the preconceived notions of Minnesota are lakes deep in the forest or vast open prairies. Here, plateaus that are dissected by four major rivers and innumerable creeks rise over 600 feet above the mighty Mississippi. This is where deep hardwood valleys hide clear running trout streams, and goat prairies grow on the steep sides of the bluffs. This is actually the northern-most extension of the driftless region that extends south to Missouri, bordering the Mississippi River. The blufflands are also known as the Paleozoic Plateau for their exposed layers of Paleozoic rock, left untouched by the last major glaciation. The bluffs themselves record a 300-million-year history from the recent glacial loess (wind-deposited silt) on the mesas to ancient layers of limestone, sandstone, siltstone, and shale underneath.

You can spend an afternoon on an oak savanna blufftop or explore the dense, thickly wooded hillsides and valleys. The blufflands contain over thirty different plant communities, providing for more variety than any other part of the state. The hikes range from towering Barn Bluff right outside of Red Wing, to several state parks nestled in the deep valleys and overlooking bluffs, to a sampling of the encompassing Richard J. Dorer Memorial Hardwood State Forest. At 2 million acres of public and private land, this is our largest state forest and a success story in land conservation. The forest was named in honor of the man who worked for the creation and protection of these deciduous woods and the lands in this region.

69 Barn Bluff Trail

General description:	Hike up the steep bluff overlooking the backwaters of the Mississippi and downtown Red Wing.
General location:	City of Red Wing.
Length:	2-mile loop.
Difficulty:	Moderate; trail angles up the bluff with stairs in the steepest sections.
Elevation gain:	About 300 feet. The bluff is about 340 feet above the river.
Special attractions:	The Mississippi river, rock climbing, and overlooks of the city.
Maps:	Trail map posted at the trailhead: USGS quad: Red Wing.
For more information:	Red Wing Parks; see Appendix B.
GPS:	44 34.080N 92 31 129W.

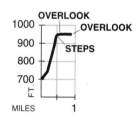

Finding the trailhead: From downtown Red Wing and U.S. Highway 61, take Minnesota Highway 58 (Plum Street) a couple of blocks to Fifth Street. Turn left on this street, which changes into East Fifth Street. Right after going under the bridge for U.S. Highway 61 you will find a small parking area for the bluff on the right. Several small, brown Barn Bluff signs lead the way.

The hike: People visiting or passing through the city of Red Wing cannot help but notice the huge bluff towering over the edge of the city. The bluff, sometimes called by its French name of *Mount La Grange,* which translates to "barn mountain," was originally named by the Dakota, who summed up the hill quite nicely by calling it *Rhemnicha* or "hill-water-wood." Today, it is commonly known as Barn Bluff. Of the thousands of bluffs in southeast Minnesota, this one is probably climbed by the most people; even Henry David Thoreau climbed it on a visit to the town. The town's residents started trail improvements in the late 1800s, with the first set of steps created in the early 1900s. The steps not only make the climb easier, but also help cut down on soil erosion.

Geologically, the bluff is a stranded island that was once in the middle of

Barn Bluff Trail

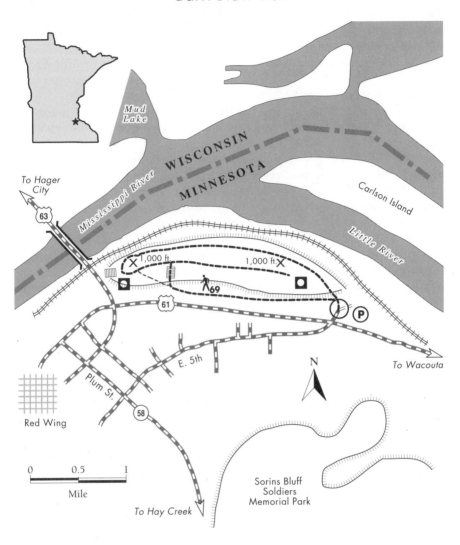

the huge glacial Mississippi. It measures 800-feet-wide, 3,100-feet-long, and has a top covered with 65 feet of till, while the remainder is made of Paleozoic bedrock. The layering on the river side, top to bottom, goes as follows: 75 feet of tough Oneota Dolomite, 120 feet of Jordan Sandstone, 45 feet of Saint Lawrence Siltstone (where fossils of trilobites are found), and Franconia Greensand (it has a greenish gray tinge) at railroad level by the river. The bluff spans a passage of a few hundred million years from top to bottom

The hike starts across the street from the parking area at the staircase landing, at the top of which is a map and an interpretive sign explaining the bluff's geology. To start the loop, take a right going straight toward the bluff

213

along the larger main trail. You want to climb up the north side of the bluff; a minor trail veers to the right. After about 0.3 mile, the loop begins, where a left goes up the road side and a right circles around to the river side of the bluff. The trail stays on the same level all along the east side, where you might also find some rock climbers climbing the steep bluff face. This is considered a mecca for climbers in the region, with fourteen technical rock climbs up the bluff's faces. At about 1 mile, climb the steps to the top of the plateau.

The top of the steps gives you the first overlook of the northern edge of the bluff. You almost feel as if you're suspended above the downtown area. The view includes a bend in the Mississippi, north Red Wing across the river, and Mud Lake by the highway. Apparently, locals come here on the Fourth of July to watch the fireworks at eye level. From this overlook platform, walk the 0.5 mile across the oak savanna prairie on the top, staying to your left at the intersection to get to the southern side of the bluff; some short side trails lead to the edge of the cliff. Exercise caution with small children. The southern overlook provides a panoramic view over Lake Pepin, Carlson Island, and the many sloughs and lakes in the back waters of the Mississippi River (at mile maker 790 on its way to the Gulf of Mexico). Looking in the other direction to the west, on the other side of U.S. Highway 61 you will see Sorin's Bluff, another ancient stranded island. Solider's Memorial Park is on top of that bluff.

Take the same trail back to near the overlook of the town; there is an unofficial shortcut down, which appears to cause erosion. At the first left, staying on the proper trail after descending a bit, you should come to more steps. Go down to the bottom trail, which parallels US 61, and back to the trailhead and the stairs to the parking lot.

70 Hay Creek Unit–R.J. Dorer Memorial Hardwood State Forest

General description:	A little known trail following the steep sides of a tucked away valley to the ruins of an old farm and overlooks of the valley.
General location:	Just south of Red Wing.
Length:	1.5 miles; there are nearly 25 miles of hiking and multi-use trails (mostly horse trails) in the entire unit.
Difficulty:	Moderate, trail is washed out in places. Steep climb up.
Elevation gain:	Nearly 300 feet.
Special attractions:	Observation platform, wildlife, and a trout stream.
Maps:	State forest trail map, USGS quad: Goodhue East and Red Wing.
For more information:	DNR Information Center; see Appendix B.
GPS:	44 30.250N 92 33.732W.

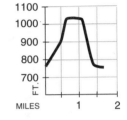

Finding the trailhead: From Red Wing, take Minnesota Highway 58 south for 2 miles to Hay Creek and Hay Creek Trail. Turn west (right) at the trailer campgrounds, go about 1.5 miles past the tree farm up to the unit. Park either at the main parking lot at the picnic area or at the intersection 500 feet beyond the main parking area, in a small space to the left, in front of a gate.

The hike: Most visitors come to Hay Creek to fly fish in the fine trout stream, or to ride horseback on the miles of equestrian trails. But within this 1,500-acre management unit are also some simple hiking paths for navigating up the easily erodible hills. While the unit does not have spectacular views, the trail does lead to a pleasant enough vista of the narrow Hay Creek valley and its small tributaries. Many hikers do double duty as they search for mushrooms or walnut trees.

The trails containing the most mileage are also the one with the most horse traffic. Just north of the picnic grounds, they follow an old railroad grade to a large looping network. The trails here can be confusing, since there are numerous unmarked access trails leading to private property. Most of the official trails keep either to the dense forest in the lower valley, or stay along farm land on the upper plateau.

The hiking loop just east of the picnic grounds goes around a constricted valley of an intermittent stream. The trail is almost down the middle of the stream on the northern half of what was, at the time, a washed-out path. This, according to the map, is a hiking-only trail, though it looks like a few horses have also traveled up here. Near the top of the valley, the trail offers views of the southern slope of a carved valley. The trail crosses to the valley's

215

Hay Creek Unit–R.J. Dorer Memorial Hardwood State Forest

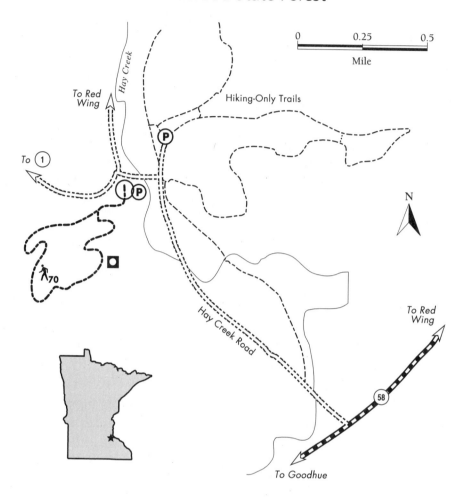

other side, providing more views, then reaches the bottom, circling a farmer's field. The loop comes out on the road near the intersection leading into the parking area and the other hiking trails.

Another shorter hiker-only loop is on the west side of the road at the trailhead about 500 feet up the road from the main parking lot. This fine loop seems to be the least used and most quiet of the trails, with most hikers choosing the closer eastern loop. The trail starts off like the others, going through the lowland mixed forest with plenty of shrubs. At about 0.5 mile, it reaches the top, where you will find the remains of an old farm house. Another 0.1 mile brings you to a pine plantation, in the middle of which is an observation platform and a small shelter. Here, the platform is built on top of an old shed, providing a view across the road to the valley of the first hiking loop. After the overlook the trail bumps along the edge of a farm field and some more pine. Then it returns to the edge of the valley, with opportunities for surveying the Hay Creek topography as you descend.

71 Kruger Unit–R.J. Dorer Memorial Hardwood State Forest

General description: Some steep going, up and down, as the trail ascends for a tour to the bluff's plateau, which offers some splendid overlooks of the meandering Zumbro River, and descends into thickly-wooded valleys.

General location: Southwest of Wabasha.

Length: About 5 miles for the big loop.

Difficulty: Moderate. Follows wide, easy-to-follow path, steep in sections.

Elevation gain: About 450 feet from the picnic area to the top of the bluff.

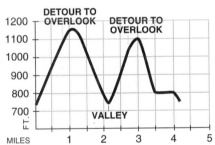

Special attractions: Overlooks of the Zumbro River; wildlife—turkeys; and camping sites.

Maps: State forest trail map; USGS quad: Wabasha South.

Camping: State forest campground.

For more information: DNR Information Center; see Appendix B.

GPS: 44 20.375N 92 04.487W.

Finding the trailhead: From Wabasha and U.S. Highway 61, take Minnesota Highway 60 southwest for 6 miles to County Road 81 and parking for the unit.

The hike: Kruger Unit is maintained as a primitive use area, which means motorized vehicles are not allowed on the trails. Instead, the unit is one of the few in the Dorer State Forest geared specifically toward campers and hikers who can spend an easy day exploring the valleys and limestone bluffs that rise above meandering rivers. The unit has two short loops near the picnic grounds and a long loop around the upper plateau.

Kruger Unit–R.J. Dorer Memorial Hardwood State Forest

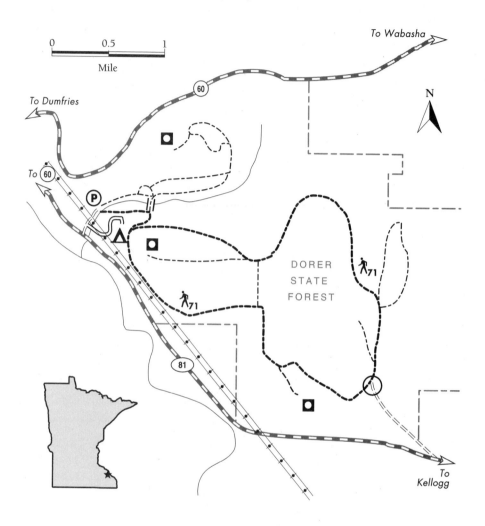

The loop by the picnic grounds, an easy paved nature trail that goes alongside a small creek, is also wheelchair accessible. The flat trail at the bottom of the valley acts as a connector with the other two loops on the upper plateau. The short one on the north side climbs up and onto a point for an overlook. Located near a well in disrepair, this spot has a scenic vista looking back into a confined echoing valley where the picnic area is located. The other longer hike requires more climbing as it explores another plateau leading to a number of overlooks, then descends into the narrow valley on the far side and returns for more overlooks along the plateau's front edge. You might also meet up with either mountain bikers or horses traveling these wide trails.

The long loop begins at the end of the paved path in the picnic area. A trail crosses the bridge leading to a climb up the bluff for the official start of the loop not too far from the campgrounds. A left at the intersection will start you climbing up a steep, rutted path, passing through an area that was clear cut in 1992. Keep climbing for about 0.6 mile until you come to an intersection for the first scenic overlook. The side trail goes across the flat-topped, but narrow, ridge of the plateau for almost 0.5 mile and yields a panoramic view of the Zumbro River bottomlands from the sparsely forested ridge. Once back on the main trail, continue with a left. Here the trail goes all the way across the wide plateau—a short cut to the other side can shorten the loop by half. Near the far side right next to a few planted pines where a snowmobile trail veers off into a farmer's field, the trail turns right to descend into the valley on the other side. This area can be confusing as you pass near the farmstead.

The return section gently slopes down the valley's side. Between the trees you can catch glimpses out across the valley. Trees of the hardwood forest that you might be able to identify include black walnut (collecting nuts is permissible on state forest land), cherry, and oak. You have a good chance to see, or at least hear, some re-introduced wild turkeys. At the bottom, entering into a lowland woods consisting of cottonwood, silver maple, and willow, a short side loop goes to the right, while the main trail continues south following an intermittent stream. At the end of this valley you come to a gate for the horse and gun club, where the trail turns right.

Next, climb through the forest and onto another arm of the plateau. A short spur goes to a wide clear area on the edge of the bluff where you get an overlook of the meandering Zumbro River and farmland. Keep to your left as you pass by the other side of the shortcut and then descend along a powerline. The trail passes by the campground and heads to the lower valley for the picnic grounds.

72 Zumbro Bottoms Unit–R.J. Dorer Memorial Hardwood State Forest

General description:	A short hike to a high windswept ridge that gives a panoramic view of the Zumbro River valley. This hike is just a small part of a larger network used mainly by horseback riders.
General location:	Southwest of Wabasha and near the Kruger Unit.
Length:	About 3 miles out to the bluff and back again.
Difficulty:	Moderate; numerous logging trails and intersections can make trails tough to follow.
Elevation gain:	About 350 feet up to the overlook.
Special attractions:	Overlooks of the Zumbro River valley; numerous side trails down to the river bottom.
Maps:	State forest trail map, USGS quad: Theilman and Wabasha South.
Camping:	State forest campgrounds in the unit.
For more information:	DNR Information Center; see Appendix B.
GPS:	44 19.268 N 92 07.842W.

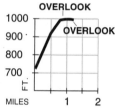

Finding the trailhead: From Wabasha and U.S. Highway 61, take Minnesota Highway 60 for 2 miles southwest to just past Dumfries at County Road 86. Take CR 86 1 mile to Zumbro Bottoms North Road. Park before Funk Ford in a small turnoff; more parking areas are on the west side in the main assembly area. The minimally maintained forest roads are in a floodplain. They might be closed during flooding or wet conditions, in which case you can still park at the gates and enter by foot.

The hike: Minnesota has four major rivers in the southwestern part of the state that dissect and carve the land, making valleys and bluffs on the way to the Mississippi River: the Cannon River, the Whitewater River, the Root River, and the Zumbro River. The name Zumbro comes from the French name *des Embarras,* which means "hindrance" and refers to the river's logjams of driftwood. The river trails in Zumbro Bottoms explore both the river's high bluffs and its meandering path in the valley bottom. This large state forest unit spreads out on both sides of the river, with miles of trails for hiking and horseback; described herein is just a small scenic section along the upper bluff.

One of the most scenic views and perhaps the driest trail lies right across the Funk Ford. The easiest route is to go up the bluff and head back down the same way. The trail system on the eastern side of the bluff is a bit confusing because of a tree plantation, which has more than a few intersecting logging trails and roads.

From the parking lot alongside the road, head down for 0.25 mile, then cross to the closed double gates on the other side of the road, right before the Funk Ford. This old iron trestle bridge was built in 1893 and was named for a local resident. The trail follows an intermittent stream part of the way to the top. At about 0.3 mile up you come to an intersection; stay to your

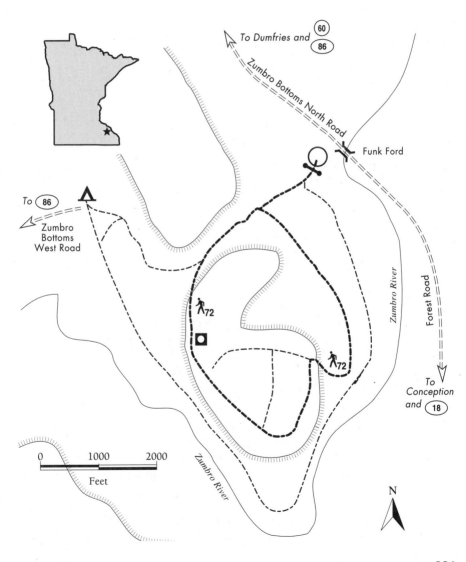

Zumbro Bottoms Unit–R.J. Dorer Memorial Hardwood State Forest

right in the flat area, consisting of pine saplings and tamarack. Next, a short steep climb brings you to another intersection, where a right leads down into the valley to the west assembly area for equestrians, and a left for the overlooks. The bluffline goes for about 0.75 mile, along which it provides a sweeping view of the river as it turns a bend in its meandering course and heads down the flat-bottomed valley. Off in the distant blufftops are farms, while here a scraggly tree shares the top on what is otherwise a steep bluff prairie leading down to the river. The bluff faces directly south, making for a warm place to bask in the sun for lunch. Behind you on the main plateau is a young oak plantation that should be quite a sight when trees fully mature. To return, either retrace your steps or go down the other side of the bluff though a more mature hardwood forest.

73 Trout Valley Unit–R. J. Dorer Memorial Hardwood State Forest

General description:	A multi-use trail on two arms of a plateau, with some fine views of the Mississippi backwaters to the east, and west to the whitewater bottoms.
General location:	Between Wabasha and Winona, just south of Weaver.
Length:	7-mile loop.
Difficulty:	Moderate. The route climbs up the plateau twice.
Elevation gain:	About 440 feet from the parking to the top of the bluff.
Special attractions:	Demonstration lot overlooks, and Trout Creek.
Maps:	State forest trail map; USGS quad: Weaver.
For more information:	DNR Information Center; see Appendix B.
GPS:	44 11.395 N 91 55.743 W.

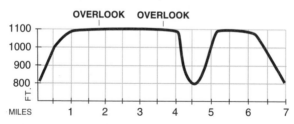

Finding the trailhead: From Wabasha and U.S. Highway 61, take Wabasha County Road 29 which changes into Winona County Road 31. Follow it for 1.8 miles to the Trout Valley Demonstration Woodland lot. This unit is about 4 miles north of John A. Latsch State Park on US Highway 61.

The hike: The Trout Valley unit of Dorer State Forest consists of 2,375 acres centered on a large plateau, bordered nearly on all sides by creeks and rivers. Along the unit's southern ravine, the spring-fed Trout Valley Creek

Trout Valley Unit–R. J. Dorer Memorial Hardwood State Forest

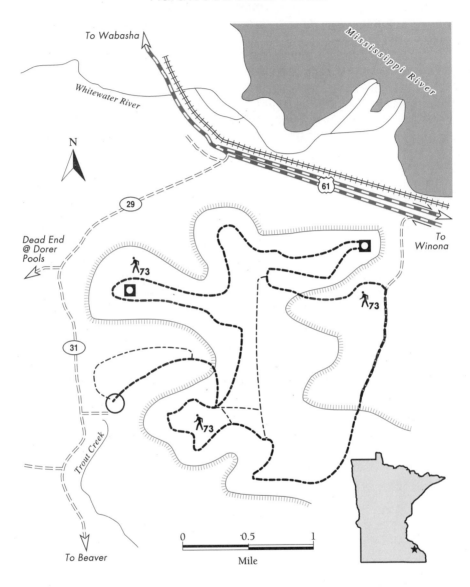

begins its short journey to the Whitewater River to the north. Bordering on the west and north sides of this unit, you have the wilderness of Whitewater Wildlife Area with 27,000 acres, and a small section of the Upper Mississippi National Wildlife and Fish Refuge, which in total spans 200,000 acres through four states. While this forest unit lacks the pristine nature of its neighbors, it does offer overlooks of each river. The trail for the most part follows the edge of this serrated bluff around its northern section, dropping down into a valley only on the east side. The path travels through forest mixed with oak, hickory, aspen, birch, and black walnut on steeply sided slopes, while flat plateau tops are mostly farm land. The multi-use trails are open to mountain bikes, motorcycles, and ATVs, though the times I visited the trails were quiet.

Hiking starts off with a steep climb of 300 feet to the top of the plateau. After a little under 0.75 mile, you come to a four-way intersection and the start of the big loop. Here a sharp right or left turn takes you around the outer loop, while the middle trails follow a shortcut through a field. Starting clockwise, another 1 mile brings you to one of the plateau's narrow arms for an overlook onto Whitewater bottoms, Hoosier Ridge, and Dorer Pools. In the fall this would make an excellent spot to enjoy foliage displays of the aspens and oaks extending off in the valley.

At 3.6 miles you reach the second overlook onto the Mississippi River Valley featuring Maloney Lake (a backwater of the Mississippi) and Weaver Bottoms. Out in the water you can see several of the boomerang-shaped islands designed for wake control. The Mississippi at this point has 743 more miles to go before reaching the Gulf of Mexico. At nearly 4.5 miles, the trail comes to the shortcut's other end, which returns across the field. The main trail then descends into the valley. At 5.6 miles in, you reach another parking spot, most often used by snowmobilers; then the trail climbs back up, for what is turning out to be a healthy workout. Once again on top, stay to the left of the field, heading to the right of the oak- and hickory-forested ravine to return to the beginning of the loop.

74 Bronk Unit–R. J. Dorer Memorial Hardwood State Forest

General description:	A good hiking trail circling a plateau's upper edge, giving vistas of the Mississippi River valley to the east and a picturesque farm valley to the west.
General location:	By Goodview and Minnesota City, just north of Winona.
Length:	About a 7-mile loop.
Difficulty:	Moderate. Easy-to-follow wide path. Steep climb to the plateau.
Elevation gain:	460-foot hike up from the lower parking lot to the top, over 550 feet above the Mississippi.
Special attractions:	Overlooks on all sides of the plateau.
Maps:	DNR trail maps; USGS quads: Winona West and Rollingstone.
For more information:	DNR Information Center; see Appendix B.
GPS:	44 03.300N 91 44.736W.

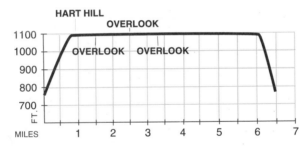

Finding the trailhead: At 0.25 mile south of Minnesota City and about 6 miles north of Winona on U.S. Highway 61, turn west on County Road 23. Continue for 2.5 miles for Hillsdale Township Road number 6. This turnoff is easy to miss, since there are no signs along the main road. The township road crosses some railroad tracks and then goes down 0.5 mile to the parking area located near a gate at the bottom of the hill. You can also reach the trail site from Winona by way of U.S. Highway 14, going to Stockton and turning west on County Road 23. Travel about 2 miles to the Township Road number 6.

The hike: The unit has only 761 acres, but it covers a narrow and much-scalloped plateau that includes Hart Hill. The land was previously farmed by Leon Bronk; a loop called the Plowline Trail follows the edge of his former fields. Both hikers and mountain bikers use this multi-use trail, and in seemingly equal numbers. Hiking around the loop, you will pass by oak savannas, bluff prairies, and several overlooks—enough to keep you looking until the shadows close in on the valleys below.

Bronk Unit–R. J. Dorer Memorial Hardwood State Forest

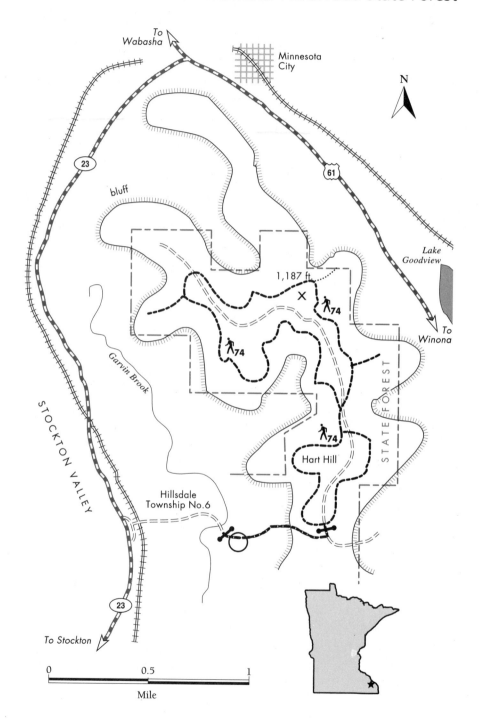

To Wabasha

Minnesota City

N

23

bluff

61

Lake Goodview

1,187 ft.

X

74

74

To Winona

Garvin Brook

74

Hart Hill

S T A T E   F O R E S T

S T O C K T O N   V A L L E Y

Hillsdale Township No. 6

23

To Stockton

0   0.5   1
Mile

Looking south toward Winona from Hart Hill.

Walk around the gate and climb to the top of the plateau for a nice vigorous start to this hike. At the top, after about 0.5 mile, you come to an intersection. Here take a left through another gate to the start of the trail loop. On the other side of the gate, a right will lead in a counterclockwise direction, which is opposite of the usual direction of mountain bikers. Following this wide grassy path, a vista yields a deep narrow canyon, looking almost like a chaparral of Southern California with a dense shrubby hillside. At about 0.75 mile you pass by a big satellite dish and a meadow. Off to the right on the Minnesota side of the river, you take in the town of Goodview, and across the Mississippi River valley in Wisconsin, the bluffs of Buffalo Ridge.

About a mile in, the top of the plateau narrows and the trail merges briefly with the forest road, which runs down the middle of the unit. At 1.5 miles you reach an intersection for the first scenic point, which walks out 100 feet or so to a little clearing on an arm of the plateau. From here you can get a clear panorama of the Mississippi River. Back on the main path, after another mile of walking through some mixed woods with oak, aspen, pines, and tamarack, you arrive at the next overlook on the edge of a steeply sloping prairie. This might be the best view of the river and also the stretch of highway leading to Winona. Out in the river and off this map is the Upper Mississippi River Wildlife and Fish Refuge, Prairie Island, Winona Slough, and many more backwaters and channels. A pair of binoculars would make a good addition to a rucksack. (This is a migration path of eagles). After this overlook, the trail turns a corner, taking you into another forested section for the most remote area in the loop.

After about 1 mile, you reach an intersection for the next overlook, this time on the west side. This one looks down on the pastoral farms in the 0.5-mile-wide Stockton Valley. In spring and fall this makes a perfect vantage point for watching the tractors plow furrows in the fields. Sitting on the edge of a goat prairie, you will find it's a good spot for a picnic.

Back along the main trail you skirt the edge of the bluff, which provides a good vantage point to the bluffs, and several vistas through young pine and oak trees, into the valley below. Nearing the end of the loop, with 1.5 miles left, you reconnect with the forest road. Here is the one spot where the panorama extends in both easterly and westerly directions. Another 0.5 mile of hiking brings you on your way back to the first intersection, with a big old oak marking the way.

75 Whitewater State Park

General description:	An exploration of the flat bottom valleys and the high towering blufftops overlooking Whitewater River.
General location:	East of Rochester, just south of Elba.
Length:	About 3 miles for Dakota trail. 10 miles total in the park.
Difficulty:	Moderate, with three steep climbs up the bluffs.
Elevation gain:	The bluffs are about 300 feet high off the valley floor.
Special attractions:	Overlooks of the narrow valleys, Chimney Rock, few if any mosquitoes and trout streams.
Maps:	State park trail map; USGS quad: Elba (one of the prettiest topographic maps in the state—maybe even suitable for framing).
Camping:	106 drive-in and 4 walk-in sites.
For more information:	DNR Information Center; see Appendix B.
GPS:	44 03.346N 92 02.664W.

Finding the trailhead: From U.S. Highway 61, turn off at Weaver to follow the winding Minnesota Road 74 as it follows the Whitewater River to the park. This gravel road changes to pavement 3 miles from the park at Elba. From Rochester, take County Road 2 east for about 21 miles to the park. From Saint Charles in the south, a straight MN 74 goes about 6 miles north to the park.

The hike: The Dakota named this river *Miniska,* which translates to "white water," for the spring runoff that washes the banks into the river, turning the water a milky white. The river has three branches: the north, south, and middle, which runs through the park. With 2,800 acres, the park covers both sides of this branch and nearly the whole watershed of Trout Run Creek, a tributary to the Middle Fork.

Whitewater State Park

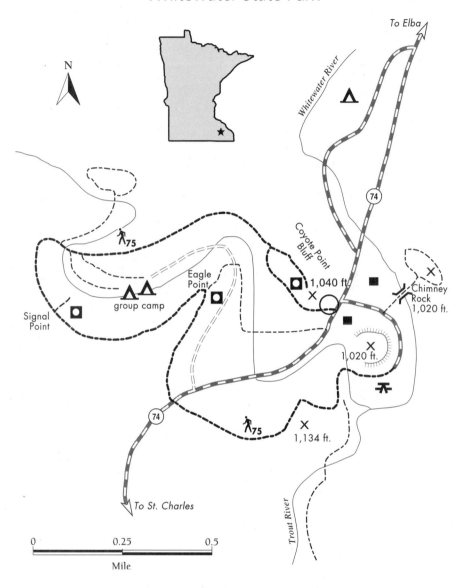

The park's two facets include both flat bottoms (where the river meanders) and steep-sided cliffs rising above the creeks. As the translated name might indicate, the valley is erosion prone and subject to flooding. However, before the park was created, this was a bigger problem as old-fashioned intensive agricultural practices, grazing, and logging removed any anchors in the soil.

Today, the problem in this popular park has shifted to excessive foot traffic, causing erosion on the steep trails. The valleys are surrounded by nearly

229

Coyote Point overlook.

vertical 200-foot dolomite cliffs, whose slopes harbor a wide and unique selection of flora and fauna. Some of the residents (which are on the edge of their normal range) include the white pine, shagbark hickory, and timber rattlesnake. Others have been reintroduced into the park; you might catch glimpses of wild turkeys.

Some have described the region as hinting of the Appalachians, with the thick hardwood forests growing in the narrow valleys. The park has three main trails, Chimney Rock, Trout Run Creek, and Dakota, which explore all reaches of the park. The short 0.75-mile Chimney Rock Trail is a visitor favorite that climbs a steep high bluff just behind the main parking areas. At the top, a rock that has a sizable hole at its base—much like a fireplace—sits precariously on the edge of the cliff. Trout Run Creek is a self-guided trail that starts from the south picnic area and follows the creek up a valley enclosed by bluffs. It's a 2-mile round-trip that might be the best birding spot of the park.

The Dakota Trail, the main loop in the park, takes a tour of the Whitewater River's bluffs, climbing the slopes three times, and then travels along the wide, level river valley bottom. The trail starts across the road from the nature store and immediately ascends a wooden staircase (over 300 steps). Climbing this bluff face really would be challenging were it not for the steps; near the end, they are more like a ladder than a staircase. Going 100 feet to the right yields one of the best overlooks of the park, as it looks back across the road toward the high bluffs. Exercise extra caution with children here. This overlook, named Coyote Point, is shared by a weathered cedar tree on a small ledge that juts out into space.

Continuing along, the trail runs the ridge with jutting points and views off the bluffs. Look for the gnarled old cedar trees hanging on the edge for dear life. Again, watch out. The cliff is steep and a wrong step could send you for a long fall. At about 0.5 mile you come to the intersection with the Coyote Trail, which started at the campground. Views look down into the narrow Whitewater River valley where the group camp is also located. From this side, you can look back as the trail curves around a point along the high bluff. At the 1-mile mark, the trail drops to the valley floor to cross the river. The crossing is easily navigable on the big limestone block stepping stones. The next intersection is with the wide Valley Trail that passes by the group camp and continues on through a meadow, back to the trailhead. On the other side of the river, the trail hugs the base of the bluff as it slants to climb back up the blufftop.

On top is a secluded platform at Signal Point. This provides a vantage spot of the steep bluffs on the other side of the valley as well as of the river almost straight below. A little farther down, Eagle Point has a panoramic view of the prairie near the road. Here take a right down the stone steps and head back to the valley floor. At about the 2-mile mark you go by the road and the intersection for the entrance to the group camp. On the other side of MN 74, climb through the oaks, which brings you to an overlook with views of the other ridge across the road and the bridge below. At 2.5 miles the trail descends to the park picnic area right by a stranded bluff. Follow the path around this bluff back to the starting point.

76 O.L. Kipp State Park

General description:	A short hike onto a narrow ridge that gives panoramic views of the Mississippi.
General location:	Near the intersection of Interstate 90 and U.S. Highway 61, northwest of Dakota.
Length:	About 2 miles; 6.5 miles of hiking trails in the park.
Difficulty:	Easy, well-maintained trail out to overlooks.
Elevation gain:	Only 50 feet; though the blufftop is over 600 feet above the river.
Special attractions:	Views of the Mississippi and goat prairies.
Maps:	State park trail map USGS quad: Pickwick.
Camping:	31 drive-in sites.
For more information:	DNR Information Center; see Appendix B.
GPS:	43 56.620N 91 24.200W.

Finding the trailhead: From U.S. Highway 61, take Interstate 90 going west until you reach the park sign for the turn-off at County Road 12. On the north side of I-90, this connects with Winona County Road 3 (Apple

O.L. Kipp State Park

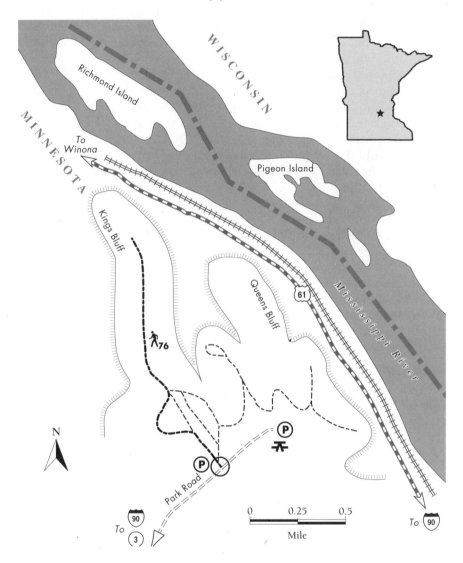

Blossom Drive). Follow this for 1 mile to County Road 2, and the park's first parking lot at 1 mile.

The hike: Situated on high bluffs alongside the Mississippi River Valley, O.L. Kipp has its fair share of overlooks: eight spots yield panoramic scenes of the river 600 feet below. Many of these spots are accessible from near the picnic area, while the path out to King's Bluff provides a river overlook, a tour through a hardwood forest, as well as visit to a unique and fragile habitat called a goat prairie.

Looking down King's Bluff and its goat prairie.

Goat prairies are the dry prairies growing on the steep southwestern slopes of the plateau's outstretched tentacles. These grasslands are named for goats, since these were the only livestock capable of grazing on the steep slopes—40- to 50-degree angles in places. Given this orientation, the slopes can get a full dose of sunlight, especially in winter; however, the sunlight also prevents trees and woody plants from growing. During the winter, the ground goes through an almost daily freeze/thaw cycle, with the slopes receiving a full dose of sunlight and heating up, then at night freezing solid, killing any tree roots. What does survive the winter are grasses and forbs that die back each year, including some fifteen rare plant species that have found this environment to their liking. On other parts of the bluff, other forest communities find a foothold; a bur oak savanna covers the plateau's top, and a deciduous forest grows on the northeast slopes and on the lower inclines below the prairies.

Start along the trail at the end of the parking lot. The trail skirts a pine plantation to the right, left over from the park's former existence as part of Richard J. Dorer State Forest, and a field to the left. Head straight at the first two intersections; the first gives access to the picnic area, while the second is the return for this loop. At 0.2 mile take the nature trail off to the left, which leads to the edge of a ravine and the first overlook on this little jaunt. The woods change from pine to a mixed oak and shagbark hickory forest. Shagbark hickory is easy to identify, as its name might indicate, with its long shaggy pealing bark.

At the end of the forest and almost 1 mile into the hike, you get a bucolic scene of the farms below, the scraggly bur oak savanna hanging onto the slopes, and a sweeping panorama of the Mississippi River Valley. Also from here you can view a perfect shot of Queen's Bluff and the tip of King's Bluff, both off limits to hiking. It is easy to see the difference between the slopes; compare the treeless south side of the bluff to the oak-rich north side.

77   Beaver Creek Valley State Park

General description:	A quick hike up the switchbacks of a bluff overlooking Beaver Creek valley.
General location:	West of Caledonia.
Length:	About 1.25 miles round-trip; a total of 7.5 miles of hiking trails in the park.
Difficulty:	Easy to moderate up bluffs. Other trails alongside the creek are easy.
Elevation gain:	Valley rises to 250 feet above the creek .
Special attractions:	Overlooks, birding, trout fishing, Big Spring, and Schech's Mill nearby.
Maps:	State park trail map; USGS quad: Sheldon.
Camping:	42 drive-in and 6 walk-in sites.
For more information:	DNR Information Center; see Appendix B.
GPS:	43 38.63N 91 34.828W.

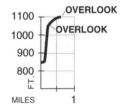

Finding the trailhead: From Caledonia and Minnesota Highway 44, go 3 miles west on Houston County Road 1 to the park entrance, and another 2 miles down a twisting road for information and parking.

The hike: A survey of Minnesota's state parks ranked Beaver Creek State Park among the best, in the same league as the much bigger Itasca and Saint Croix state parks. In its 1,214 acres, the park makes the grade by offering unique plant life and wildlife along its steep bluff walls, a bit of historical significance from 1876 with Schech's Mill, and interesting geology showcasing the heart of the driftless area. Spanning both sides of the east branch of Beaver Creek, the park encompasses most of the creek's watershed, including its main source at the Big Spring.

The valley's walls, top to bottom, are composed of Oneta Dolomite—Jordan Sandstone—Saint Lawrence Formation. The bottom two layers are porous enough to let water seep through. In the case of Big Spring enough water gushes out to basically form a creek. This clear water makes an ideal trout habitat, high in minerals needed for aquatic life. In fact, the creek has

Beaver Creek Valley State Park

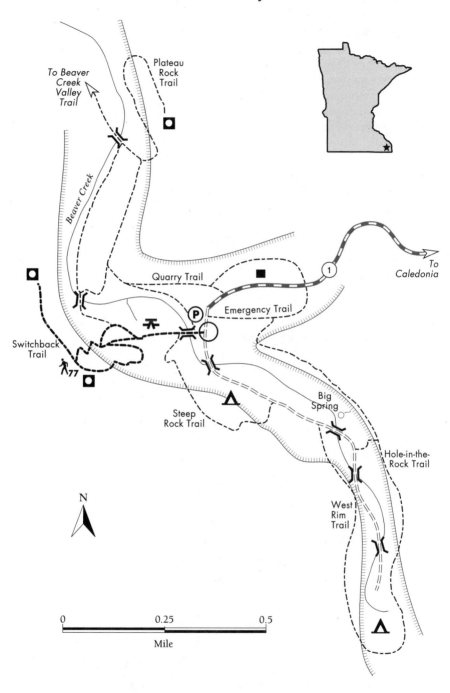

To Beaver Creek Valley Trail

Plateau Rock Trail

Beaver Creek

Quarry Trail

Emergency Trail

To Caledonia

1

P

Switchback Trail

77

Steep Rock Trail

Big Spring

Hole-in-the-Rock Trail

West Rim Trail

N

0   0.25   0.5

Mile

a natural reproducing stock of wild trout. Flash flooding is enough of a possibility in the narrow confined valley that there are emergency trails if you need to get out in a hurry. Around the bottoms, you'll find an assortment of willow and cottonwood trees, while farther up the hill, flora changes to a mixture of oaks and big woods with prairies on the edges. Beaver Creek is one of the best birding spots of the southeast—the park placed a birding board at the picnic area to note the most recent sightings.

One of the shortest hikes in the park, this gives a great view 220 feet above the valley floor and brings you through all the plant communities hugging the steep bluff. The trail begins at the parking lot for the picnic area, next to the birding information sign. Cross the swinging bridge and stay on the paved trail past the picnic grounds. At about 0.2 mile take a left for the switchback trail to start the climb. Almost immediately, you pass a small spring, which is a great place to see marsh marigolds in springtime. Take a right for the steeper of the switchbacks, a steep climb through the moist bluff vegetation habitat. Near the top, a dolomite bedrock ledge juts out of the cliff. On top, the bedrock ledge provides a vista down the narrow forested creek valley. As you continue a bit farther down, hugging the edge of the cliffline, you will reach another overlook before turning back.

78 Brightsdale Unit–R. J. Dorer Memorial Hardwood Forest

General description:	Easy interpretive trail that drops to the Root River and climbs again to give an educational tour of the woods.
General location:	Northwest of Lanesboro in Fillmore county.
Length:	1.7 miles; About 6 miles of trails in the unit.
Difficulty:	Easy to moderate on well-maintained trails with a couple of steep hills.
Elevation gain:	About 200 feet.
Special attractions:	Overlook, Forest Resource Center (on private land in the heart of the unit), and a forest interepretive trail.
Maps:	State park trail maps USGS quads: Arendahl and Pilot Mound.
For more information:	DNR Information Center; see Appendix B.
GPS:	43 45.7 N 92 00.1W.

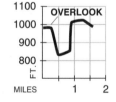

Finding the trailhead: From Lanesboro go north on Minnesota Highway 250. Travel for about 2 miles until a dirt road appears on the left, marked by a small inconspicuous Forest Resource Center sign. Follow this twisting road

Brightsdale Unit–R. J. Dorer Memorial Hardwood Forest

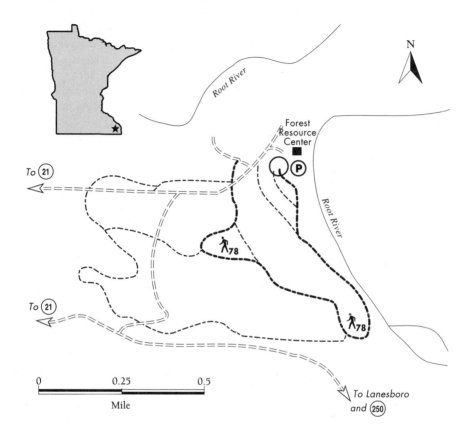

west for another 2 miles to the center. The Root River Bike Trail also runs through Lanesboro.

The hike: The Brightsdale is a 900-acre management unit of the Dorer Hardwood State Forest located along the north branch of the Root River. At the heart of the unit is also the Southeastern Minnesota Forest Resource Center, a non-profit organization who's main goal is promoting reforestation of the neighboring hillsides. The center has other activities, such as seminars on growing Shittake mushrooms, brunches with a naturalist, and even tests of daring with rope bridges that cross ravines. The state's forest demonstration plot might be one of the best, since it showcases trees common in the warmer south, as well as cold weather northern species. For just a sampling, black ash, wild grape, and walnuts, as well as several species of oaks and pines can be found here. There are two interconnected trail loops in the unit; this is the shorter one, which goes through the forest and alongside the river. Stationary ecological plaques identify the trees and interesting features.

Start at the end of the parking lot where the trail immediately goes into a Y intersection, with both paths path leading to an overlook and the rest of the trail system. The overlook is at the end of the first short loop. At about 150 feet off the river, the viewing platform offers a vista down the winding valley of the Root River. The scene reminds me slightly of New England with the sloping bluffs thickly covered with hardwoods (which also must produce a decent show of fall colors) and a gently flowing stream.

Follow the trail down the hill, which will take you close to the river. At the bottom, you reach an intersection where a sharp right (north) will take you back to the center, or straight ahead (south) continues on a bigger loop. About 500 feet after the intersection, look for the Hazel spring, a small trickle coming from the bottom of the bluff. After another 500 feet the trail heads back up the valley side, passing through a pine plantation. From here either hike along a field heading back to the center or follow an intermittent creek for a longer loop back.

79 Forestville State Park

General description:	A short hike through a mostly equestrian park. The trail travels along a wooded ridge and then alongside a trout creek. Side trips to the historic town of Forestville.
General location:	Between Preston and Spring Valley.
Length:	2-mile loop; part of the park's 16-mile network of trails.
Difficulty:	Easy to moderate. Trails alongside the creek are flat and easy.
Elevation gain:	About 160 feet.
Special attractions:	Historic town of Forestville, trout fishing, and Big Spring.
Maps:	State park trail map. USGS quads: Fountain and Greenleafton.
Camping:	73 drive-in sites.
For more information:	DNR Information Center; see Appendix B.
GPS:	43 37.988N 92 13.558W.

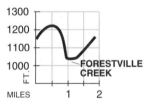

Finding the trailhead: From U.S. Highway 52 and Preston, take Minnesota 16 west 9 miles to County Road 5. Turn south (left) and travel 4 miles to County Road 12 going east. Drive 2 more miles for parking, either at the picnic grounds by the river or up by the campgrounds.

The hike: Back in the mid-1800s when train companies were deciding where to lay the railroad lines through the countryside, they chose to bypass

Forestville State Park

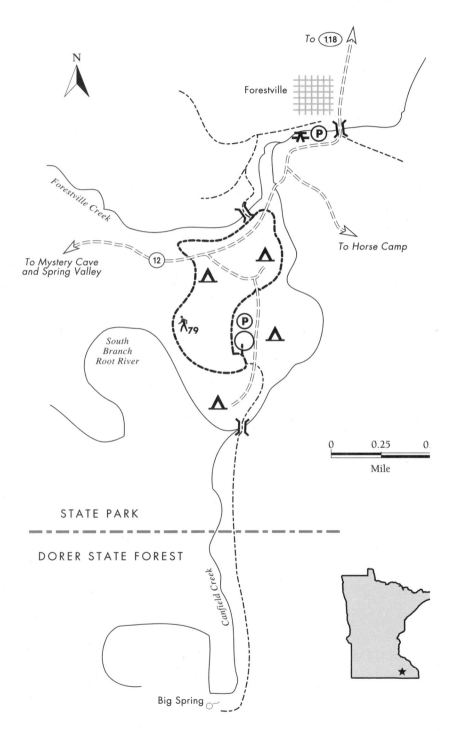

To (118)

N

Forestville

P

Forestville Creek

To Horse Camp

To Mystery Cave
and Spring Valley

12

🚶79

South
Branch
Root River

P

0   0.25   0.
Mile

STATE PARK

DORER STATE FOREST

Canfield Creek

Big Spring

Forestville. After this decision, the once thriving town was bought out by a local merchant, who slowly closed up shop. Today, only a few buildings remain, which have been preserved to their turn-of-the-century appearance. The town's main feature is Meighen Dry Goods store, operated by the Minnesota Historical Society. It's open to everyone, and staff even wear period dress, fitting for the age. This is said to be the most heavily used park by equestrians, though hikers are also welcome. Trails explore the old town plat lines (where only the street corners remain), follow the creeks, and climb into the surrounding hills.

This hike starts off at the visitors parking near the state park's information building and next to the campgrounds. Follow the limestone trail that parallels the parking lot and then goes into the woods to the right (west). The trail runs up the ridge for the only real climb of the route, and for about the next 0.25 mile, the trail strolls through a mixed forest of oak, maple, pine, and aspen, which changes into a higher concentration of maple at the lower sections. At about 1 mile, the trail crosses the road and then parallels the road alongside Forestville Creek. When I visited the park in early spring, the lowlands next to the creek were covered with wildflowers of hepaticas, bloodroot, spring beauties, and trout lilies. This path leads to the road, where you can either check out the former street corners of the town or climb to the scenic overlook on the trails above the town. (These trails might be soggy and closed in spring.)

Another loop on the east side of town, called the Sinkhole Ridge Trail, offers itself for hiking. Otherwise, head south and follow the path for hikers as it continues alongside Canfield Creek. The creek is picturesque, with the bluffs rising on the far side of the creek. The trail cuts through the campground on the way back to the start. The Big Spring Trail starts at the end of the campground following the Canfield Creek for about 1.5 miles down to its source.

Note: Mystery Cave is also located 5 miles from Forestville. This is probably the state's best cave, with over 12 miles of passage through limestone and dolomite bedrock. Guided tours are given; the cave is open seasonally. Call or write for more details.

Prairie Grasslands

For many people, the word grasslands conjures up scenes of endless fields of tall grasses waving in the wind, and of wildflowers blooming in the sun. Just a century ago much of Minnesota looked like this, with the prairies still covering 18 million acres, roughly a third of the state. Today, less than one percent remains—only 150,000 acres. This small area of grassland exists only as small islands or remnants tucked in among what is very productive farmland. These places include the shores of Albert Lea Lake in Big Island State Park, the upper plateau of Camden State Park, and the prairie corridor of Wild Indigo Scientific Natural Area.

The prairie grasslands are broken up by two features: the creeks and rivers cutting through the glacial till and the *Couteau des Prairies*. Several state parks lie within the grasslands; you can explore the forested valleys from the double waterfall at Mineopa, the rolling oak savanna hills at Kilen Woods, the floodplain forest at Flandrau, and the woods and prairies at Camden. The other feature of the grasslands is the quartz outcropping, called *Couteau des Prairies,* which translates from French to "highland of the prairie." Here the land rises, in a slow incline to the southwest, nearly 1,000 feet from the Minnesota River valley. In a few spots the underlying Sioux quartzite juts through in dramatic fashion as seen at Blue Mounds and Pipestone.

This section does not include all the prairies; elsewhere in this guide, you can find prairies at Buffalo River State Park, Glacial Lakes State Park, O.L. Kipp State Park, plus smaller segments in the Hayes Lake State Park, Louisville Swamp Preserve, Crow-Hassan Park Reserve, William O'Brien State Park, and Richardson Nature Center.

80 Wild Indigo Scientific Natural Area (SNA)

General description:	A tallgrass prairie trail following a narrow old railroad right-of-way that splits the farmland.
General location:	Northeast of Austin, between Ramsey and Dexter.
Length:	6.2 miles one way (County Road 19 to Dexter).
Difficulty:	Easy to moderate. Long hike on an easy-to-follow nearly level path
Elevation gain:	108 feet over the 6 miles (only a 0.4 percent grade).
Special attractions:	Wildflowers and tallgrass prairie.
Maps:	USGS quads: Brownsdale and Dexter.
For more information:	DNR Information Center; see Appendix B.
GPS:	43 44.074N 92 49.75 at County Road 19.

Finding the trailhead: From Interstate 90 and Minnesota Highway 56, travel north to Brownsdale and County Road 2. Go east for 2 miles to County Road 19. Take this dirt road 0.2 mile for parking on the west (right) in a small lot off the road. The trail starts on the other side of the road to go to Dexter. There is also parking off of CR 16, 2 miles west of Brownsdale. Street parking is available in Dexter, which might also make good place for a bike drop and an easy return trip.

The hike: As one of the best examples of mesic tallgrass prairie in southeastern Minnesota, Wild Indigo can be a great hike for a true prairie enthusiast. However, since it lacks the scenic vistas or challenging terrain, some might not appreciate it as much. The beauty of the hike is directly at your feet, with the grasses and forbs growing along the trail. Take along your wildflower field guide to help identify some 340 native plants that have been noted growing along the path. These include the compass plant with its yellow flowers, common Indian plantain, the blooming purple stalks of blazing stars, the small white flowers of wild quinine, the butterfly loving milkweeds, and, of course, the shrub-like white wild indigos.

This hike divides prime farm land by following an abandoned Chicago, Milwaukee, Saint Paul, and Pacific Railroad right-of-way. Unlike the surrounding land, it never was put into crop production, but was fenced in, with passing trains providing the only disturbance. The hike can be started anywhere on the tracks from Dexter in the east to Cedar River in Ramsey in the west, which spans a 12-mile round-trip. The eastern portion is pure prairie with only an occasional invading tree finding a foothold. On the western end, the trail follows alongside Wolf Creek, traveling through a savanna with small scrub oaks scattered along the path. The trail has no signs or trail markers except at the marked parking spots on CRs 16 and 19. However, it is easy to follow, as farm fields line both sides of the trail, and just about every mile the trail crosses a country road.

Wild Indigo SNA

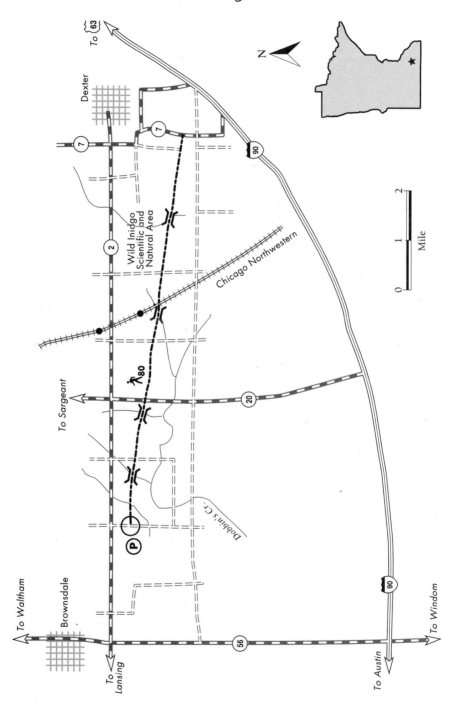

Outlined is just the eastern half, which ranges from CR 19 to Dexter for the prairie section. From the parking area, head across the road for an eastward journey. This is not a wilderness area, as you can see from the farms abutting both sides of the path, but still, in the 0.5 mile, I saw a deer, a skunk, and three grouse. After 1 mile of travel through the grassland you come to an intersection with a small dirt road; at about 2 miles you come to a small creek and a bridge, which looks as if it has seen a fire. Here the trail is almost on a plateau with a number of small intermittent creeks draining into Dobbins Creek to the south. Then the trail crosses County Road 20, where you need to go around the gated path. At 3 miles the next crossing of a dirt road awaits, which is about where Dexter's water tower comes into sight off in the distance. After another 0.5 mile, you pass the remains of an overpass for the Chicago Northwestern Railroad line. From there on to the end, cross over one more dirt road and a bridge over a creek (which drains into the North Branch of the Root River). At the trail's end you come to a thick grove of trees and turn off on Front Street, a residential street, which is about 0.2 mile off of Main Street.

81 Myre Big Island State Park

General description:	A loop that follows a point out into Albert Lea Lake through a prairie and up into an esker in the northern section.
General location:	Right outside of the city of Albert Lea.
Length:	2.5 miles; part of the parks 16-mile network of trails.
Difficulty:	Easy, follows a wide grassy path.
Elevation gain:	70 feet.
Special attractions:	Birding, eskers, and the Owen Johnson Interpretive Center.
Maps:	State park trail map; USGS quads: Albert Lea East and Glenville.
Camping:	99 drive-in and 4 hike-in sites.
For more information:	DNR Information Center; see Appendix B.
GPS:	43 38.242N 93 18.476W at park entrance.

Finding the trailhead: From Albert Lea, follow signs from either Interstate 35 or Interstate 90. From I-35 going north, take County Road 46 (Exit 11) east 0.5 mile to County Road 38 and about 1 mile south to the park entrance.

The hike: Most islands are an anomaly and Myre Big Island is no exception. On this island in the middle of Albert Lea Lake there is a hardwood forest, far south of its range, in the middle of the prairie. The lake acts as a moat, protecting the woods from the once common prairie wildfires that swept through the region. You will also find marshes that bring all sorts of waterfowl, and rolling lakeside prairies. With the lake and marshes and various habitats, the park is also one of the best birding spots in the region. Hawks might be spotted circling overhead, bluebirds darting back and forth on the prairie, and pelicans searching for fish in the water. Geologically, the whole county is completely covered by the Bemis Moraine till. Within the park, glacier remnants can be found in the shallow (maximum 6-feet-deep)

Myre Big Island State Park

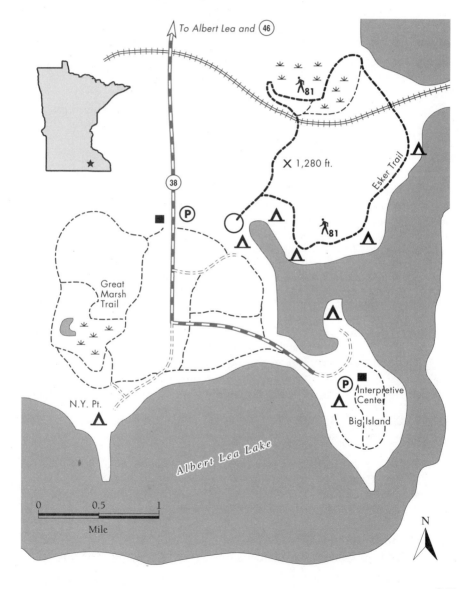

Albert Lea Lake, which rests in an old glacial riverbed, and the esker in the park's northwest corner.

The park has several trails: the Big Island Trail, the Great Marsh Trail, and the Esker Trail, which is accessed by a trail that goes along the western shore of Albert Lea Lake. On the Big Island, the trail circles the island that is really a peninsula, while passing through a northern hardwood forest (a forest type uncommon to this region). The trail connects the campground, the picnic area, and the Olson Interpretive Center. The center has what is said to be the state's largest prehistoric artifact collections. The Great Marsh Trail, appropriately enough, provides a 1.5-mile tour of a marsh near the New York Point group camp.

To reach the Esker Trail, start at the White Fox Campground (the upper campground), right across from the Big Island. The trail begins by passing oak trees and prairie to reach the main loop at about 0.2 mile. At this intersection, a right will bring you alongside several walk-in campsites and a patch of prairie. There are also several benches perched about 20 feet above the lake along the grassy path, making this a pleasant spot to relax.

The grassy path then veers off, heading for the northern section and the Esker Trail. It's a short steep climb up the esker, which rises about 30 feet above the surrounding marshes and runs for a total of about 0.5 mile (An esker, by the way, is a high sinuous ridge of gravel that was left by rivers that flowed within a glacier). After the trail descends from the esker, pass through an oak savanna and cross the railroad tracks. A shaded picnic area, complete with hand pump, is just to the left after the tracks. Finally, before ending the loop, one last prairie panorama appears at the park's high spot.

82 Minneopa State Park

General description:	A short hike around the largest waterfall (a double waterfall at that) in southern Minnesota.
General location:	Just west of Mankato.
Length:	0.4-mile loop around the falls; part of the park's 4.5-mile network of trails.
Difficulty:	Easy.
Elevation gain:	45 feet from the top to the base of the falls.
Special attractions:	Double waterfall, erratic strewn prairie, and the Seppman windmill.
Maps:	State park trail map; USGS quad: Mankato West.
Camping:	62 drive-in sites.
For more information:	DNR Information Center; see Appendix B.
GPS:	44 08.919N 94 05.536W.

Finding the trailhead: From Mankato, take U.S. Highway 69 for 5 miles west to Minnesota Highway 68 and follow the park signs to the entrance.

Minneopa State Park

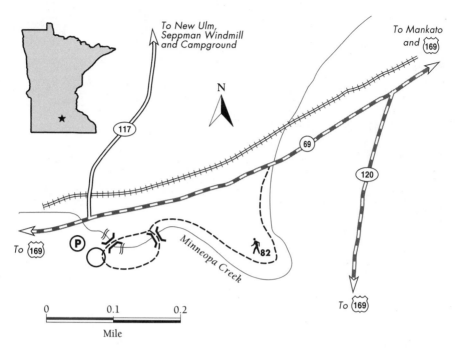

Park by the waterfalls or in the park's other section along the Minnesota River.

The hike: Something about waterfalls attracts people. It might be the sound of water splashing, the cool mist, or the blur of the water as it drops. Minnesota has its share, whether along the North Shore, in the city, or here in the south; but in Minneopa you see, feel, and hear it twice with a double falls. The falls have been bringing people here since the late 1800s, when literally thousands of people showed up to attend picnics, relax, hike in the glen, and, of course, see the falls.

The name *Minneopa* is a Dakota word for "water that falls twice." And this actually happens here as the creek first plunges over a small falls, then drops over a second in what is the largest waterfall in the southern part of the state. On its way to the falls, Minneopa Creek cuts a small valley through glacial till before making the first plunge of about 15 feet. The second falls appears a bit downstream where a hard layer of sandstone is undercut by the softer sandstone, to create the drop of about 30 feet. At the base, a sandstone amphitheater makes a great place to listen and watch the falls splash. A staircase leads down to the bottom of the falls, and bridges cross the creek both above and below. The trail at the bottom continues on down the glen for a tour of the lush valley, which was cut by the waterfall. Numerous goat paths line the sides, resulting in even more trails to explore.

The second drop of Minneopa Falls.

The park is really broken up into two sections: the small park here at the falls and a larger section north along the Minnesota River, leading to the Seppman Windmill. The latter section includes a riverside trail that might be seasonally closed due to flooding. It also features a long trail, passing through a former sheep pasture, currently in stages of prairie restoration. The prairie is strewn with glacier erratics, making it almost seem like a gardener's landscaping work in progress. Follow the road up to the large round Seppman Windmill (without the wind vanes), which was built of stone in 1864, modeled after a traditional German design.

83 Flandrau State Park

General description:	An easy walk along the floodplain forest in the valley of a meandering prairie river.
General location:	Right on the edge of New Ulm.
Length:	About a 3-mile loop; part of the park's 8-mile network of trails.
Difficulty:	Easy.
Elevation gain:	90 feet from the river up the bluff, stairs in steepest section.
Special attractions:	Overlooks of Cottonwood River.
Maps:	State park trail map; USGS quad: New Ulm.
Camping:	90 drive-in sites.
For more information:	DNR Information Center; see Appendix B.
GPS:	44 17.50N 94 28.1W.

Finding the trailhead: On the edge of New Ulm, just off Minnesota Highway 15, take 10th Street south to the top of the hill and turn left on Summit Avenue. Look for the park's sign.

The hike: Flandrau State Park is one of the more urban hikes in the book, bordering the well laid-out city of New Ulm. Many visitors follow the paths leading to the pool or up the bluff to take in the sunset over the Cottonwood River, but a few other paths explore the lowlands alongside the river.

The trails start at the visitor center, a massive WPA building built during the 1930s located next to the swimming pool. The park is located in a floodplain forest (replanted for the park) and the Cottonwood River's old meanders. For hiking, there are a couple of starting points. To the north behind the main building a trail leads up to Indian Point and a popular scenic overlook 100 feet over the river. This trail is short and accessible directly from

Flandrau State Park

town. Farther to the west, the trail system has an interpretive loop along the river, which leads to the oxbow meadows in the back of the park and the Prairie Trail, along the bluff.

The quietest hike in the park (farthest away from the other activities) is probably the River Trail, which leads to the site of the former dam in the park's eastern half. This section, featuring a couple of loops, also has the longest set of trails in the park.

From the visitor's center, keep to your right to start the River Trail. A short, steep staircase climbs the bluff, where burr oaks cling to the upper slopes. On the top, the trail briefly borders a golf course, then angles back down into a floodplain forest. At the bottom the trail divides for the 1-mile Old Island Loop, which goes around a stranded island left dry when the river's meandered course changed. Next you'll find the intersection for the River Loop at the end of which is a former dam site. The park originally had a lake backed up behind this dam, until floods overwhelmed it and made it unfeasible to maintain. The only thing left is the rampart of the dam, leading to the water. A trail runs along the top of the rampart to head back and finish off this 0.75-mile loop.

84 Kilen Woods State Park

General description:	A hike from the oak grove down the 150-foot valley of the Des Moines River and back up to a rolling prairie.
General location:	Between Jackson and Windom in Jackson County.
Length:	1.5 miles round-trip; part of the park's 5-mile network of trails.
Difficulty:	Easy. Steep climb up from the river, otherwise easy going on a wide grassy path.
Elevation gain:	About 150 feet from the river to the top of the valley.
Special attractions:	Prairie Bush Clover SNA and Dinosaur Ridge overlook.
Maps:	State park trail map; USGS quad: Lakefield NE.
Camping:	33 drive-in and 4 walk-in sites.
For more information:	DNR Information Center; see Appendix B.
GPS:	43 43.830N 95 04.124W.

Finding the trailhead: From Interstate 90, take Minnesota Highway 86 for 5 miles, past Lakefield and on to County Road 24. Turn east (right) and go 5 miles to the park entrance.

The hike: With only 200 acres, Kilen Woods is a small park, though the park actually feels much bigger and more remote than one might imagine. By taking a short hike around the park, you can find lowland forest along the river, some unique prairies (where the endangered prairie bush clover resides), and a peaceful oak savanna in the rolling hills. No doubt the deep 150-foot Des Moines River valley and a couple of tucked away ravines help give a sense of remoteness to this heavily farmed region. (The river valley resulted, not from the slow moving present day Des Moines, but from the draining of the Des Moines ice lobe during the Wisconsin glaciation.)

This hike starts at the interpretive center in the midst of an oak forest at the Rock Creek Trail. Follow the hiking club sign to the left, which quickly leads to a watch tower. The tower was built in 1957, but today it's in a state of disrepair and inaccessible. Take the trail down the forested ravine where it follows an intermittent creek to the river's edge. At the bottom, take a right to cross the winter sledding hill. On the other side, the path leads through a forest where a few large basswoods can be seen. Cross a small creek and go up the Ox Cart Trail. (The rest of the Rock Creek Trail was closed due to erosion.) Toward the top the woods slowly change to an oak

Kilen Woods State Park

The oak savanna in Kilen Woods State Park.

forest and then to prairie. Once on top you will meet the intersection for the Dinosaur Ridge Overlook, which gives one of the better vistas of the quaint and meandering river valley far below. Through the trees, one can also see on the opposing plateau a barn to complete the pastoral scene.

From this point turn around and take the connector trail, which leads to the prairie and oak savanna. The Prairie Bush Clover SNA, which is classified as dry gravel hill prairie, occupies a small portion of the park along this trail. The SNA is one of the largest sites for this federally threatened plant. The plant (a member of the pea family) has a silver green color and pink to white flowers that bloom in mid-July. Next, cross a bridge, passing by a fen along the stream bed, and hike onto the Sioux Trail for the oak savanna. If there is any spot in Minnesota that looks like it came out of "The Little House on the Prairie," it might be here. The land has gently rolling hills, covered with wide spreading oaks. On top of the knoll near the end of the trail is an overlook, which is about 100 feet above the creek. With the bench and the bluebird houses, this makes a perfect place for bird watching or taking in a sunset.

85 Camden State Park

General description:	The trails loop around the park, descending into the Redwood River valley and topping off onto a large open prairie.
General location:	Southwest of Marshall.
Length:	2-mile loop; part of the park's 15-mile network of trails.
Difficulty:	Easy to moderate. Follows on wide path on the upper plateau.
Elevation gain:	About 100 feet.
Special attractions:	Scenic vistas, cool refreshing river valley, trout fishing, and a beach.
Maps:	State park trail map; USGS quad: Russel.
Camping:	80 drive-in sites.
For more information:	DNR Information Center; see Appendix B.
GPS:	44 21.667N 95 55.611W at the picnic area.

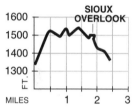

Finding the trailhead: From Marshall, travel 10 miles southwest on Minnesota Highway 23 to the park road entrance on the right. Park at the north picnic area, the beach, or, for this hike, at the south picnic area.

The hike: Nestled in the valley of Redwood River, Camden State Park provides a cool refuge in the midst of the Minnesota Prairie. This conjures up images of dangling your feet in cool waters and relaxing in the shade after the heat and sun of the open prairie. The park is somewhat of an oasis, with a clear cool stream, lakes, a dense forested valley, and a patch of prairie on the upper plateau. The valley has a long human history. Historical sites in the park record the park's inhabitants ranging from the Native Americans to settlers from New Jersey who formed and named a town in the valley—now long gone.

The trails form a large network of loops spreading throughout the park, although some might be closed in spring due to erosion or flooding. The various seasons all have something to offer in this park—morels and blooming spring ephermals, a multitude of summer flowers, and a tremendous hardwood display of fall colors. Some of the trails are also multi-purpose, so you might have to share a path with mountain bikers or equestrians.

The trails in the park are really of two types: the lower valley trails pass through dense forests and the upper plateau trails skirt the edge of the scalloped valley on a prairie. There are several loop options here and I have not had the chance to try them all. However, I found a short loop by the south picnic area well worth the visit. This loop radiates to the southwest as you first cross the Redwood River on a small footbridge, and then climb a densely

Camden State Park

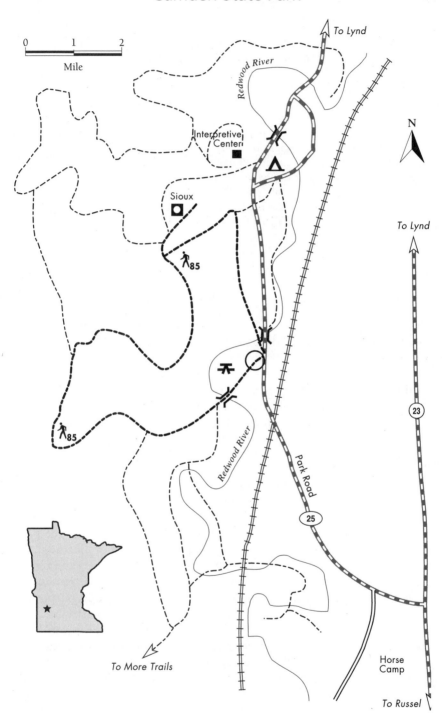

0   1   2
Mile

To Lynd

N

Redwood River

Interpretive Center

Sioux

85

To Lynd

23

Park Road

Redwood River

85

25

To More Trails

Horse Camp

To Russel

forested ravine.

At the top of the ravine is a big transition from the lower densely-forested valley to the expansive upper rolling prairie. During a springtime visit, this plateau area was scorched black from a prescribed burn, giving the place a charcoal smell and a slightly eerie look. Only a few scattered shoots of grasses sprouted through the charcoal grass to provide some green, while animal tracks, which were vegetation-free and did not burn, crisscrossed the ground in a intricate network. This loop circles the upper section of the ravine where you began, then enters the woods again.

A short spur leads up to Sioux overlook, which is also one of the historical sites in the park. As the story goes, here was a lookout spot that was used to guard against attacks. The view is encompassing, taking in the narrow valley of the Redwood River, which some have described as being a bit like the Appalachians. The overlook is complete with a deck and a bench for a comfortable viewing situation. To return to the picnic grounds, either take the trail down to the interpretive center, or keep to your left for the next intersection down to the trail that parallels the road back to the picnic grounds. The path shares the car bridge over the Redwood River.

86 Pipestone National Monument

General description:	A guided tour along prairie, bluff, and quarry alongside Pipestone Creek.
General location:	Just north of the city of Pipestone.
Length:	About a 1-mile loop.
Difficulty:	Easy. Follows a guided tour.
Elevation gain:	Nominal, with a short optional climb up the 30-foot ledge.
Special attractions:	Waterfall, leaping rock, interpretive center, and quarry.
Maps:	Maps available at the monument; USGS quad: Pipestone North.
For more information:	Pipestone National Monument; see Appendix B.
GPS:	44 00.724N 96 19.561W.

Finding the trailhead: From Pipestone, take U.S. Highway 75 north for about 1 mile. Watch for monument signs. Park at the interpretive center.

The hike: The mineral known as catlinite, or pipestone, has played a significant role in Native American culture. Upon first entering the Pipestone National Monument and being greeted by the Three Maidens, you realize this is a special place. The Three Maidens, actually six large boulders left by the glaciers, was the traditional place to leave offerings to ensure good quar-

Pipestone National Monument

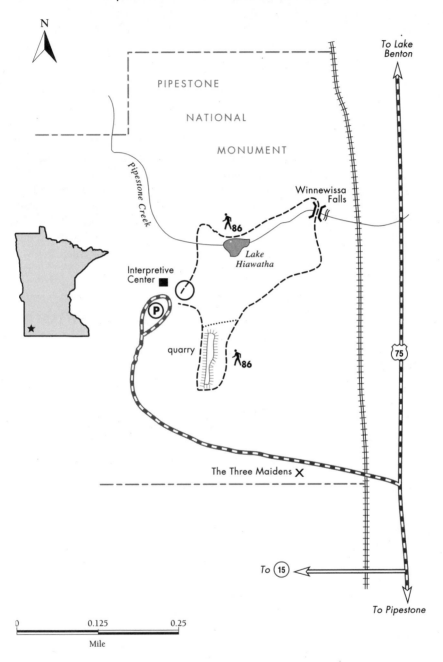

N

PIPESTONE

NATIONAL

MONUMENT

Pipestone Creek

Winnewissa Falls

Lake Hiawatha

⊼86

Interpretive Center ■

Ⓟ

quarry

⊼86

The Three Maidens ✗

To Lake Benton

US 75

To ⑮

To Pipestone

0   0.125   0.25

Mile

Winnewissa Falls.

rying of pipestone. The visitor center near the end of the road is a good place to learn more about native culture. Inside the center you find the human history of the native people of the area, the geologic history of the mineral, and the material most often used to create pipes and totems.

The trail loop starts out the back door, but first pick up a Circle Trail brochure for a self-guided tour of the monument. You will walk along Pipestone Creek past Lake Hiawatha to the grove of trees, which hides a 30-foot Sioux quartzite ledge. This section holds some of the park's favorite features, including some early graffiti scratched into the rock by Joseph Nicollet when he was on his mapping expedition. One tall pinnacle called "Leaping rock" is—as legend has it—the rock from which braves would prove themselves by jumping from the ledge across the gap to the pinnacle. The Winnewissa (or "jealous maiden") Falls of Pipestone Creek tumbles off the ledge. These falls were actually lowered by 8 feet back in the early 1900s, in order to gain additional land agriculture (only 18 acres). Imaginative minds have found a couple of faces in the cliff, including the Old Stone Face, a large visage of an old man, and the Oracle, best viewed from on top of the bluff through a looking hole.

The trail returns to the center by way of a small prairie, which was never plowed but partially used as a grazing pasture. Within this field wildflowers bloom in summer, adding color to the scene. Finally, just before you reach the center, a side loop leads to the actively-mined pipestone quarries. The narrow trench of the quarry runs the length of this loop, bordered and shaded on one side by trees. Since no mechanized tools can be used in the quarry, all the digging is by hand, with shovels, picks, and buckets used to haul out water. While the pipestone is relatively soft, it is the overlying layers of extremely hard quartzite that have to be excavated away before hitting the pipestone layer. The pipestone also slants downward, so to remove more rock, the digging must be progressively deeper, which means the pipestone gets harder to reach. When you return to the center, check out the demonstration pit where you can easily walk down to the thin pipestone layer under the many feet of Sioux quartzite.

87   Blue Mounds State Park

General description:	A prairie hike on top of the mound, which rises 100 feet from the surrounding landscape.
General location:	North of Luverne.
Length:	About a 4-mile loop; part of the park's 13-mile network of trails.
Difficulty:	Easy to moderate on a general flat sloping trail, except for the one steep path leading up to the Upper Cliffline Trail.
Elevation differential:	234 feet from the lake to the top of the mound.
Special attractions:	Minnesota's stonehenge, overlooks, and a buffalo round-up every fall.
Maps:	State park trail map; USGS quad: Luverne.
Camping:	73 drive-in and 14 walk-in sites.
For more information:	DNR Information Center; see Appendix B.
GPS:	43 42.92N 96 11.213W at picnic grounds.

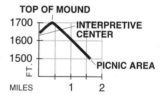

Finding the trailhead: From Luverne, which is just north of Interstate 90, go 4 miles north on U.S. Highway 75. Park at either the interpretive center or the picnic grounds.

The hike: When French explorers first came to the area known as Minnesota, this is one of the regions that impressed them enough to give it a name, *Couteau des Prairies*, or "Highlands of the Prairies." And the mound is impressive at a distance, as it rises nearly 100 feet off the flat surrounding landscape, taking on a bluish tint in the evening. The park offers more than just the mound's blue tint; you can get a panoramic view of three states, buffalo roaming the prairie (behind a fence), and what is believed to be a prehistoric stonehenge.

The mound is made of pink to purplish Sioux quartzite, estimated to be about 1.5 billion years old. The most striking feature of the mound is the bluff on the eastern side that runs for 1.5 miles and rises 90 feet. Legend has

Blue Mounds State Park

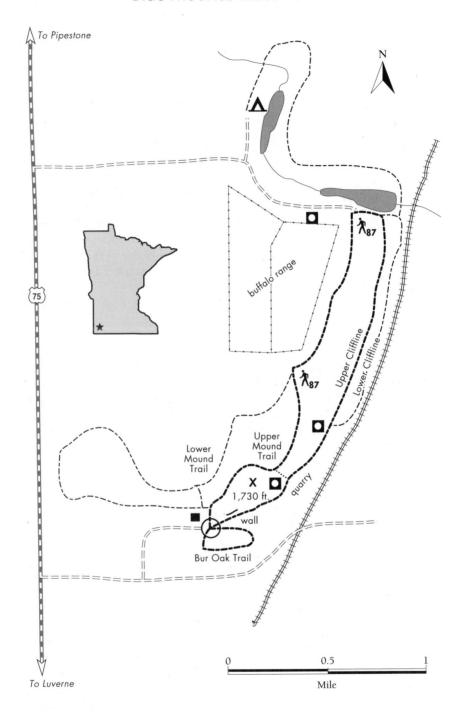

To Pipestone

N

75

To Luverne

buffalo range

87

87

Upper Cliffline

Lower Cliffline

Upper Mound Trail

Lower Mound Trail

quarry

X
1,730 ft.

wall

Bur Oak Trail

0   0.5   1
Mile

it that animals were herded over the edge, though no bones have been discovered below. This cliff face, a local mecca for rock climbers, has along the vertical faces some extremely technical climbs of up to 5.11. The best hiking is up and around the mound itself, with a starting point from either end, next to the swimming beach/picnic area or at the park's southern end at the interpretive center.

During the park's development, a road was planned to run on top of the mound through the middle of the prairie. Fortunately, this plan was dropped, and today only footpaths cross the upper plateau. The plateau is like an island removed from the roads and noise below, where one can meditate out over the landscape. One of the favorite spots up here seems to be the old quarry on the mound's southeastern edge. The excavation took what is really just a small bite out of the mound, leaving for us what is now a large amphitheater. The main trail on top is the Upper Cliffline Trail, which extends from the Interpretive Center down a gentle slope to the swimming beach. The panorama spans the numerous geometric farms off in the distance, as well as the meandering Rock River and its tributaries. The Lower Cliffline Trail follows, logically enough, the base of the cliff for about half its distance. This is a good place to watch birds, since it has the only tree cover on the mound.

Prairie covers the majority of the park's 1,500 acres, making it one of the state's largest grassland parks. Though not farmed, the land here was grazed at one time; the Department of Natural Resources is working to reintroduce native species. One plant that does make a home here among the rocks, is the prickly pear cactus, which blooms in mid-summer. The Upper Mound Trail leads to Eagle Rock, which at 1,730 feet is the area's highest point. Here you can have a 360-degree panoramic view and literally see into two other states: Iowa 14 miles to the south, and South Dakota 13 miles to the west. Directly to the south, the vista takes in the town of Luverne, sitting nearly 300 feet below. To the east you see Rock River as it makes its way into the Missouri.

Near the Interpretive Center, there are a couple of shorter loops. One goes down the slope, exploring an oak savanna on the Burr Oak Trail. This trail clings to the bluff for a tour of these gnarly trees. The other goes up a short distance to the 1,250-feet-long ancient stone wall, sometimes referred to as the Minnesota Stonehenge. During the vernal and autumnal equinoxes, the walls apparently line up with the sun at sunrise and sunset. The wall itself, at first sight, looks like a long, straight foundation where big rocks are firmly planted in the ground. Tall grasses obscure it in places as it runs along this southeast corner of the mound.

The park also provides a large enclosed grazing area for buffalo. Their own private section of prairie is accessible from either the picnic grounds, where there is a viewing platform, or along the Mound Trail, which follows the fenced-in prairie on the eastern side. The grazing area spans enough land that the scene might not include a closeup view of the herd, but the panorama, nevertheless, with even a far-off herd, still hints at what the prairies once must have been like.

Appendix A—
Suggested Reading

ACTIVITIES

Beymer, Robert. *Superior National Forest*. Seattle: the Mountaineers, 1989.

Buchanan, Jim. *The Minnesota Walk Book*. 3 vol. Minneapolis: Nodin Press, 1974 -1989.

DuFresne, Jim. *Voyageurs National Park*: Water Routes, Footpaths, and Ski Trails. Seattle: Mountaineers, 1986.

Hagen, Kai J. *Parks and Wetlands*: A guide to 170 special places in and around the Twin Cities. Minneapolis: Nodin Press, 1989.

Malach, Jim and Mary Jo. *Walking Minnesota*. Stillwater: Voyageurs Press, 1991.

Scott, Marcia and Rudy Hargesheimer. *The Border Route Trail: a Trail Guide and Map*. Minneapolis: Minnesota Rovers Outing Club, 1987.

Slade, Andrew. *Guide to the Superior Hiking Trail*. Two Harbors: Ridgeline Press, 1993.

Umhoefer, Jim. *A Guide to Minnesota Outdoors*. Minocqua: Northword Press, 1984.

ECOLOGY

Benyus, Janine M. *Northwoods Wildlife*. Minocqua: Northword Press, 1989.

Daniel, Glenada. *A Sierra Club Naturalist's Guide to the Northwoods*. San Francisco: Sierra Club Books, 1981.

Hazard, Evan B. *The Mammals of Minnesota*. Minneapolis: University of Minnesota Press, 1982.

Oberle, Frank. *Tallgrass Prairie Wildflowers*. Helena: Falcon Press, 1995.

Minnesota Department of Natural Resources. A *Guide to Minnesota's Scientific and Natural Areas*. Saint Paul: DNR, 1995.

Moyle, John B. *Northland Wildflowers: A Guide for the Minnesota Region.* Minneapolis: University of Minnesota Press, 1982.

Strangis, Jay M. *Birding Minnesota.* Helena: Falcon Press, 1996.

Tester, John R. *Minnesota's Natural Heritage.* Minneapolis: University of Minnesota Press, 1995.

Wocha, Daniel S. *Minnesota's St. Croix River Valley: A Guide to Native Habitats.* Minneapolis: University of Minnesota Press, 1995.

Wright, H.E., ed. *The Patterned Peatlands of Minnesota.* Minneapolis: University of Minnesota Press, 1992.

GEOLOGY

Ojakangas, R.W. and C.L. Matsch. *Minnesota's Geology.* Minneapolis: University of Minnesota Press, 1982.

Sansome, Constance J. *Minnesota Underfoot.* Edina: Voyageur Press, 1983.

Waters, Thomas F. *The Streams and Rivers of Minnesota.* Minneapolis: University of Minnesota Press, 1977.

HISTORY

Meyer, Roy W. *Everyone's Country Estate.* Saint Paul: Minnesota Historical Society Press, 1991.

Upham, Warren. *Minnesota Geographic Names: Their Origin and Historic Significance.* Saint Paul: Minnesota Historical Society Press, 1969.

Appendix B—
For More Information

STATE

Minnesota Travel Information Center
100 Metro Sq., 121 7th Place East
Saint Paul, MN 55101-2112
612-296-5029
or 800-657-3700

Minnesota Department of Natural Resources
Information Center
500 Lafayette Road
Saint Paul, MN 55155-4040
Web Site: http://
www.dnr.state.mn.us/outdoor/
parks/parks.htm

For general information for all state parks, state forests, and scientific and natural areas call:
612-296-6157 or 800-652-9747;
and TDD: 612-296-5484
or 800-657-3929

For camping reservations in a state park call: 612-922-9000
or 800-246-2267

FEDERAL

Chippewa National Forest
For general information on any of the districts:
Chippewa National Forest
Route 3 Box 219
Cass Lake, MN 56633
218-335-2283
http://www.fs.fed.us/recreation/
states/mn.html

Superior National Forest Supervisor
For general information on any of the districts:
Superior National Forest
Box 338, Duluth MN 55801
218-720-5324
http://www.gis.umn.edu/snf
or http://www.fs.fed.us/recreation/
states/mn.html

To make reservations:
BWCAW Reservation Service
PO Box 450
Cumberland, Maryland 21501
800-745-3399

Grand Portage National Monument
PO box 668
Grand Portage, MN 56604
http://www.nps.gov/grpo/

Pipestone National Monument
PO Box 727
Pipestone, MN 56164
http://www.nps.gov/pipr/

Voyageurs National Park
3131 Highway 53
International Falls, MN 56649-8904
http://www.nps.gov/voya/

Minnesota National Wildlife Refuge
3815 East 80th Street
Bloomington, MN 55425-1600
612-335-2299
http://ww.fws.gov/~r3pao/index.html

CITY AND COUNTY
Duluth Convention and Visitors Bureau
100 Lake place Drive
Duluth, MN 55805-2326
800-438-5884 (800-4-DULUTH)

Grand Portage Lodge and Casino
PO Box 233
Grand Portage, MN 56605
800-543-1384

Hennepin Parks
12615 county Road 9
Plymouth, MN 55441
612-559-9000

Minneapolis Park and Recreation Board
200 Grain Exchange
400 South 4th Street
Minneapolis, MN 55415
612-661-4800

Orr Tourist Information Center
PO Box 236
Orr, MN 55771
218-757-3932 or 800-357-9255

Red Wings Parks
PO Box 34
Red Wings, MN 5506
612-385-3674

ASSOCIATIONS AND CLUBS
Kekekabic Hiking Club
1627 West County Road B, Suite B
Roseville, MN 55113
http://205.243.221.9/ktc.html

Minnesota Rovers Outing Club
PO Box 14133
Minneapolis, MN 55414
612-522-2461

North Country Trail Association
49 Monroe Center NW, Suite 200B
Grand Rapids, MI 49503
http://people.delphi.com/wesboyd/ncnst.htm

Superior Hiking Trail Association
PO Box 4
23 Waterfront Drive
Two Harbors, MN 55616

HIKING MINNESOTA
Web Site - http://www.tc.umn.edu/~puk/hike.html
e-mail: pukite@daina.com
or Falcon Press: http://www.falconguide.com

Glossary

Anorthosite—A common igneous rock in northern Minnesota made up of feldspar.

Blue diamond sign—Indicates across-country skiing trail, often follows a hiking trail.

Blazes—Red or orange plastic tape tied to branches or trees to mark trails.

Bog—Wet peatland with black spruce, Labrador tea, and sphagnum mosses.

Coniferous—Trees with cones, usually an evergreen tree, though, as an exception, the tamarack loses all its leaves each year.

Corundum—A hard form of alumina; used as the grit for sandpaper.

Deciduous—Trees that lose their leaves annually.

Delta—The mouth of a river.

Diabase—Medium-grained mafic volcanic rock.

Dike—A volcanic rock that enters the bedrock perpendicularly.

Dolomite—A limestone-like rock composed primarily of the mineral calcium magnesium carbonate.

Drumlin—A hill composed of glacial fill, stretched in the direction of glacial movement.

Ephemerals—Wildflowers that appear in the spring in the big woods.

Erratic—A big rock left by glaciers.

Esker—A long, narrow ridge of sand and gravel deposited by glacial meltwaters.

Fen—Wet peatland fed by groundwater; without sphagnum moss.

Formation—A sequence of rocks, usually from the same epoch.

Gabbro—A coarse-textured igneous rock.

Gneiss—Pronounced "nice," a hard igneous rock; Minnesota's gneiss is some of the world's oldest.

Goat Prairie—Dry bluff prairies that grow on steep southwestern slopes.

GPS—Global Positioning System; a navigation system that uses satellites and computers to determine coordinates.

Kame—A mound or knoll of sand or gravel deposited by glacial meltwaters.

Kettle—A small lake formed from buried ice blocks.

Krummholz effect—Name given to the climatic conditions that result in low-growing, stunted trees.

Marsh—Grassy, low-lying wetland.

Mesic—Land that is moist but well drained.

Moraine—Gravel left by glaciers.

Orange diamond sign—Indicates snowmobile trail.

Oxbow Lake—A meander of a river that is stranded to form a lake.

Peatlan —Land where plants decompose only partially and accumulates to form brown to black organic material called peat; two main types: bogs and fens.

Portage—A trail for carrying boats; often measured in rods, which equal 16.5 feet.

Prairie—An area where tree cover makes up less than 10 percent of land.

Precambrian—prior to 570 million years ago.

Rod—16.5 feet; used to measure portages.

Sedimentary rock—Layered rock.

Sill—Volcanic rock extrudes parallel to dominate bedrock; compare dike.

Slough—A swampy area or backwater.

Swale—A wide, low depression.

Till—Sand, gravel, and rocks carried and deposited by a glacier.

Volcanic—Rock from molten lava.

White diamond sign—Indicates a hiking trail.

ABOUT THE AUTHOR

John Pukite was a Peace Corps volunteer in the Central African Republic from 1988–1990, promoting agricultural diversity in a small region near the Ubangi River.

His Peace Corps service was followed by five years aboard dozens of fishing boats as a National Marine Fisheries Service biologist, which entailed the collection of fishery management data while battling the elements off the Oregon coast, in the Bering Sea, and around the Gulf of Alaska.

John is a graduate of the University of Minnesota and the author of the Penguin book *A Field Guide to Cows*. He is currently at work on *A Field Guide to Pigs*.

Index

Page numbers in *italics* refer to maps. Page numbers in **bold** refer to photos.

get
FALCON GUIDED

FALCON GUIDES® are available for where-to-go hiking, mountain biking, rock climbing, walking, scenic driving, fishing, rockhounding, paddling, birding, wildlife viewing, and camping. We also have FalconGuides on essential outdoor skills and subjects and field identification. The following titles are currently available, but this list grows every year. For a free catalog with a complete list of titles, call FALCON toll-free at 1-800-582-2665.

HIKING GUIDES

Hiking Alaska
Hiking Alberta
Hiking Arizona
Hiking Arizona's Cactus Country
Hiking the Beartooths
Hiking Big Bend National Park
Hiking California
Hiking California's Desert Parks
Hiking Carlsbad Caverns &
    Guadalupe Mtns. National Parks
Hiking Colorado
Hiking the Columbia River Gorge
Hiking Florida
Hiking Georgia
Hiking Glacier & Waterton Lakes National Parks
Hiking Grand Canyon National Park
Hiking Great Basin National Park
Hiking Hot Springs
    in the Pacific Northwest
Hiking Idaho
Hiking Maine
Hiking Michigan
Hiking Minnesota
Hiking Montana
Hiking Nevada
Hiking New Hampshire
Hiking New Mexico
Hiking New York
Hiking North Carolina
Hiking North Cascades

Hiking Northern Arizona
Hiking Olympic National Park
Hiking Oregon
Hiking Oregon's Eagle Cap Wilderness
Hiking Oregon's Three Sisters Country
Hiking Pennsylvania
Hiking South Carolina
Hiking South Dakota's Black Hills Country
Hiking Southern New England
Hiking Tennessee
Hiking Texas
Hiking Utah
Hiking Utah's Summits
Hiking Vermont
Hiking Virginia
Hiking Washington
Hiking Wyoming
Hiking Wyoming's Wind River Range
Hiking Yellowstone National Park
Hiking Zion & Bryce Canyon National Parks
The Trail Guide to Bob Marshall Country

BEST EASY DAY HIKES

Beartooths
Canyonlands & Arches
Best Hikes on the Continental Divide
Glacier & Waterton Lakes
Glen Canyon
Grand Canyon
North Cascades
Yellowstone

■ *To order any of these books, check with your local bookseller*
or call FALCON ® *at **1-800-582-2665**.*

Visit us on the world wide web at:
www.falconguide.com

get
FALCONGUIDED

BIRDING GUIDES
Birding Arizona
Birding Minnesota
Birder's Guide to Montana
Birding Texas
Birding Utah

FIELD GUIDES
Bitterroot: Montana State Flower
Canyon Country Wildflowers
Great Lakes Berry Book
New England Berry Book
Plants of Arizona
Rare Plants of Colorado
Rocky Mountain Berry Book
Southern Rocky Mtn. Wildflowers
Tallgrass Prairie Wildflowers
Western Tree
Wildflowers of Southwestern Utah
Willow Bark and Rosehips

FISHING GUIDES
Fishing Alaska
Fishing the Beartooths
Fishing Florida
Fishing Maine
Fishing Michigan
Fishing Montana

WALKING
Walking Colorado Springs
Walking Portland
Walking St. Louis

PADDLING GUIDES
Floater's Guide to Colorado
Paddling Montana
Paddling Oregon

ROCK CLIMBING GUIDES
Rock Climbing Colorado
Rock Climbing Montana
Rock Climbing New Mexico & Texas
Rock Climbing Utah

ROCKHOUNDING GUIDES
Rockhounding Arizona
Rockhound's Guide to California
Rockhound's Guide to Colorado
Rockhounding Montana
Rockhounding Nevada
Rockhound's Guide to New Mexico
Rockhounding Texas
Rockhounding Utah
Rockhounding Wyoming

HOW-TO GUIDES
Bear Aware
Leave No Trace
Mountain Lion Alert
Wilderness First Aid
Wilderness Survival

MOUNTAIN BIKING GUIDES
Mountain Biking Arizona
Mountain Biking Colorado
Mountain Biking New
 Mexico
Mountain Biking New York
Mountain Biking Northern
 New England
Mountain Biking Southern
 New England
Mountain Biking Utah

LOCAL CYCLING SERIES
Fat Trax Bozeman
Fat Trax Colorado Springs
Mountain Biking Bend
Mountain Biking Boise
Mountain Biking
 Chequamegon
Mountain Biking Denver/
 Boulder
Mountain Biking Durango
Mountain Biking Helena
Mountain Biking Moab

FALCON®

■ *To order any of these books, check with your local bookseller
or call FALCON ® at **1-800-582-2665**.*

Visit Falcon on the world wide web at:
www.falconguide.com

get
FALCON GUIDED

Hiking the National Parks

The national parks have some of the very best hiking in the world, and just because it's in a national park doesn't mean it's crowded. In many parks, the roads are clogged with traffic, but the trails are nearly devoid of people.

As part of the **FALCON** GUIDES series, Falcon plans to publish a complete set of hiking guides to every national park with a substantial trail system. If your favorite park isn't on the following list of books currently available, you can plan on it being available soon. Each book comprehensively covers the trails in the parks and includes the necessary trip planning information on access, regulations, weather, etc., to help you put together a memorable adventure.

AVAILABLE NOW:
Hiking Big Bend National Park
Hiking California's Desert Parks (includes Death Valley and Joshua Tree National parks,
    Mojave National Preserve, and Anza-Borrego State Park)
Exploring Canyonlands & Arches National Parks
Hiking Carlsbad Caverns & Guadalupe Mountains National Parks
Hiking the Columbia River Gorge
Hiking Glacier & Waterton Lakes National Parks
Hiking Grand Canyon National Park
Hiking Great Basin National Park
Hiking North Cascades
Hiking Olympic National Park
Hiking South Dakota's Black Hills Country (includes Wind Cave, Badlands and
    Mount Rushmore national parks, and Custer State Park)
Hiking Yellowstone National Park
Hiking Zion & Bryce Canyon National Parks

COMING SOON: Redwoods, Glen Canyon/Escalante, Grand Teton,
and Rocky Mountain

ALSO AVAILABLE: 26 state-wide hiking guides

TO ORDER:
Check with your local bookseller or
call Falcon at **1-800-582-2665**
www.falconguide.com

FALCON®

WILDERNESS FIRST AID

By Dr. Gilbert Preston M.D.

Enjoy the outdoors and face the inherent risks with confidence. By reading this easy-to-follow first-aid text, all outdoor enthusiasts can pack a little extra peace of mind on their next adventure. *Wilderness First Aid* offers expert medical advice for dealing with outdoor emergencies beyond the reach of 911. It easily fits in most backcountry first-aid kits.

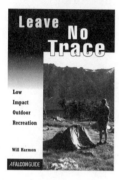

LEAVE NO TRACE

by Will Harmon

The concept of "leave no trace" seems simple, but it actually gets fairly complicated. This handy quick-reference guidebook includes all the newest information on this growing and all-important subject. This book is written to help the outdoor enthusiast make the hundreds of decisions necessary to protect the natural landscape and still have an enjoyable wilderness experience. Part of the proceeds from the sale of this book go to continue leave-no-trace education efforts. The Official Manual of American Hiking Society.

BEAR AWARE

by Bill Schneider

Hiking in bear country can be very safe if hikers follow the guidelines summarized in this small, "packable" book. Extensively reviewed by bear experts, the book contains the latest information on the intriguing science of bear-human interactions. *Bear Aware* can not only make your hike safer, but it can help you avoid the fear of bears that can take the edge off your trip.

MOUNTAIN LION ALERT

By Steve Torres

Recent mountain lion attacks have received national attention. Although infrequent, lion attacks raise concern for public safety. *Mountain Lion Alert* contains helpful advice for mountain bikers, trail runners, horse riders, pet owners, and suburban landowners on how to reduce the chances of mountain lion-human conflicts.

To order these titles or to find out more about this new series
of books, call FALCON® at **1-800-582-2665.**